# NOLO Products & Services

### ⇨ Books & Software

Get in-depth information. Nolo publishes hundreds of great books and software programs for consumers and business owners. Order a copy—or download an ebook version instantly—at Nolo.com.

### ⇨ Legal Encyclopedia

**Free at Nolo.com.** Here are more than 1,400 free articles and answers to common questions about everyday legal issues including wills, bankruptcy, small business formation, divorce, patents, employment and much more.

### ⇨ Plain-English Legal Dictionary

**Free at Nolo.com.** Stumped by jargon? Look it up in America's most up-to-date source for definitions of legal terms.

### ⇨ Online Legal Documents

Create documents at your computer. Go to Nolo.com to make a will or living trust, form an LLC or corporation or obtain a trademark or provisional patent. For simpler matters, download one of our hundreds of high-quality legal forms, including bills of sale, promissory notes, nondisclosure agreements and many more.

### ⇨ Lawyer Directory

**Find an attorney at Nolo.com.** Nolo's consumer-friendly lawyer directory provides in-depth profiles of lawyers all over America. From fees and experience to legal philosophy, education and special expertise, you'll find all the information you need to pick the right lawyer. Every lawyer listed has pledged to work diligently and respectfully with clients.

### ⇨ Free Legal Updates

**Keep up to date.** Check for free updates at Nolo.com. Under "Products," find this book and click "Legal Updates." You can also sign up for our free e-newsletters at Nolo.com/newsletters.

6th Edition

# How to Make Patent Drawings

## A *Patent It Yourself* Companion

Patent Agent Jack Lo &
Patent Attorney David Pressman

| Sixth Edition | AUGUST 2011 |
|---|---|
| Editor | RICHARD STIM |
| Illustrations | JACK LO & TERRI HEARSH |
| Cover Design | SUSAN PUTNEY |
| Production | MARGARET LIVINGSTON |
| Proofreader | SUSAN CARLSON GREENE |
| Index | MEDEA MINNICH |
| Printing | BANG PRINTING |

Lo, Jack.
 How to make patent drawings : a patent it yourself companion / by Jack Lo and David Pressman. —
6th ed.
      p. cm.
 Includes index.
 Summary: "Explains preparing formal patent drawings that comply with the rules of the U.S. Patent
and Trademark Office. The 6th edition contains the latest forms, plus new patent rules for application
and prosecution."— Provided by publisher.
 ISBN-13: 978-1-4133-1257-7 (pbk.)
 ISBN-10: 1-4133-1257-8 (pbk.)
 ISBN-13: 978-1-4133-1648-3 (epub e-book)
 1. Patents—United States—Drawings.  I. Pressman, David, 1937-  II. Title.
 T223.U3L6 2011
 608.022—dc23

2011017131

**Please note**

We believe accurate, plain-English legal information should help you solve many of your own
legal problems. But this text is not a substitute for personalized advice from a knowledgeable
lawyer. If you want the help of a trained professional—and we'll always point out situations in
which we think that's a good idea—consult an attorney licensed to practice in your state.

## Acknowledgments

I am most grateful to David Pressman for being a friend and mentor, whose generous support has been truly invaluable.

   I also thank the staff at Nolo, including Stephanie Harolde and Steve Elias for their suggestions and Terri Hearsh for her help in incorporating the drawings.

**—Jack Lo**

Thanks to Jack Lo for his excellent drawing skills, computer knowledge, sound ideas, and friendship. Thanks also to everyone at Nolo for their invaluable help and suggestions.

**—David Pressman**

# Table of Contents

## Index

# Your Legal Companion for
## *How to Make Patent Drawings*

If you're familiar with the Nolo book *Patent It Yourself,* you're already aware that most patent applications require detailed drawings showing the inventions. Although *Patent It Yourself* provides the basic guidelines for making patent drawings, its primary focus is on the written portion and the formal paperwork of an application. As a result, many readers of *Patent It Yourself* asked for a more detailed guide to, and explanation of, patent drawings. This is it.

Why do your own drawings?

Professional patent draftspersons typically charge $75 to $150 per sheet of patent drawings (each sheet may contain several figures or separate drawings). Most patent applications typically have between two and ten sheets of drawings. By reading this book and making your own patent drawings, such as the ones shown later, you can save between about $150 and $1,500 per patent application. Once you learn the skills, you can do all the drawings yourself for any subsequent patent applications you file.

You'll see by reading this book that it's not essential to have drawing skills to create suitable patent drawings. Some knowledge of cameras and computers may be all that's required to prepare formal patent drawings that meet strict Patent Office requirements.

This book shows you:
- the basics of drawing (Chapter 1)
- how to draw with pen, rulers, and other tools (Chapter 2)
- how to "draw" with a computer (Chapter 3)
- how to "draw" with a camera (Chapter 4)
- the basics of patent drawings (Chapter 5)
- different types of patent drawings (Chapters 6 and 7)
- PTO drawing standards (Chapter 8), and
- how to respond to PTO examinations or Office Actions (Chapter 9).

Furthermore, using the skills you acquire in this book, you will be able to make drawings for a promotional brochure for marketing your invention to prospective manufacturers or customers. In short, you may be able to save hundreds, or even thousands, of dollars in the years to come.

You will also be able to make drawings that more accurately reflect your intentions than a hired professional, because you know your invention best. By doing your own drawings, you do not have to take the time to make someone else understand your invention or to send the drawings back and forth for corrections. Also, if you've already prepared your application using *Patent It Yourself,* you will have the great satisfaction of properly completing the entire patent application by yourself—an impressive accomplishment for any inventor. ●

# General Introduction to Drawing

This chapter provides the background information you need to understand the more advanced concepts that are presented in later chapters. Basic drawing principles, including the different types of drawing views and foreshortening (a technique for making realistic views), are presented here. We also provide an overview of several drawing methods, to show you that making patent drawings is probably easier than you may have anticipated.

## Different Drawing Views

Any physical object can be seen from a great variety of view angles—for example, head-on, from the side, from the top, and from the back. Of course, a single drawing, also known as a drawing view or a figure, may show an object only from one view angle. Typically, a single figure cannot show all of the important features or parts of an object, because some of them may be on an opposite side that is not visible in the view. Therefore, when you need to clearly explain the structure of an invention in a patent application, several drawing views may be necessary to show the object from different angles.

Certain view angles have conventional names, so that they can be immediately understood when referred to. Let's look at the most common of these views.

### Orthogonal Views

An orthogonal, or engineering, view is one in which the viewer's eyes are centered over a particular side of the object. Put another way, the viewer's line of sight is perpendicular, or orthogonal, to such side. A special object—especially created to look different from every side—is shown in perspective at the top of Illustration 1.1 and is shown below the perspective view in all possible orthogonal views, as described here.

**Front Side or Front Elevational View.** Shows the front side from a viewpoint centered over the front side.

**Rear Side or Rear Elevational View.** Shows the rear side from a viewpoint centered over the rear side.

**Left Side View or Left Elevational View.** Shows the left side from a viewpoint centered over the left side.

**Right Side View or Right Elevational View.** Shows the right side from a viewpoint centered over the right side.

**Top Side View or Plan View.** Shows the top side from a viewpoint centered over the top side.

**Bottom Side View.** Shows the bottom side from a viewpoint centered over the bottom side.

Orthogonal views are relatively difficult to understand because they do not convey a sense of depth, so the shapes of many surfaces appear ambiguous. Despite such a shortcoming, orthogonal views are commonly used in patent drawings because they are relatively simple to make. If one of the orthogonal views is considered alone, without the benefit of the other views, the true shape of the object cannot be deciphered. Such ambiguity is shown in Illustration 1.2. An object that appears as a rectangle in an orthogonal view may have many possible true shapes. Therefore, if an orthogonal view does not convey the shape of an object clearly enough, it should also be shown in one or more perspective views.

### Perspective Views

A perspective view is one that shows the three dimensions of an object on a two-dimensional surface; it is not orthogonal to or centered over any side. When the view angle is properly selected, it presents an object as it would be seen in real life by a casual observer. It conveys

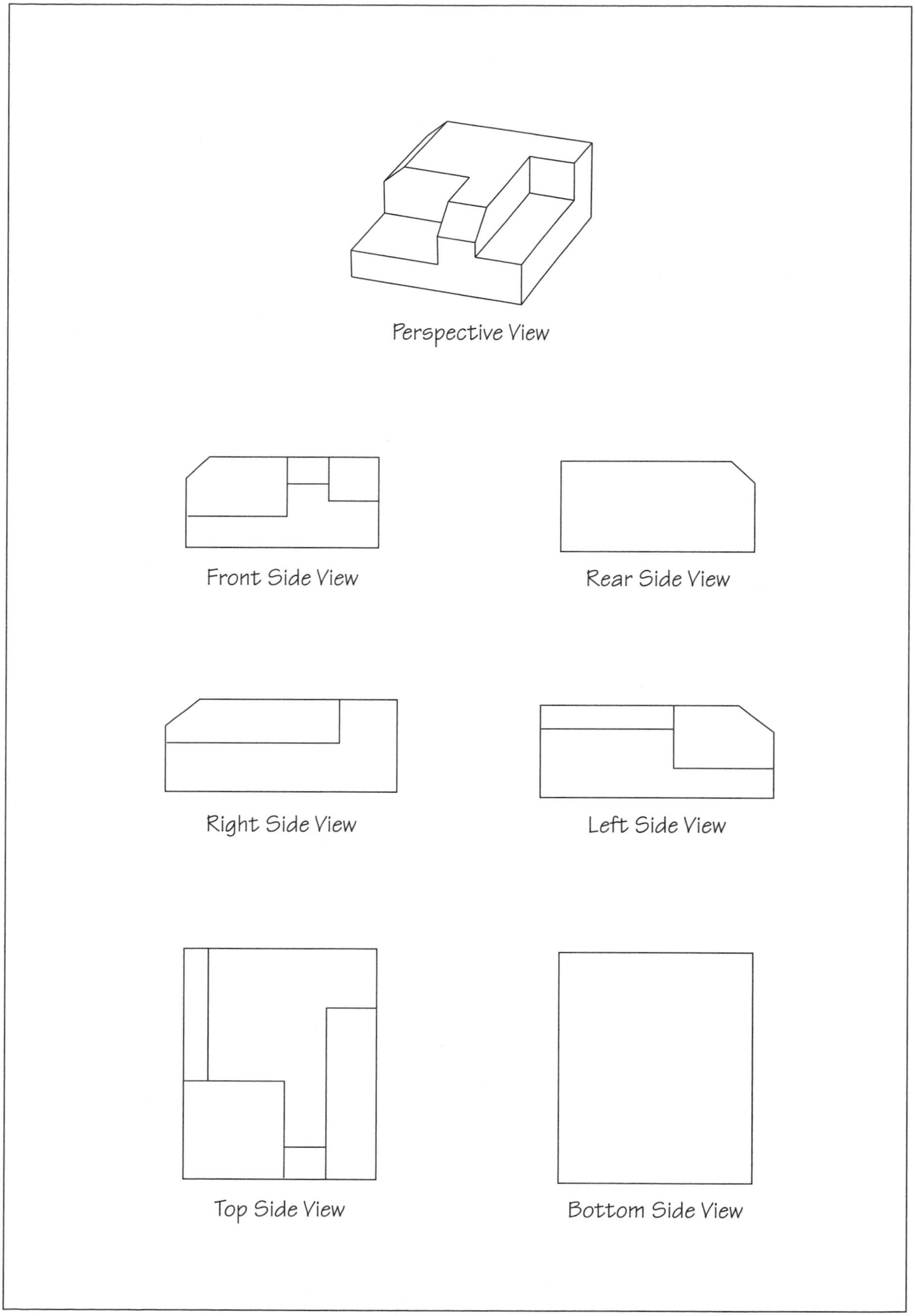

Perspective View

Front Side View

Rear Side View

Right Side View

Left Side View

Top Side View

Bottom Side View

**Illustration 1.1—Orthogonal Views**

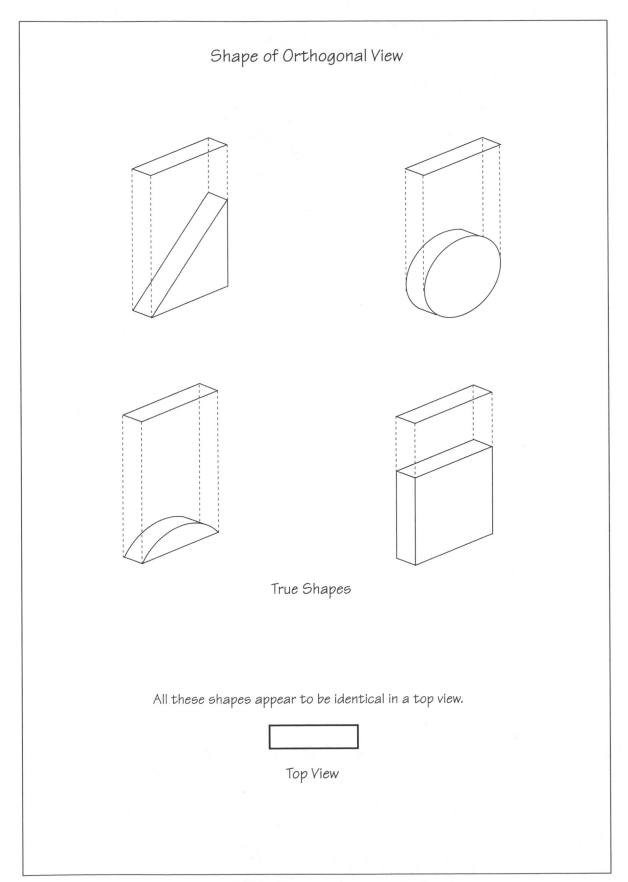

Shape of Orthogonal View

True Shapes

All these shapes appear to be identical in a top view.

Top View

**Illustration 1.2—Orthogonal View May Be Ambiguous**

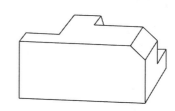

Front Perspective View

Rear Perspective View

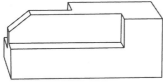

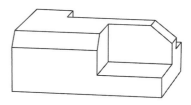

Right Perspective View

Left Perspective View

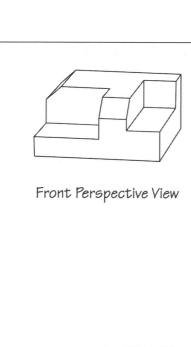

Top Perspective View

Bottom Perspective View

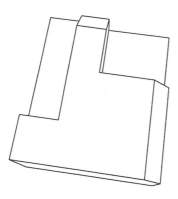

**Illustration 1.3—Perspective Views**

a good sense of depth, so that it is much easier to understand than orthogonal views. The special object of Illustration 1.1 is shown in typical perspective views in Illustration 1.3, which includes those described below.

**Front Perspective View.** Shows the front side somewhat angled away.

**Rear Perspective View.** Shows the rear side somewhat angled away.

**Right Perspective View.** Shows the right side somewhat angled away.

**Left Perspective View.** Shows the left side somewhat angled away.

**Top Perspective View.** Shows the top side somewhat angled away.

**Bottom Perspective View.** Shows the bottom side somewhat angled away.

## Variations of a Perspective View

If the two sides of an object are equally visible—for example, the top and front—then it may be called either a top perspective or a front perspective view. The view angle of any particular perspective view may be varied. Using the same special object of Illustration 1.1, some variations on the front perspective views are shown in Illustration 1.4, including those described below.

**Front Perspective View (from above).** Shows the front from a higher viewpoint off to one side.

**Front Perspective (from the same level).** Shows the front from a viewpoint off to one side, but at the same level. Such a view is almost as ambiguous as the front orthogonal view, so it is not recommended.

**Front Perspective (from below).** Shows the front from a lower viewpoint off to one side.

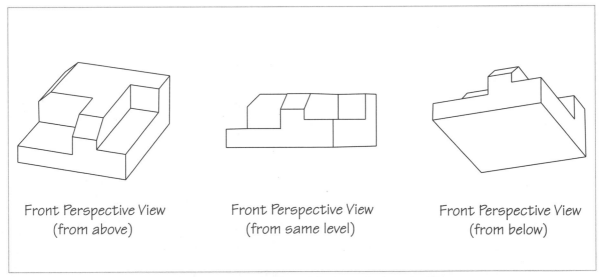

Front Perspective View
(from above)

Front Perspective View
(from same level)

Front Perspective View
(from below)

**Illustration 1.4—Variations of the Same Perspective View**

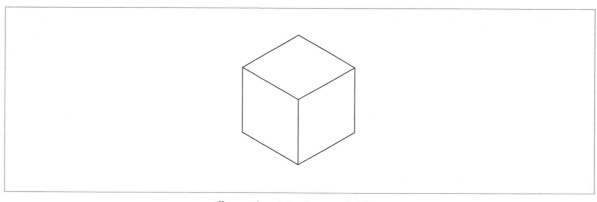

**Illustration 1.5—Isometric View**

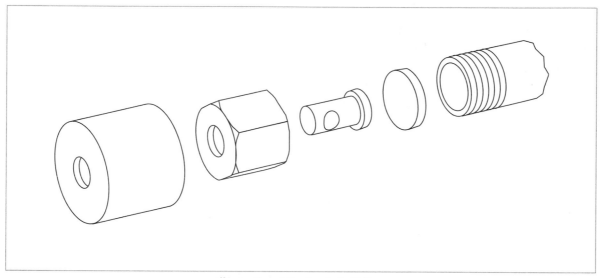

**Illustration 1.6—Exploded View**

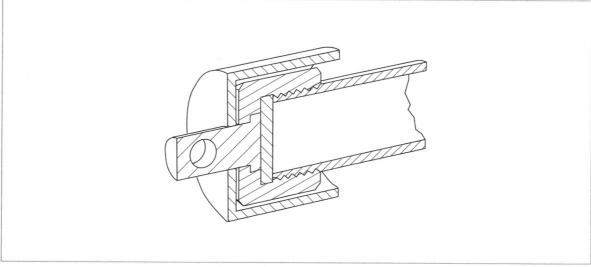

**Illustration 1.7—Sectional View**

One particular type of perspective view is the isometric (iso = equal; metric = measurement) view, from which the viewer's eyes or viewpoint is positioned exactly between three orthogonal views, as illustrated by the simple cube in Illustration 1.5.

Other types of drawing views include the following two.

**Exploded View.** The parts of a device can be disassembled and spread apart in space to show otherwise hidden features, as pictured in Illustration 1.6, a water pipe fitting. Exploded views may be orthogonal or perspective. For example, there can be a front exploded view, a side exploded view, and so on.

**Sectional View.** Part of an object can be sliced away to show interior structures. Sectional views may also be orthogonal or perspective. For illustration, there can be a front sectional view, a side sectional view, a front perspective sectional view, and so on. The view shown in Illustration 1.7 is a side perspective sectional view of the water pipe fitting of Illustration 1.6.

## Perspective Foreshortening

In real life, objects in the distance appear smaller than similar objects up close. The same principle also applies to a single, three-dimensional object: Its far end appears smaller than its near end, and its parallel edges appear to converge. The closer you are to the object, the greater the effect appears. To see the effect very clearly, put a long rectangular object, such as a toothpaste box, very close to your eyes. You will notice that its far end appears much smaller than its near end, and that its parallel edges appear to converge.

The technique of representing such an effect in a drawing is known as foreshortening. It is applied to perspective views to make them more realistic. The next time you go to a museum or look at an art book, compare earlier medieval paintings, which were done without foreshortening (it hadn't been invented yet!), to the later Renaissance paintings, which were done with foreshortening. You will see that the medieval paintings appear flat and somewhat cartoon-like, whereas Renaissance paintings are much more realistic representations of people and things.

The degree of foreshortening is inversely proportional to the viewing distance. That is, an object seen from a short distance is drawn with more foreshortening, and an object seen from a greater distance is drawn with less fore-shortening. Using the same toothpaste box, you can see that it appears highly foreshortened when it is very close to your eyes and not foreshortened at all when it is far away.

## No Foreshortening Versus Excessive Foreshortening

Illustration 1.8 shows a square box drawn without foreshortening, and also with different degrees of foreshortening. The box drawn without foreshortening represents its appearance as seen from a great distance. Its parallel edges are drawn as perfectly parallel lines, so this view is also known as a parallel view. Without foreshortening, the box actually appears slightly distorted.

The middle box, drawn with excessive fore-shortening, represents its appearance as seen from an extremely short viewing distance, such as when it is positioned right up against your eyes. Although excessive foreshortening causes the box to appear greatly distorted, it clearly shows how foreshortening is applied: The parallel edges of the box are drawn as con-verging lines that, if extended, will intersect at points known as "vanishing points." The vanishing points on the sides lie on the horizon (a horizontal line), and the central vanishing

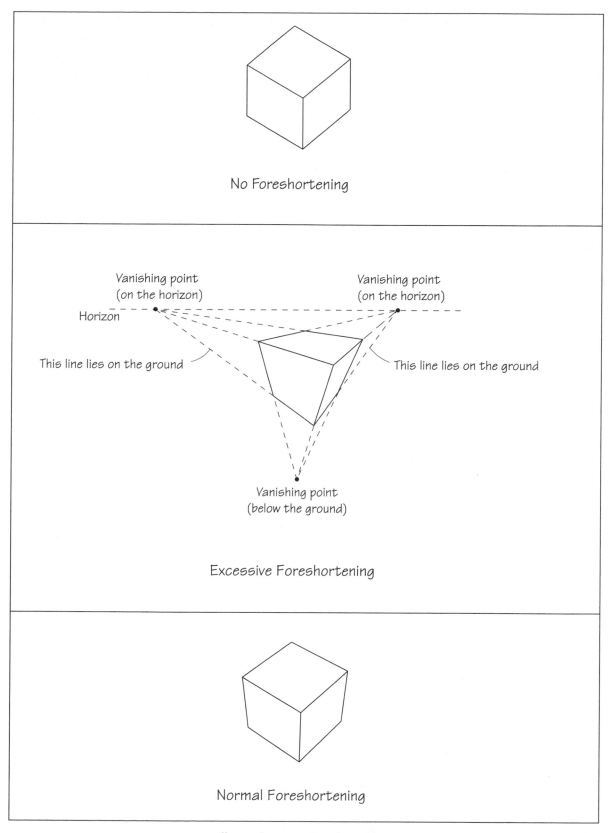

**Illustration 1.8—Foreshortening**

point lies below "ground level." In the illustration shown, the box is being seen from above.

## Realistic Foreshortening

The bottom box is most realistically illustrated with normal foreshortening, that is, a small degree of foreshortening, which represents the object as seen from a normal viewing distance. The parallel edges are drawn as slightly converging lines. The vanishing points of such slightly converging lines are far off the page, so they are not shown.

The rule of thumb is that the greater the foreshortening, the closer the vanishing points are positioned, and the lesser the foreshortening, the farther the vanishing points are positioned. A drawing without foreshortening has no vanishing points, because parallel edges are drawn as parallel lines, which do not converge.

Drawings done with normal foreshortening are the most realistic, but drawings done without foreshortening (parallel views) are perfectly acceptable for patent drawings. Foreshortening is a difficult technique to apply with pen and rulers, but as discussed in Chapter 3, it is extremely easy to apply with a computer. You can forego foreshortening in patent drawings, but you can make much more attractive marketing brochures if you use it.

## Drawing With Pen, Ruler, and Instruments

There are two methods for making patent drawings: the traditional or old way with pens and rulers; and the modern way, with a computer. A set of basic tools for the traditional method can be assembled relatively inexpensively, and making simple drawings is fairly easy. However, with pens and rulers, there is little room for mistake, because, except for very small marks,

it is very difficult to correct misplaced ink lines. Nevertheless, with careful planning of drawing positioning (layout) and great care in laying down ink lines, drawing with pens and rulers is still a viable technique. Some professional patent draftspersons still make drawings this way, but most now use computers.

## Necessary Tools

The necessary tools include pencils for preliminary sketches, ink drafting pens for drawing ink lines, rulers for making straight lines, triangles for making angled lines, templates for making certain standard shapes, compasses, curve rules for drawing curves, an optional drafting table, and high-quality ink drawing paper.

## Pen and Ruler Drawing Techniques

Pens and rulers may be used to make patent drawings in the ways described below.

**Drawing From Scratch.** You can draw an object by visualizing in detail what it should look like, carefully sketching that image on paper with a pencil, correcting it until it looks about right, and finally inking in the lines. Drawing from scratch requires some basic drawing skills. If you need to learn such skills, you can do some additional reading as suggested at the beginning of Chapter 2, or you can draw with a computer instead, which eliminates the need for traditional drawing skills.

**Tracing.** Tracing is much easier than drawing from scratch. An obvious method is to trace a photograph of an object that you wish to draw, as shown in Illustration 1.9. An actual, three-dimensional object can also be traced by using a device called a camera lucida, available at art supply stores, which projects an image of the object onto a drawing surface. As shown in Illustration 1.10, you may also

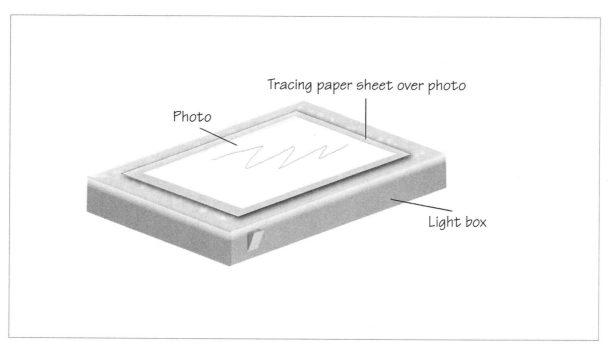

**Illustration 1.9—Tracing a Photo**

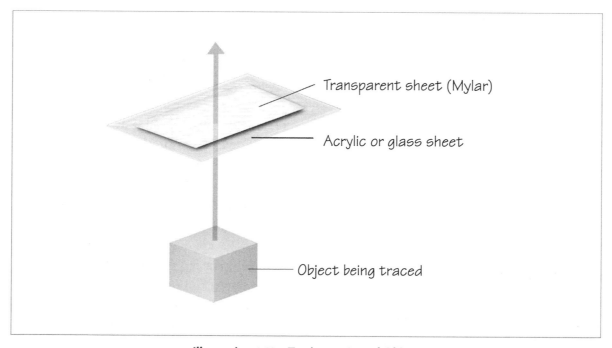

**Illustration 1.10—Tracing an Actual Object**

trace an actual object—again, we use a simple box to illustrate—by positioning a transparent drawing sheet on a transparent sheet of glass or acrylic, looking at the object through the glass, tracing the lines of the object on the drawing sheet, and photocopying the tracing onto a sheet of paper. This technique is discussed in greater detail in Chapter 2. Tracing requires very little skill other than a steady hand.

**Drawing to Scale.** You can also draw by scaling —that is, reducing or enlarging—the dimensions of an object to fit on a sheet of paper and draw the lines with exact scale dimensions. For example, if an object has a height of 20 inches and a width of 12 inches, you can reduce those dimensions by 50%, so that you would draw it with a height of 10 inches and a width of 6 inches on paper, as shown in Illustration 1.11. All other dimensions of the object are scaled accordingly for the drawing. One easy way to scale an object is to photograph it and then reduce or enlarge the print using a photocopier. Making a drawing that looks right is easier by drawing to scale than by drawing based on only a mental image.

The techniques and tools for drawing with pens and rulers are explained in greater detail in Chapter 2.

# Drawing With a Computer

CAD (computer-aided drafting or design) has been around since the early 1970s. When we refer to CAD (sometimes known as CADD), we're talking about software programs used by inventors, architects, and other design professionals to visualize inventions, products, tools, machinery, and other devices. CAD programs provide a way of modeling these products in 2D or 3D perspectives. Originally, these programs were affordable only to design professionals, but nowadays, powerful CAD

software programs are within the price range of just about anyone who owns a computer. In addition, modern CAD software is easier to use than earlier versions.

CAD allows you to produce accurate drawings even if you consider yourself to have little or no artistic ability. In fact, no drawing skills in the traditional sense are needed at all. Furthermore, CAD enables you to correct mistakes as easily as a word processor enables you to edit words in a document. Even if you discover a mistake after you print a drawing, you can easily correct the mistake and print a new copy. To use CAD, you will need some computer skills, but if you know how to type letters on your computer, you can easily learn how to draw with it.

## Equipment

You will need a computer, an ink jet or laser printer, a CAD program, an optional scanner, and an optional digital camera.

## Computer Drawing Techniques

A computer may be used to make patent drawings in the ways described below.

**Tracing.** If you have a scanner, you can scan a photograph of an object, import (load) the scanned image into a CAD program, and trace it easily, as shown in Illustration 1.12, a photo of an aircraft. (Although difficult to see in a black-and-white book, the black outlines are the tracing lines.) If you have a digital camera, you can take a photograph of the object and download (transfer) the image directly into your computer through a cable, without having to print and scan the photograph. Once it is in your computer, tracing the image is very easy. Since you use a mouse instead of an ink pen, you don't even need a steady hand.

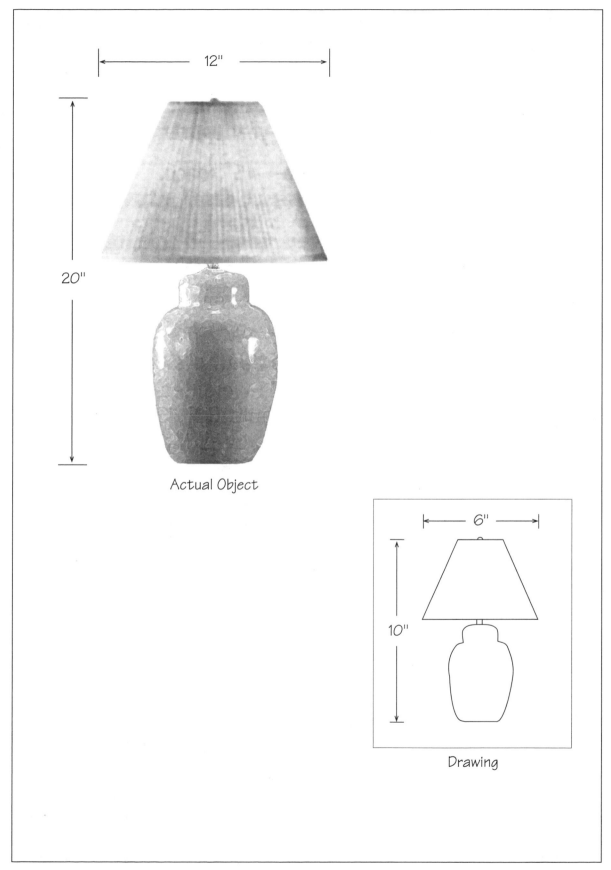

Actual Object

Drawing

**Illustration 1.11—Drawing to Scale**

**Illustration 1.12—Tracing a Photo on a Computer**

**Drawing From Scratch.** A CAD program will enable you to construct an accurate, three-dimensional (3D) representation of your invention within the computer. A 3D model is typically made by using and modifying basic geometric building blocks, such as boxes, cylinders, planes, and custom-defined shapes. You may create each part with specific dimensions, or you may simply draw a shape that looks about right. You can easily rotate the finished model to see it from any angle. You can also easily zoom in or out to adjust the viewing distance, which is equivalent to adjusting the degree of foreshortening (in CAD, the term "viewing distance" is used instead of "foreshortening"). Once you are satisfied with the view, you can print it as a line drawing (a drawing of dark lines on a light background). Therefore, you can make wonderful looking drawings with a computer, even if you consider yourself to be a terrible artist.

These techniques and tools are explained in greater detail in Chapter 3.

## Using a Camera

Almost everyone has some degree of familiarity with photography. Obviously, a camera can take an accurate photograph or "drawing" of an object. While photographs may no longer be submitted as patent drawings (except in special circumstances that will be explained in Chapter 4), they can be converted into suitable patent line drawings by tracing them. To do so, you must have a basic understanding of photographic lighting and exposure.

## Equipment

To take accurate photographs, you will need a digital (preferred) or 35 mm film camera. Your camera should have optical zoom and macro (close up) capabilities. You will also need a tripod.

## Taking Pictures

There are mountains of books on photographic techniques, and cameras typically come with booklets on basic techniques, so we will not go into great detail. We will cover a few simple techniques in Chapter 4 that will enable you to take pictures good enough for tracing (and for filing as patent drawings when permitted).

## Tracing Pictures

A photograph can be converted into a line drawing by putting a piece of paper over it and tracing it with a pencil, or by scanning it into a computer and tracing it with a CAD program.

## Summary

As you can see, there are two ways to make patent drawings. If you favor one of them, you may go directly to the chapter that discusses it in detail. Otherwise, a reading of the following chapters will help you select the technique that is right for you. ●

# Drawing With Pen, Ruler, and Instruments

This chapter provides general instructions for making drawings with pen, ruler, and instruments. However, it is beyond the scope of this book to go into great detail on basic drawing skills, which are already covered in many other books. The advantage of making drawings with pens and rulers is that the tools are relatively inexpensive. The drawback is that, because ink marks cannot be easily corrected, there is little room for making mistakes. If you can be very careful in laying down ink lines, drawing manually is still a viable technique.

### Additional Reading

For basic drawing skills, we suggest:

- *Basic Drawing Techniques*, by Greg Albert and Rachel Wolf (North Light Books)
- *Keys to Drawing*, by Bert Dodson (North Light Books)
- *The New Drawing on the Right Side of the Brain*, by Betty Edwards (HarperCollins), and
- *Learn Cartooning and Drawing the Easy Way*, by Bruce Blitz (Art Products, Inc.).

## Necessary Tools and Supplies

All the traditional drawing tools and supplies you will need can be found at an art supply store. If there is no such store in your area, you can request catalogs or shop online at art supply outlets, such as Blick art supplies (www.dickblick.com) and Flax Art & Design (www.flaxart.com).

Generally, a drawing of a physical object requires the greatest number of tools because of its complex lines, whereas a drawing of graphical symbols, such as flowcharts and electrical schematics, requires fewer tools because of the simple, regular shapes. Usually, you will not need a complete set of drawing tools; what you need depends on what you want to draw and how you want to draw it. You can determine the tools and supplies you need after you have read this chapter. You also may try drawing in pencil after reading this chapter to see if you can produce satisfactory drawings before you invest in new tools and supplies.

## Essential Tools and Supplies

The following tools and supplies are essential for traditional, manual drawing techniques:

- **Pencils, either wood or mechanical, for making light, erasable sketches.** A soft lead pencil, such as 2B, is usable as long you draw lightly with it. A medium lead pencil, such as HB or F, is probably more suitable. A hard lead pencil, such as H or above, is generally not suitable, because too much pressure is needed to make a visible line, and the pressure will tend to score grooves in the paper.

- **A soft or kneaded eraser for erasing pencil marks without harming paper.** A good brand of soft eraser is Staedtler, by Mars Plastic. Soft erasers are easier to handle, but they leave debris on the drawing that must be brushed away. Kneaded erasers, which are usually available only at art supply stores, are pliable and do not leave debris. They must be kneaded, like dough, to push in the dirtied parts and bring the clean inner parts to the surface. You may also wish to get an electric eraser, which is handy for erasing long ink lines.

- **Technical pens for drawing ink lines.** Technical pens are ink pens made specifically for precision ink drawings. They come in different sizes; you should have at least the 0.13 mm and 0.25 mm sizes. Well-known brands include Koh-I-Noor Rapidograph and Rotring Rapidograph, which cost about

$20 each. Alternatively, good quality, extra fine to medium point, felt-tip or plastic-tip pens, which are only about $2 to $3 each, may be used. A good brand is Tech-Liner Pens by Alvin. Do not use ballpoint pens, rollerball pens, or fountain pens, because they do not make lines that are sharp and black enough to meet Patent and Trademark Office (PTO) standards.

- **Nonclogging black ink for the pens, unless you use the prefilled models.** Some good brands include Higgins Black Magic and Rapidograph Ultradraw.

- **White correction fluid with a pen-type applicator.** A good brand is Pentel Quick Dry correction fluid. We recommend the pen type, rather than the brush applicator because the fluid in a pen-type applicator is less likely to thicken or dry out.

- **A drafting board with a built-in parallel ruler and protractor.** A drawing board can be plain or can have a built-in ruler that slides in a parallel fashion up and down or left and right on the board. This enables you to accurately draw parallel lines, vertical lines, horizontal lines, or lines at any other angle. A board with a built-in ruler is practically an essential tool. Rotring sells an inexpensive model (about $60) under the trademark Koh-I-Noor Portable Drafting System. Alternatively, a T-square (a T-shaped device for sliding up and down or left and right along the edges of a plain, rectangular drafting board) may be used. You may also dispense with the drafting board by using the corner of a table with a smooth surface to guide the T-square. If you use a T-square, you will also need a set of triangles and a protractor for drawing lines of different angles. The overall cost of assembling these components may not

be lower than the Koh-I-Noor Portable Drafting System, depending on the quality of the components, and they are definitely more difficult to use, because you have to keep the T-square and the triangle aligned properly while you control the pen.

- **Lettering guides (templates) for writing text.** To print neat text, ⅛" and ¼" letter guides are available for use with a drawing pen. Alternatively, transfer type (rub-on lettering) of a simple typeface or style in the same sizes may also be used. The guides cost about $5 each, and transfer type costs about $13 per sheet.

- **Masking tape.** To tape down drawing paper on the drafting board, use only tape that does not damage paper. Post-It® brand or regular masking tape will do.

- **Parchment tracing paper for tracing photographs or sketches.** Any brand will do.

- **Vellum or Mylar for finished drawings.** Vellum is a tough, matte (frosted), translucent paper that takes ink very well, and can be repeatedly erased without damage. Mylar is a very tough plastic film; use the kind that has a matte rather than glossy surface. A proper ink drawing paper must be used, because other papers will cause the ink to feather—that is, seep between the paper fibers—and spread out. Vellum costs about $18 for 100 sheets. Since it is difficult to erase lines on bristol board, we do not recommend using it for finished patent drawings. Always keep the originals of your drawings and send high quality photocopies on bond paper to the PTO.

- **An electric eraser.** To erase ink lines, a rotary electric eraser with a lightly abrasive eraser works best. About $15 to $60.

## Additional Tools Recommended for Drawing Physical Objects

In addition to the tools listed above, the following are useful for drawing physical objects:

- **An engineer's triangular scale (a six-sided ruler) for drawing to scale.** One side of the triangular scale is marked with full-size inches with ten divisions each, and other sides are marked with ½, ⅓, ¼, ⅕, and ⅙ scale inches. For example, on the ½ scale side, each inch mark is ½ the size of an actual inch. Scales are as low as $5 each.

- **Various circle templates (plastic sheets with holes) for drawing circles of different, fixed sizes.** These cost about $7 each.

- **Various ellipse templates for drawing ellipses of different, fixed sizes and shapes.** An ellipse is the shape a circle takes when seen at an angle. These cost about $7 each.

- **Triangles with beveled edges.** Triangles (30° and 45°) with beveled edges are necessary for preventing ink from seeping under them. They are as low as $4 each.

- **A compass capable of holding a technical pen for drawing circles and arcs of custom sizes.** Such a compass costs about $25.

- **An ellipsograph for drawing ellipses of custom sizes and shapes.** Although it will enable you to draw an ellipse with the exact shape desired, an ellipsograph is more difficult to use than an ellipse template, because it has to be carefully adjusted and positioned to get the desired results. It has reportedly been discontinued by the manufacturer, but some vendors may still have them in stock.

- **Various French curves (templates with many curved edges of fixed shapes) for drawing uneven curves.** French curves require a lot of practice to use, because it is often difficult to find an edge with the desired curvature (about $8 for a set).

- **A flexible (adjustable) curve for drawing custom-shaped curves.** A flexible curve or spline (about $6) may be used instead of a French curve, but you will have to adjust it every time you need a different shape.

- **A transparent grid overlay.** This is a transparent plastic sheet with a grid etched on it for plotting difficult shapes.

- **Preprinted grid paper.** Available in various sizes, including inch, metric, isometric, and perspective, this is used under a sheet of tracing paper to serve as a guide.

## Additional Templates for Drawing Graphical Symbols

To draw graphical symbols, you may want to have one or more symbol templates. They are available for a variety of specialized symbols, such as electronics, architectural, and flowchart symbols.

## Additional Tools for Tracing Photographs or Sketches

For tracing photographs or sketches, you may want these additional tools:

- **A light box.** A box with internal light and translucent white top (about $80).

- **Clear polyester film.**

The pantograph (a mechanical parallelogram device) is also available for tracing drawings. It may be adjusted to make a drawing at various scales to the original. However, it produces very inaccurate results, so it is not recommended. A photocopier may be used to make enlargements or reductions much faster and more accurately.

## Additional Tools for Tracing Actual Objects

You may want these additional tools for tracing actual objects:

- **A camera lucida.** This clever device includes a lens mounted on an adjustable arm for projecting an image of an actual object onto a drawing surface at selectable magnification or reduction, so that the image size on the paper may be adjusted. Interestingly, this device was invented back in 1807. It is available at Flax Art & Design for several hundred dollars. It is relatively difficult to use. (See Illustration 2.5.)

- **A homemade, direct-view tracing device that includes a 12" × 24" sheet of ⅛" thick transparent acrylic or Plexiglas, and a device for supporting the transparent sheet above the object being traced.** The acrylic sheet is available at plastic supply stores, such as Tap Plastics (www.tapplastics.com). Avoid using glass, which may break and cause injuries. There is no commercially available supporting device suitable for this purpose, so you will have to create your own with your inventive ingenuity. Below, we provide some suggested solutions.

- **Clear polyester film.** This is for use with the homemade, direct-view tracing device (not the camera lucida, which projects an image onto paper).

## Total Cost of Tools

The cost of a set of tools and supplies may range from as little as $100 to several hundred dollars, depending on your particular needs and how frugal you are. Note that some simple CAD (computer aided drafting) programs are free while more complex CAD programs cost several hundred dollars. If you already have a computer, you may want to read Chapter 3, which deals with computerized drafting, to see if you prefer to use the computer instead. If you do not have a computer, then drawing with pens and rulers is the most economical way to go.

# Basic Drawing Rules and Techniques

Everyone planning to make a patent drawing with pens and rulers should review the rules and techniques described in this section.

## A List of Rules and Techniques

To produce good drawings, you will need to apply the following basic rules and techniques:

- Always sketch a drawing lightly in pencil first, then apply ink lines over the final pencil marks.

- All ink lines should be drawn with the aid of guides, such as rulers, templates, and French curves. Use freehand drawing only when there is no alternative.

- Position the pen substantially vertically, and apply even pressure when moving it for a smooth and even line. Do not tilt the pen when you move it; otherwise the line width will be uneven.

- Avoid going over a line for a second pass; otherwise the line will become too thick or uneven due to the slightly changed position of the pen on the second pass.

- Position the pen so that the point of its tip does not touch the edge of rulers and other guides, or the ink will touch and spread under the guides.

- After drawing a line, pull or lift the guide straight up without crossing over the line to avoid smearing the ink.

- Wait patiently until ink lines dry completely before putting anything over them, erasing pencil marks near them, or erasing misplaced ink lines; otherwise you will smear the ink. Generally, ink takes a few seconds to a minute to dry completely. Look closely at the ink lines; if they are shiny, they are still wet.

- Avoid erasing ink lines as much as possible, because erasing roughens the paper. Subsequent ink lines drawn over the roughened area will feather or bleed out. If you do have to erase ink lines, use an electric eraser *very lightly*, taking a long time and repeated passes to erase the ink lines.

- Use white correction fluid for covering unwanted ink marks. Make sure the ink is dry before applying the correction fluid. Dab the fluid on quickly and sufficiently so you don't have to go over the same area again, because that tends to roughen the fluid as it dries. This surface may not take ink well and may show up as blotches in photocopies. Do not rub the fluid on, because this may mix the ink with it.

- Lines that meet to form sharp corners must touch precisely without overlap, as shown in Illustration 2.1.

- Rounded corners should be created by drawing the curved segment first, then drawing the straight lines from the ends of the curved segment, as shown in Illustration 2.2.

- Erase pencil marks by holding down the paper with one hand, and stroking an eraser along the paper away from the hand holding the paper. Do not stroke the eraser back and forth, because—unless the paper is secured all around—the eraser will push the paper toward the hand holding it and wrinkle it.

- Make full use of the space on each sheet of paper to make a drawing as large as necessary to show all details clearly.

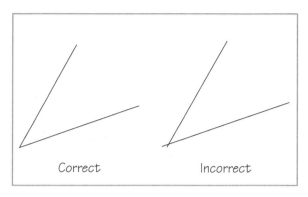

**Illustration 2.1—Lines Forming Corners**

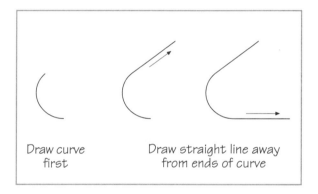

**Illustration 2.2—Drawing Rounded Corners**

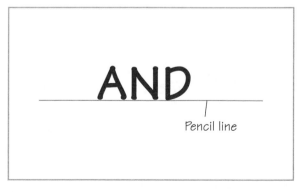

**Illustration 2.3—Applying Lettering**

- Unless you are an expert calligrapher, always use a lettering set to write text, or use transfer type for applying lettering to drawings. If you use a lettering set, use a pencil line for aligning the letters, as shown in Illustration 2.3. Do not use a pencil line for aligning transfer type, because the line cannot be erased later without also rubbing off the letters. Misplaced transfer type may be lifted off with tape, but be careful not to damage the paper. Be careful not to rub off the letters after they are applied.

- Do everything with great care and patience.

## Practice, Practice, Practice

If you are unfamiliar with doing high-quality ink drawings, you should not make your drawing project your first ink-drawing experience. If you do, you will make mistakes right from the start, get discouraged, and give up. Instead, you should practice drawing basic shapes—such as straight lines, rectangles, circles, and corners—with the techniques presented above, so that you become familiar with the tools and medium

(ink and paper). Reading one of the books recommended at the beginning of the chapter will be helpful. Next, you should practice drawing more complex shapes, such as the more difficult portions of the drawing you ultimately want to do. By becoming familiar with the tools and techniques first, you will avoid becoming discouraged before you start your project.

## Tracing Photographs and Objects

You can produce accurate drawings with relative ease by either tracing photographs of an object, or by tracing the actual object.

## Tracing Photographs

To trace a photograph or other printed graphics, follow these steps:

1. Take close-ups of the object. It should appear as large as possible in the photos. Make 4" × 6" or larger prints, so that the image of the object is large enough to produce the right

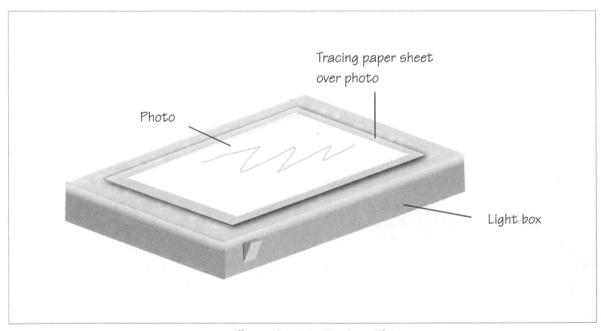

**Illustration 2.4—Tracing a Photo**

sized drawing. See Chapter 4 for details on how to take suitable photographs.

2. Tape the photograph on a light box and tape a piece of vellum over it, as shown in Illustration 2.4.

3. Trace the photograph very carefully and lightly with a pencil. Avoid making dark lines or pressing too hard and scribing grooves in the paper.

4. Mount the paper on a drafting board, ink over the pencil lines, and erase the pencil marks. Always draw ink lines with the aid of rulers and templates. When inking circles, ovals, or curves, select a template that most closely matches the shape desired.

5. After the ink is completely dry, erase any pencil marks that remain visible outside the ink lines.

## Tracing an Object With a Camera Lucida

To trace an actual object with a camera lucida, follow these steps:

1. Mount the arm on a table, and position the lens over a sheet of paper, as shown in Illustration 2.5.

2. Position the object on the table.

3. Look through the lens at the paper with one eye, and adjust the positioning of the lens and the object until an image of the object appears on the paper.

4. Adjust the distance of the object, or change the lens to adjust the image size on the paper.

5. Trace the image lightly with a pencil. You may trace freehand or with the aid of rulers and templates. Keep your head steady to

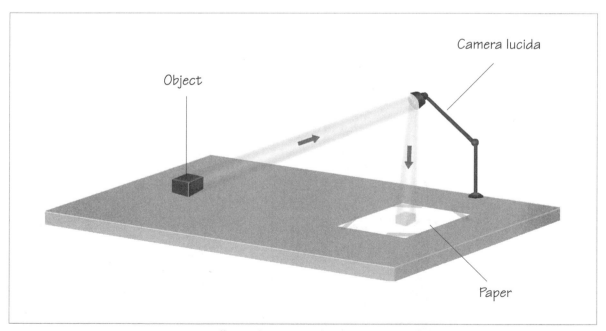

**Illustration 2.5—Using a Camera Lucida**

maintain the image's position on the paper at all times. Every time you move your head away from the lens and go back later, you must realign the image with the lines on the paper.

6. After you finish tracing, mount the paper on a drafting board and ink over the pencil lines. Always draw ink lines with the aid of rulers and templates. When inking circles, ovals, or curves, select templates that most closely match the shapes desired, or use an adjustable curve. If you trace freehand, the pencil lines will be somewhat crooked, so you should apply the ink lines for a best fit.

7. After the ink is completely dry, erase any stray pencil marks that remain visible outside the ink lines.

### TIP

**Tracing with the camera lucida is relatively difficult,** because you must keep your head very still while your hand moves. Tracing a photograph is much easier.

## Tracing an Actual Object With a Direct-View Device

To trace an actual object with a direct-view device, as discussed above, follow these steps:

1. Position the object on the ground, and orient it for a suitable view (front, side, top, and so on.) when seen from above. Use tape, blocks, modeling clay, earthquake wax, or whatever is suitable to fix it in the desired position, as shown in Illustration 2.6.

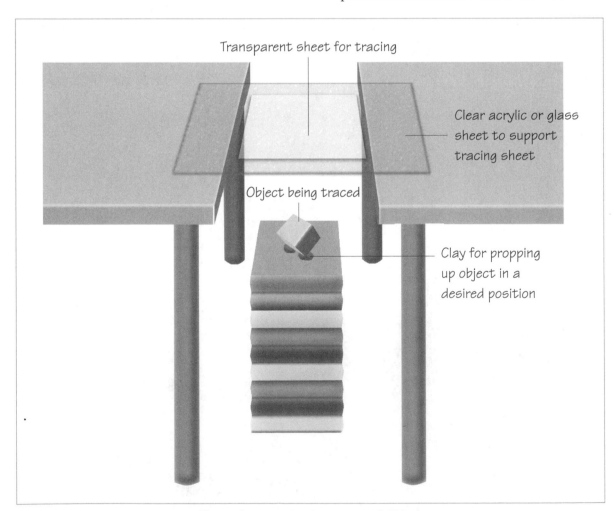

Transparent sheet for tracing

Clear acrylic or glass sheet to support tracing sheet

Object being traced

Clay for propping up object in a desired position

**Illustration 2.6—Tracing an Actual Object**

2. Tape a sheet of polyester film on a sheet of transparent acrylic.

3. Position the acrylic sheet over the object and adjust the height or distance of the sheet so that the object fits within the desired drawing area of the polyester film. There is no commercially available device for supporting the acrylic sheet for this purpose, so you will have to use your ingenuity to devise a solution. One possibility is to support the acrylic sheet between two tables of identical height (or in the gap made when the leaf is removed from a pull-apart table), and position the model below the acrylic sheet (Illustration 2.6). The object can be lifted off the ground with a stack of magazines or encyclopedias to adjust its distance from the acrylic sheet. Another possibility is to support the sheet between the heads of two camera tripods, which can be easily adjusted to support the sheet at a range of different heights. For a larger object that requires a greater distance to fit within the tracing film, the acrylic sheet may be positioned vertically and spaced horizontally from the model. This may be done on a long table, as shown in Illustration 2.7, or with tripods, as shown in Illustration 2.8.

4. Close one eye. Position yourself so that you see the object within the desired part of the polyester film. Select two opposite corners of the object and mark them. Whenever you are tracing, you must keep the same

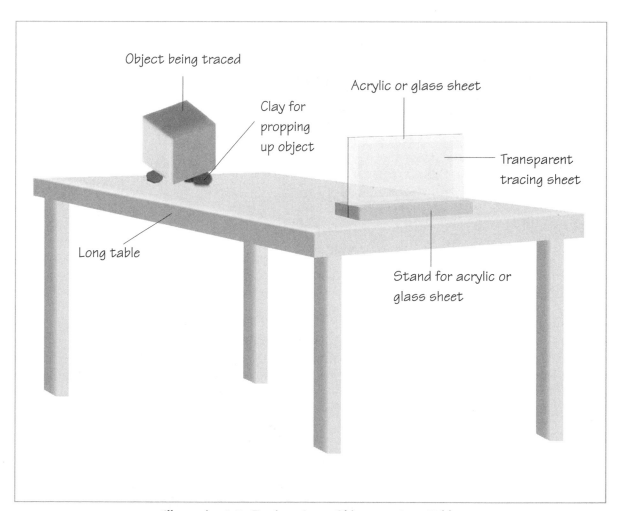

Object being traced

Clay for propping up object

Acrylic or glass sheet

Transparent tracing sheet

Long table

Stand for acrylic or glass sheet

**Illustration 2.7—Tracing a Large Object on a Long Table**

eye closed and see with the other eye, or parallax will cause substantial errors in the drawing.

5. Trace the model very carefully with a pencil. You must hold your head steady to keep the object lined up with the marks when you are tracing. Whenever you move away from—and later come back to—the model, you must adjust your head's distance and lateral position to line up the object with the marks again.

6. After tracing is completed on the polyester film, tape it on a light box, tape a sheet of vellum over it, as shown in Illustration

2.4, and lightly trace the drawing onto the vellum with a pencil. Be careful not to press too hard and scribe grooves into the paper.

7. Mount the vellum on a drafting board, and ink over the pencil lines. Always draw ink lines with the aid of rulers or templates. When inking circles, ovals, or curves, select templates that most closely match the shapes desired. If you trace freehand, the pencil lines will be somewhat crooked, so you should apply the ink lines for a best fit.

8. After the ink is completely dry, erase any pencil marks that remain visible outside the ink lines.

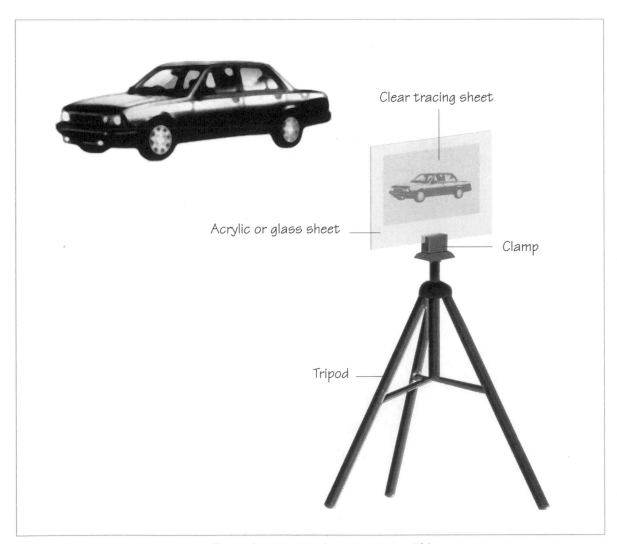

**Illustration 2.8—Tracing a Very Large Object**

**TIP**

Although it is a very inexpensive technique, tracing with the direct-view device is about as difficult as using the camera lucida, because you must also keep your head very still while your hand moves. Tracing a photograph is much easier, but relatively more expensive.

## Enlarging or Reducing a Tracing

In patent drawings, each figure should be large enough to show essential details clearly without crowding, but should not be unnecessarily large. If your tracing is not of a suitable size, you may resize it with the following method:

1. Enlarge or reduce the tracing with a photocopier. You can enlarge an enlargement or reduce a reduction to make even bigger or smaller copies, respectively.

2. Mount the photocopy on a light box and mount another sheet of paper over it.

3. Trace the photocopy lightly in pencil.

4. Mount the second tracing on a drafting board and ink over the lines. Always draw ink lines with the aid of rulers or templates. When inking circles, ovals, or curves, select templates that most closely match the shapes desired. If you trace freehand, the pencil lines will be somewhat crooked, so you should apply the ink lines for a best fit.

5. After the ink is completely dry, erase any stray pencil marks that remain visible outside the ink lines.

## Drawing From Your Imagination

If the object you wish to draw does not exist, you cannot base the drawing on its actual shape as you can when tracing and will have to base the drawing solely on a mental image.

## Sketching the Figures

To create a drawing from your imagination, sketch the figures as follows:

1. Use a sheet of vellum, and start by lightly sketching a rough shape of the object you have in mind, as shown in Illustrations 2.9 and 2.10. For long objects, such as airplanes, human limbs, or table legs, start by drawing centerlines, then add the outline around the centerlines. Don't worry about the details. Concentrate on getting the proportions and perspective right. If you fuss with the details, you will lose sight of the overall proportion and shape of the object and come up with something distorted. The pencil marks must be light enough so that they can be completely erased later.

2. Sketch the major features of the object to refine the drawing a little more.

3. Fine-tune the lines and add small details.

This technique is akin to seeing an image through a pair of binoculars that are initially out of focus for you. At first, you can see only a rough shape, but as you adjust the focus, the image slowly becomes sharper to reveal more of its shape, until the focus is perfectly adjusted and you can see all the details clearly.

## Study Similar Objects for Clues

If you have trouble making a drawing look right, study an object—or a drawing or photo of an object—that is shaped similarly to the one you wish to draw, or the portion of the object you are drawing. For example, if you have trouble drawing a box in perspective, find a similar box, position it in the same view angle that you are drawing, and study its lines to get an idea of what they should look like, as shown in Illustration 2.11. Photos and drawings of many objects can be found in a visual dictionary

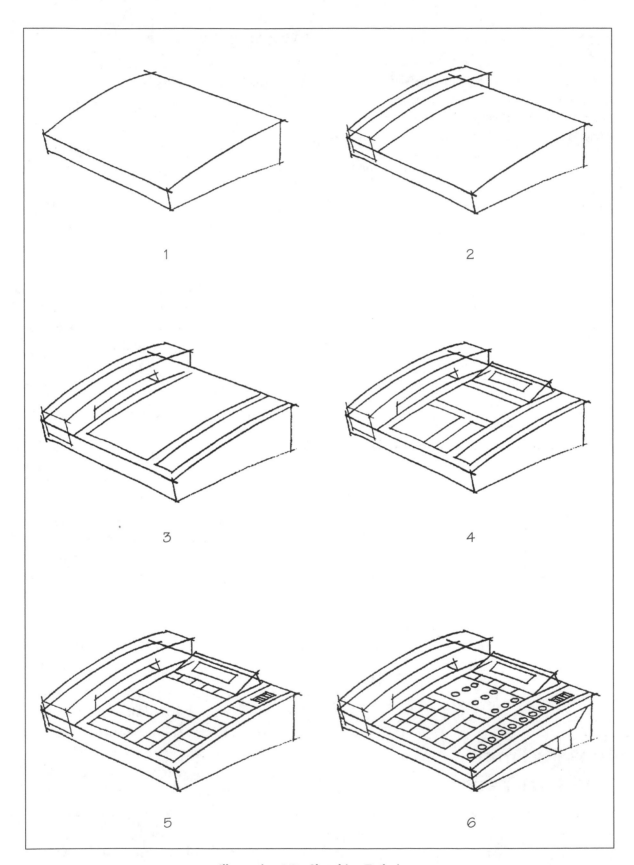

**Illustration 2.9—Sketching Technique**

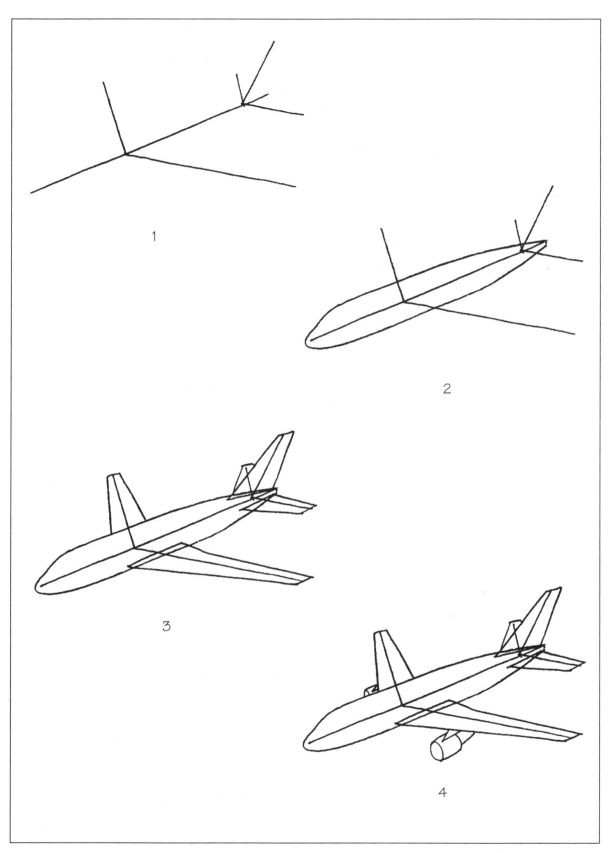

**Illustration 2.10—Sketching Technique**

such as *The Firefly Visual Dictionary* by Corbeil and Archambault (Firefly).

When studying the lines, look for qualities such as their angles relative to the vertical or horizontal, angles relative to other lines on the same object, and the relative length of each line with respect to other lines on the same object. If you are careful in making these observations, you should be able to create satisfactory drawings. However, if you are still having a great deal of difficulty, you may consider making a model and tracing it, as described above, or using a computer. (See Chapter 3 on drawing with a computer.)

Since patent drawings are not art, but technical illustrations, your drawings do not have to be artistically perfect or beautiful. However, they do have to be reasonably accurate and communicative in depicting the structure of the invention.

## Page Layout

Each figure (drawing) should be big enough to show all of its details clearly. If several different figures are still small enough, they should be placed on the same sheet of paper to avoid using too many sheets. If you know the drawings will fit on the same sheet, but you have difficulty positioning them during the sketching process, you can draw them on different sheets, cut them out, paste them on one sheet, and then make a photocopy. If the figures are too large to fit on one sheet, just use as many additional sheets as necessary.

## Ink in the Lines

After the sketch is complete, trace over the pencil lines with ink. You should always use rulers and templates to guide the ink pen, and avoid drawing anything freehand as much as possible. When you are sure the ink is completely dry (the ink is still wet if it is shiny), carefully erase any stray pencil marks that remain visible outside the ink lines. If you are impatient and start erasing too soon, the eraser will smear the wet ink lines.

## Trace Over the Sketch If Necessary

A sketch is sometimes so rough that its lines are each formed by a jumble of pencil marks, so that the exact placement of the final ink line is unclear, as shown in Illustration 2.12. Instead of risking a permanent mistake by inking over a rough sketch, you can put a fresh piece of paper on it, and trace the sketch carefully with a pencil on a light box. The tracing should be much clearer, so that you can apply ink lines on it with confidence.

# Drawing to Scale

Although the PTO does not require that drawings be scaled proportionately, it is best to do so. Doing the drawings is much easier if you have some idea about the dimensions of the object you wish to draw, because such dimensions will enable you to draw the object with the correct proportions. If you have the object available, you can use a ruler to measure all of the critical dimensions and a protractor to measure the angles of angled lines and surfaces. But then again, if the object is available, tracing it is easier. If you don't have the object, you can create some estimated measurements.

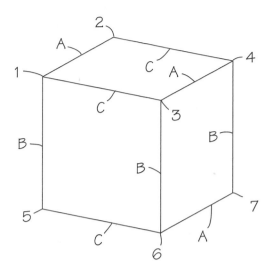

Note that:

Lines A are about 30 degrees above horizontal and parallel to each other.

Lines B are vertical and parallel to each other.

Lines C are about 10 degrees below horizontal and parallel to each other.


Point 1 is positioned about midway between Points 3 and 4 along the vertical direction.

Point 2 is positioned about midway between Points 1 and 3 along the horizontal direction.

Point 4 is positioned about midway between Points 1 and 2 along the vertical direction.

Point 6 is positioned about midway between Points 2 and 4 along the horizontal direction.

**Illustration 2.11—Studying Objects for Clues**

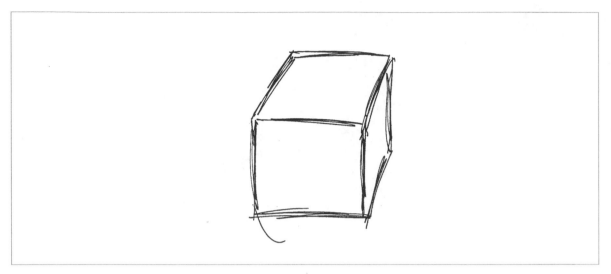

**Illustration 2.12—Rough Sketch Makes Final Line Placement Unclear**

## Use Metric Measurements If Possible

If you can immediately tell whether 2⁵⁄₁₆" or 2¹¹⁄₃₂" is longer, you are very familiar with the U.S./English measurement system (inches, feet, and so on). Otherwise, you should use metric units, such as millimeters (mm), centimeters (cm), and meters (m), which are based on multiples of ten. For example, 10 mm equals 1 cm, 100 cm equals 1 m.

With the metric system, it is immediately apparent to anyone that, for example, 6.24 cm is longer than 6.22 cm. Also, the millimeter, which is about the thickness of a dime, is a fine enough measurement for most tasks. The centimeter is equal to 0.39 inch, which is roughly equal to the diameter of a typical pen. As long as you remember visually how long the millimeter and the centimeter are, adapting yourself to work with the metric system is easy.

## Converting Dimensions With a Scale Rule

Drawing to scale is easy with a scale rule. For example, if an object is 46 cm (18.1") tall and 20 cm (7.9") wide, you can use a 1:2 scale rule to draw it at half its actual size, so that it is about 23 cm (9") tall and 10 cm (4") wide to fit on a sheet of letter-size paper.

## Converting Dimensions Manually

If there is no suitable scale rule for an object —that is, if you need to reduce or enlarge it at some odd scale—you can convert the dimensions manually. For example, if an object is 30 cm (11.8") tall, and you want to scale it down to about 23 cm (9") tall to fit on a sheet of letter-size paper, you would divide 23 by 30 to get a reduction ratio of 0.77, then multiply all other actual dimensions by 0.77 to get the scaled-down dimensions of the drawing. Conversely, if an object is only 3.4 cm (1.3") tall, you can enlarge it to make a clearer drawing. You can scale it up to, say, 20 cm (7.9") tall by dividing 20 by 3.4 to get an enlargement ratio of 5.88, then multiply all other actual dimensions by 5.88 to obtain the drawing dimensions.

Use the following steps to scale dimensions manually:

1. Determine the maximum height and width of the object to be drawn—for example, 20 cm tall and 30 cm wide.

2. Determine the maximum height and width of the desired drawing area—for example, 23 cm tall and 18 cm wide.

3. Determine the scaling factor. In this example, although the object is not as tall as the drawing area, it is wider than the width of the drawing area, so it has to be reduced to fit. Therefore, divide the width of the drawing area (18 cm) by the width of the object (30 cm) to obtain 0.60, which is the scaling factor.

4. Multiply all the actual dimensions of the object by the scaling factor to obtain the scaled dimensions. In this example, multiply all the actual dimensions of the object by 0.60 to obtain the scaled dimensions. For example, multiply 20 cm (height of object) by 0.60 to obtain 12 cm as the height of the drawing, multiply 30 cm (width of object) by 0.60 to obtain 18 cm as the width of the drawing, and multiply all other dimensions accordingly.

## Actual or Reduced Scale

If the object is just the right size to fit on a sheet of paper, it may be drawn at actual size—that is, a scale of 1:1. If your drawing is to a different scale after you have scaled all the important dimensions, draw the object by drawing each line with the scaled dimension, as shown in Illustration 2.13, which illustrates a vacuum sander.

# Drawing Different View Angles

You may choose to illustrate an object with only orthogonal views (front, side, top, and so on), because these are relatively easy to do. However, if they do not illustrate the object clearly enough, you should also draw one or more perspective views, which may be drawn with foreshortening if desired.

## Orthogonal Views

In an orthogonal view, the object is drawn as if one side of it is parallel to the drawing surface. A tapered block is used to illustrate the point in Illustration 2.14. Imagine positioning a sheet of paper parallel to the front side of the block, and projecting an image of the block onto the paper. Any surface that is parallel to the paper appears at full size. For example, the size of the front side's image is the same as that of the actual block's—that is, height "B" of the image is the same as height "B" of the actual block. Orthogonal views typically include many vertical or horizontal lines that represent the sides, top, and bottom of an object.

## Angled Lines in Orthogonal Views

Surfaces that are angled relative to the drawing sheet do not appear at full size: The more angled the surface is to the drawing sheet, the smaller its image appears. For example, the slanted surface of the block in Illustration 2.14 is at a large angle relative to the drawing sheet. It is quite long on the actual block, but its image on the drawing sheet appears much shorter: The size "A" of the slanted surface on the drawing sheet is the same as height "A" on the actual block.

Surfaces that are at a right angle to the drawing sheet appear to have zero height—that

**Actual Object**

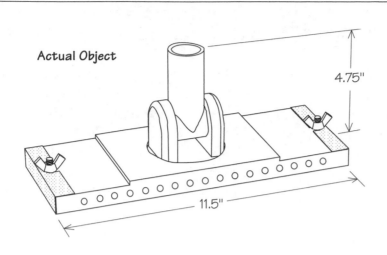

4.75"

11.5"

Simple calculations converting dimensions:

Actual Dimensions x Scale Factor = Drawing Dimensions

| | | |
|---|---|---|
| 11.5" | 0.6 | 6.9" |
| 4.75" | 0.6 | 2.85" |

**Scale Drawing**

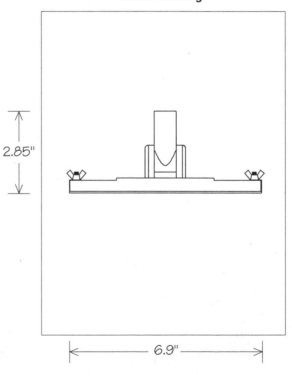

2.85"

6.9"

**Illustration 2.13—Scale Drawing**

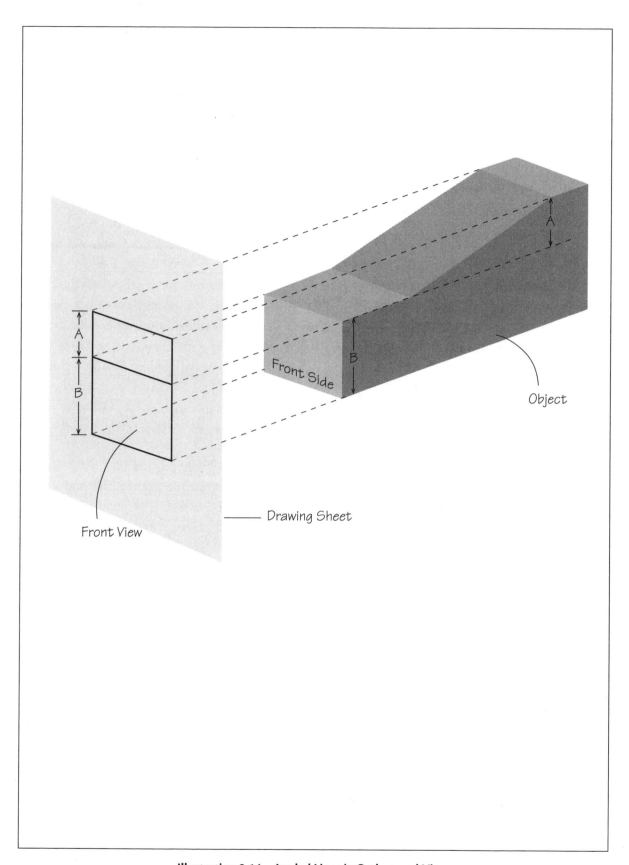

**Illustration 2.14—Angled Lines in Orthogonal View**

is, they appear as single lines. For example, the bottom surface of the block is precisely at a right angle to the drawing sheet, so that it appears as a single horizontal line on the drawing sheet. The same goes for the sides and top of the block.

## Perspective Views

Illustration 2.15 shows a box and a cylinder as viewed from different angles to illustrate what objects in perspective look like. Note that the views taken from the same height as the objects are not as clear as those that are taken above or below. Also note that the sides of the objects appear at full height when seen at the same level, but they appear shorter when the objects are seen from slightly below or slightly above—and even shorter when the objects are seen from almost directly below or almost directly above. The inverse is true for the tops and bottoms, which are not visible (having a zero height) when seen at the same level, but they appear larger when the objects are seen from slightly below or slightly above, and even larger when the objects are seen from almost directly below or almost directly above.

It is not possible to show in this book what every possible shape would look like from different angles. Illustration 2.15 serves as a rough guide to help you imagine how your drawing should look. If you still have trouble, study similar objects for clues.

## Circles in Perspective

Circles appear as ellipses (squashed circles) in perspective views. An ellipse has a major axis (the line extending across the widest part of the ellipse) and a minor axis (the line extending across the narrowest part of it). The drawing of a cylindrical rod and a hole on a box are shown in Illustration 2.16. The dashed lines are all temporary lines that should be sketched lightly in pencil and erased later.

### Drawing a Cylindrical Rod

1. Draw the parallel sides of the cylinder.

2. Sketch the major axis of the ellipse between the ends of the sides. The major axis is the same as the diameter of the cylinder.

3. Sketch the minor axis perpendicular to and through the midpoint of the major axis. The more perpendicular the cylinder is to the drawing surface (the more the end of the cylinder is seen straight on), the longer the minor axis; whereas the more oblique (angled) the cylinder is to the drawing surface (the more the end of the cylinder is angled away), the shorter the minor axis. The length of the minor axis is difficult to determine exactly, so simply use a length that makes the ellipse look "about right."

4. Draw the ellipse so that it is symmetrical about the major axis and symmetrical about the minor axis.

### Drawing a Hole on a Box

1. Determine the center of the hole and draw the centerline, which is perpendicular to the front side of the box, and parallel to the horizontal edges of the box.

2. Sketch the major axis of the ellipse through the center and perpendicular to the center-line. The midpoint of the major axis should coincide with the center of the hole.

3. Sketch the minor axis perpendicular to and through the midpoint of the major axis. The more perpendicular the hole is to the drawing surface (the more the hole is seen straight on), the longer the minor axis; and the more oblique the hole is to the drawing surface (the more the hole is seen angled away), the shorter the minor axis. Again, the length of the minor axis is difficult to determine exactly, so simply use a length that makes the ellipse look "about right."

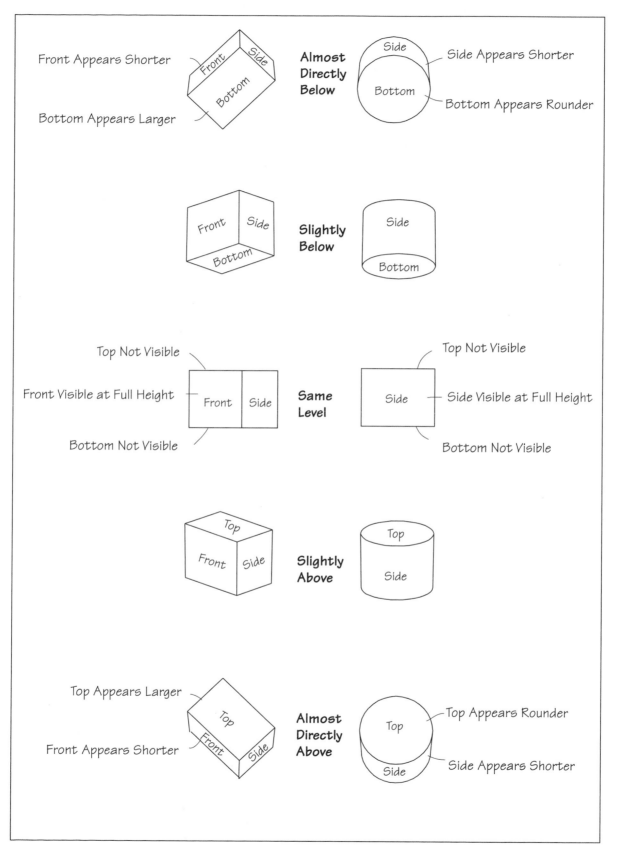

**Illustration 2.15—Perspective Views**

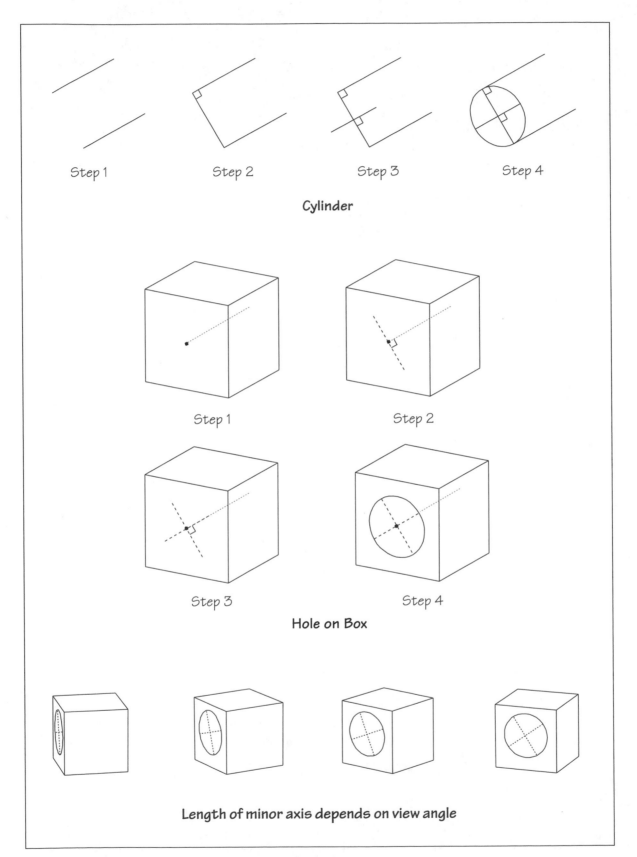

Step 1 Step 2 Step 3 Step 4

**Cylinder**

Step 1 Step 2

Step 3 Step 4

**Hole on Box**

**Length of minor axis depends on view angle**

**Illustration 2.16—Circles in Perspective**

4. Draw the ellipse so that it is symmetrical about the major axis, and symmetrical about the minor axis.

Sketching an accurate ellipse is difficult to do freehand, so you should use an ellipse template that most closely matches the desired shape. If you have an ellipsograph, you can draw a more precise ellipse.

## Translating Views by Plotting

A method for translating an orthogonal view into a perspective view comprises covering the orthogonal view with a grid, then plotting and connecting points on another grid drawn in perspective, as shown in Illustration 2.17. The finer the grid, the higher the plotting accuracy. The grid may be applied on the orthogonal view in pencil or by covering it with a transparent grid overlay. The grid for the perspective view may be lightly drawn in pencil, so that it may be erased later.

## Approximated Perspective Views

A perspective view may be easily approximated by basing it on an orthogonal view, as shown in Illustration 2.18. The perspective view is done by simply drawing oblique (slanted) lines from the orthogonal view, which may be a front, back, top, bottom, or side view. This is akin to making an extrusion of the object, like squeezing toothpaste out of a tube. The oblique lines should be relatively short—much shorter than their actual dimensions—otherwise the perspective view will appear distorted. Such approximated views are not truly perspective, but they are usually acceptable for patent drawings.

## Drawing Graphical Symbols

Graphical symbols, such as flowcharts and electrical schematics, are relatively easy to draw. There are many other types of graphical symbols used in patent drawings, including fluid-power, architectural, chemical, genetic, and so on. It is beyond the scope of this book to discuss the meaning and use of such symbols. If you are unfamiliar with them, you must refer to the literature in the relevant field for guidance.

When drawing graphical symbols, the only problem is arranging the elements of the drawing so that they fit onto a sheet. Use the following method:

1. Sketch the drawing roughly in pencil first to get an idea of its layout on the sheet.

2. If the position of the drawing needs adjusting, you can trace it onto another sheet in the desired position.

3. If the sketch grows too large to fit onto a single sheet, make another sketch by packing the elements closer together. If that is not possible, or if it makes the elements too crowded, the drawing may be spread over multiple sheets. See Chapter 6 for instructions on making multiple-page drawings.

4. When you have a satisfactory rough sketch, carefully sketch in the details, using suitable guides to ensure that they are aligned properly. There are templates available for a variety of different symbols, so use them whenever possible. They will make drawing much faster and more accurate.

5. Ink in the lines, and erase any stray pencil marks that remain visible after the ink is completely dry.

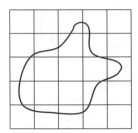

Step 1: Position grid on object.

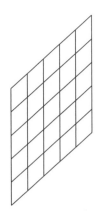

Step 2: Sketch grid in perspective.

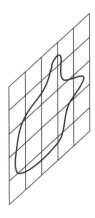

Step 3: Plot object on grid.

**Illustration 2.17—Translating Orthogonal View Into Perspective View by Plotting**

**Illustration 2.18—Approximated Perspective View**

## Practice, Practice, Practice

Remember that if you have never done high-quality drawings before, you should learn and practice basic drawing techniques before starting on your patent drawing project. If you follow this simple and obvious bit of advice, you will ultimately achieve much better results. Again, refer to the books listed at the beginning of this chapter for basic drawing techniques. ●

# Drawing With a Computer

This chapter provides general instructions for making drawings with a computer. Because there are many different types of computers available, each capable of running many different drawing programs, we cannot provide complete instructions on drawing with a computer: You must rely on the user's manual of your drawing program. Nevertheless, since most drawing programs work in similar ways, we can provide you with a good idea of the necessary equipment and software, how they are used, and the impressive results you can achieve.

> ! **CAUTION**
>
> **If you need help with using a computer or software,** please call the computer or software vendor. Neither Nolo nor the authors can provide such help.

## Necessary Equipment and Software

As you are probably aware, a computer includes two distinct elements: equipment (hardware) and software. The hardware includes a processor, a monitor or display screen, a keyboard, a mouse, and other physical components. Software includes an operating system, such as Windows or Mac OS, that controls the basic functioning of the computer, and application programs, such as word processors and drawing programs, that allow you to do useful work.

### Bitmap Painting Programs

There are two primary types of drawing programs: bitmap and vector. Bitmap programs, also known as image editing programs, manipulate bitmapped images, which are made up of individually controllable pixels or dots. Microsoft *Paint*, which comes with Windows,

and Adobe *Photoshop*, by Adobe Systems Inc., are examples of image editing programs. Because they are mainly designed for editing photographs or making artistic renderings, image editing programs are unsuitable for making patent drawings. However, they are useful in a particular method, discussed in Chapter 7, for making design patent drawings.

### Vector Drawing Programs

Vector drawing programs manipulate lines that are defined by spaced-apart points, like connect-the-dots drawings. The lines can be edited by moving the points. There are two main types of vector drawing programs: graphic design and CAD (computer-aided drafting or design). *CorelDraw*, Adobe *Illustrator*, and *Freehand* are examples of graphic design programs. Such programs are primarily designed for drawings with color-filled areas, such as those used in brochures and magazine ads. Their tools (functions) are not designed for making line drawings, such as patent drawings. Although they can be used to make patent drawings, most are not very good at the task. There are some exceptions, such as programs for making drawings of graphical symbols such as flowcharts. Besides dedicated flowchart programs, Microsoft *Word* and *PowerPoint* can also make flowcharts.

### CAD Programs

CAD programs are especially designed for making engineering drawings, which are dimensionally accurate line drawings, so they are the type of drawing program that is most suitable for making patent drawings. CAD programs are further divided into 2D (two-dimensional) and 3D (three-dimensional) programs.

## Two-Dimensional (2D) CAD Programs

Drawings done in a 2D program are simply computerized versions of paper drawings, so they do not include depth information. Each view or figure must be drawn separately. Creating a 2D CAD drawing is roughly similar to making a drawing on paper, except different tools are used in the process. However, even a 2D CAD program has huge advantages over traditional ink drawing techniques: It allows you to construct drawings more easily and with greater precision, and it allows you to edit (modify) them with great ease.

The interface (computer screen display) of a typical 2D CAD program is shown in Illustration 3.1, and includes the following important elements:

- the workspace or drawing area
- tool buttons that may be clicked to perform operations
- a movable cursor for setting points, pressing tool buttons, selecting drawing objects, and so on, and that is controlled by a mouse, and
- coordinate displays that show the position of the cursor in terms of its horizontal (X) position and vertical (Y) position relative to a reference point. The cursor may be moved a specific distance by dragging it until the desired coordinates are displayed, or by typing the desired X and Y positions in the coordinate displays.

Some 2D programs are listed later in this chapter.

## Three-Dimensional (3D) CAD Programs

Drawings done in 3D CAD programs are three-dimensional representations of actual objects. Although a drawing can be visualized in only two dimensions on the monitor screen and printed output, the drawing file includes the information that describes an object in three dimensions. Because creating a 3D drawing is equivalent to building a model of your invention in cyberspace (computer-generated world), such drawings are also called 3D models. A 3D CAD model can be rotated for viewing from any angle, sliced apart to show interior parts, and disassembled, just like the real thing. Thus, the main advantage of 3D drawings is that, by making only one 3D drawing of your invention, you can get a variety of 2D views out of it with great ease and print them as patent drawings.

The interface of a typical 3D CAD program is shown in Illustration 3.2, and includes the following important elements:

- the workspace, which is the drawing area. The particular program shown has four views of the workspace: the main view on the right being a perspective view, and the three views on the left being (from top to bottom) front, top, and side views.
- tool buttons that may be clicked to perform operations
- a cursor for setting points, pressing tool buttons, selecting drawing objects, and so on. The different views clearly show the exact position of the cursor in relation to the drawing object, so that additional objects may be created at precise positions with respect to the object.
- coordinate displays that show the position of the cursor in terms of its horizontal (X) position and vertical (Y) position relative to a reference point, as well as its depth (Z) position in front of or behind the reference point. The cursor may be moved a specific distance by dragging it until the desired coordinates are displayed, or by typing the desired X, Y, and Z positions in the coordinate displays.

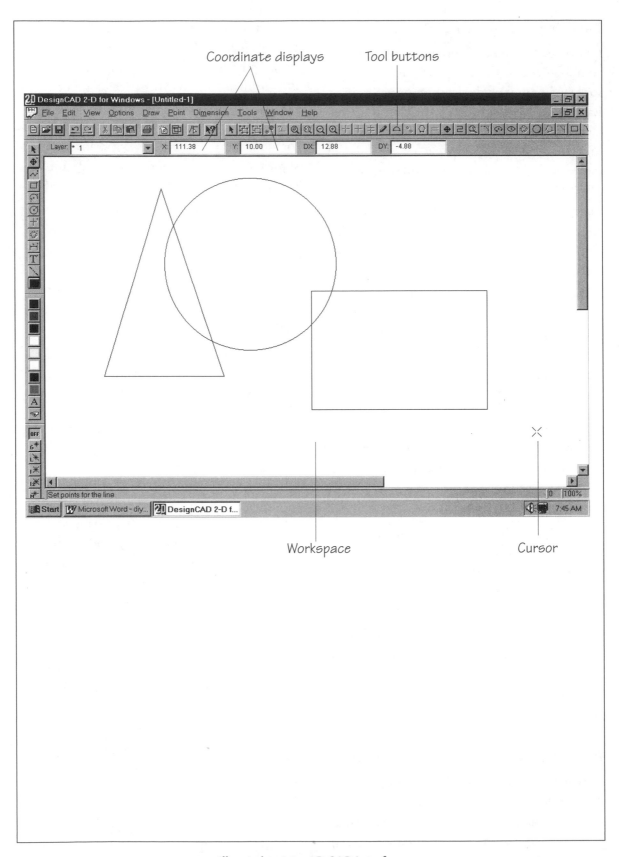

**Illustration 3.1—2D CAD Interface**

Tool buttons   Coordinate displays

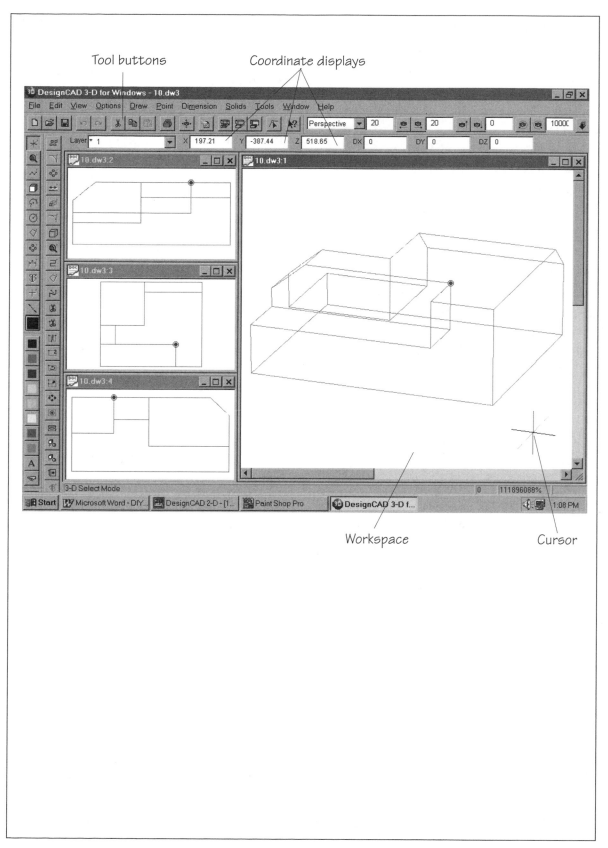

Workspace   Cursor

**Illustration 3.2—3D CAD Interface**

### 2D Necessary for Doing 3D

While some low-cost CAD programs are 2D only, some are 3D only, and some are both. A 3D-only program lacks the editing tools necessary to turn drawings into final form, so it must be used in conjunction with a 2D program. In that case, the 3D drawing must be converted into 2D format and imported (loaded) into a 2D program for editing, which is inconvenient and may not function due to incompatibility problems—particularly if the programs are from different publishers. Therefore, it is best to use a program with both 2D and 3D capabilities. Nevertheless, there are good programs that are either 2D only or 3D only. If you like a program that is 3D only, it is best to get a 2D program from the same publisher to ensure compatibility.

## Charting and Schematic Programs

Most graphic design programs, in addition to being able to make line drawings of objects, are also capable of making flowcharts, electronic schematics, and other drawings of graphical symbols. As discussed earlier, there are also specialized programs that are even more capable of making drawings of such charts, schematics, and symbols. If you want to draw graphical symbols as well as physical objects, you should try a CAD program first to see if it is adequate. If you are interested only in drawing graphical symbols, or if you plan on making many such drawings, you should consider using a program specialized for such symbols.

## List of Software

The following inexpensive programs are perfectly suitable for making patent drawings of simple inventions. They are available through the online stores of their publishers and through many other online retailers.

As a very rough general rule, the more expensive programs are more capable. However, for most patent drawings, the inexpensive programs suggested here are adequate. Each of these programs has its strengths, weaknesses, and even bugs (problems). Some publishers offer downloadable free trials or demos on their websites, so try before you buy. For other programs without demos, try to find reviews of these programs on the websites of computer magazines.

You can find some reviews at CAD-Reviews (www.cad-reviews.com), CADInfo (www.cadinfo.net), and Digital CAD (www.digitalcad.com).

### Autosketch

Functionality: Use to create 2D drawings.

Compatibility: Windows XP, Vista, Windows 7

Price: about $250

Website: www.autodesk.com

Note: From the maker of AutoCAD. File format compatibility with AutoCAD.

### DesignCAD

Functionality: Use to create 2D drawings.

Compatibility: Windows XP, Vista, Windows 7

Price: about $50

Website: www.imsidesign.com

Note: Easy to use. File format compatibility with AutoCAD.

### DesignCAD 3D Max

Functionality: Use to create 2D and 3D drawings.

Compatibility: Windows XP, Vista, Windows 7

Price: about $100

Website: www.imsidesign.com

Note: More powerful and still relatively easy to use.

### SmartDraw

Functionality: Use to create flow diagrams and block diagrams.

Compatibility: Unspecified

Price: About $200, downloadable free trial

Website: www.smartdraw.com

Note: Not for making line drawings.

### TurboCAD

Functionality: Use to create 2D and 3D drawings.

Compatibility: Windows XP, Vista, 7

Price: About $300 for Windows version, $200 for Mac version

Website: www.turbocad.com

Besides these inexpensive programs, you can also try the free CAD programs listed on these web sites:

- www.freebyte.com/cad/cad.htm, and

- www.techsupportalert.com/best-free-cad-program.htm.

In addition to the above CAD programs, more expensive CAD programs are available. These are mainly used by professionals and their price and learning curve is not usually justified unless you expect to do many patent drawings or unless you have access to a computer which contains one of these programs. Two of the professional CAD programs are *Canvas 12* (about $600) and *AutoCAD* (about $4000).

> ⚠ **CAUTION**
>
> **The above list of software is provided for your convenience.** Nolo and the authors do not endorse any of these products and have not tested them, except for an early version of *DesignCAD*.

## Computers

Most CAD or flowchart programs are made for PCs with Microsoft Windows XP, Vista or Windows 7. The less expensive programs have relatively low system requirements and run easily on virtually any personal computer with these operating systems. A few programs, such as *TurboCAD*, are available in separate Mac versions. Keep in mind that a program may run under the minimum requirements established by the manufacturer, but the performance is usually sluggish and exasperating because the system resources are strained. Fortunately, most new PCs exceed these specifications.

## Printers

A printer is necessary for putting your drawing on paper. Inkjet printers produce satisfactory patent drawings if you use high quality inkjet paper. (See Chapter 8 for details on inkjet papers.) Only color inkjets with a separate black ink cartridge have the potential to produce the truly black output required by the PTO. (**Note:** Dot matrix printer quality is considered unacceptable by the PTO.)

The PTO sometimes objects to drawings produced by inkjets (even those with a separate black cartridge) as not being black enough or sharp enough. This problem can be avoided by submitting a photocopy of the printer output. Any inkjet with a separate black cartridge that prints at 600 dpi (dots per inch) or higher is suitable for outputting black line drawings. The PTO no longer accepts photos for patent drawings (except for photomicrographs). However, if you need to print any photographic images, a higher resolution inkjet is required, such as one of the Epson Stylus Photo line of printers. Expect to pay $200 or more for a photo inkjet printer.

Low-cost laser printers that print at 600 to 1200 dpi output produce suitable quality patent drawings. Do not use older 300 dpi laser printers since PTO examiners and drawing inspectors sometimes object to their output as being too rough. Expect to pay approximately $200 or more for a typical 600 to 1200 dpi laser printer.

## Peripherals

Optional peripherals (add-on components) can expand your computer's capabilities and make drawing easier. These peripherals include:

- a digital camera for taking pictures of your invention and transferring the images to a computer for tracing in a CAD program. Higher resolution cameras produce sharper images with more details for easier tracing. The minimum recommended resolution is 4 megapixels. An optical zoom lens is a must for sharpness. Avoid phone and pocket cameras with digital-only zoom that produce blurry images.
- a flatbed scanner for scanning photographic prints of your invention for tracing in a CAD program. A digital camera is far better, but if you already have a film camera and do not plan to get a digital camera, a scanner may be used to transfer the photos into the computer. The Canon CanoScan series are very inexpensive and easy to use. Scanners cost roughly $50 to $200.

## Total Cost

If you are buying everything new, the total cost of a computer setup can vary tremendously, from $1,000 to sky's-the-limit, depending upon the number and caliber of components you get. Although the cost is higher than a set of traditional drawing tools (see Chapter 2), a computer may be used to perform a variety of other tasks in addition to making drawings, including writing your patent application, writing letters, bookkeeping, desktop publishing, playing games, and surfing the Internet. Therefore, the portion of the computer's cost attributed to patent drawing activities may be relatively low. On the other hand, you may already have all or most of the necessary equipment.

## Learning the Software

Each program works in different ways, so we cannot provide specific detailed instructions on how to use a (CAD) drawing program. You must therefore refer to the documentation of your particular program for specific instructions. A drawing program typically comes with a manual that explains all of its functions and usually also offers a tutorial that leads you through training exercises on creating simple drawings. There are enough similarities between most drawing programs that we feel safe in providing some guidelines and examples that are generally applicable to them.

## Drawing From Scratch With 2D

If the object you wish to draw does not presently exist, you will have to base the drawing solely on a mental image. Making a drawing from scratch with a drawing program is still much easier than doing it with pens and rulers, because of the large variety of shape-creating and editing tools (functions) provided by most drawing programs.

---

### CAD Terms and Concepts

The following are terms and concepts most often used in the CAD world.

**Entities.** The individual, basic elements that make up a drawing include lines, curves, text, and so on. Except for text, entities comprise lines connecting spaced-apart points, like a connect-the-dot drawing.

**Layers.** A layer is an imaginary horizontal slice of an object of any desired thickness. All CAD programs allow a drawing to be separated into different layers. Entire layers may be selected and manipulated at the same time. Layers may be made invisible or visible and may be locked to prevent them from being affected when other layers are manipulated.

**Entity Color.** Entities can be created in different colors.

**Line Types and Widths.** Entities can be created in different types, such as continuous and dashed, and different widths, such as 0.1 mm, 0.2 mm, and 0.3 mm.

**Snap Grid.** This option, when enabled, makes the cursor move only in selectable increments in the vertical and horizontal directions. It is very useful for aligning points with one another and for setting points at precise distances apart with ease.

**Cursor Step Size.** This is the amount of selectable cursor movement that is possible when moving the cursor with the arrow keys.

**Wire Frame.** A "see-through" drawing of an object, this resembles a wire frame, so that even lines on the back of the object are visible.

**Hidden Lines.** Lines that are visible when the drawing is shown in wire frame mode, but would be hidden by other parts of an object if it were shown as a solid.

## Available Tools

A typical 2D CAD program includes shape-creating tools. For example, the Box tool can be used to draw a rectangle of any desired size and height-to-width ratio on the screen. Other tools include Circle, Ellipse, Line, Parallel Line, Polygon, and so on. The shapes and lines created by such tools are called "entities," which may be edited (modified) with editing tools such as Point Move, Duplicate, Trim Line, Section Cut, Distort, and so on. The names of editing tools may vary among different programs, but their functions are basically the same. All entities may be created with any desired dimensions.

Entities may be created by selecting a tool and setting points by pressing the mouse button (each press of the button sets one point). For example, as shown in Illustration 3.3, a triangle is created by selecting the Line tool, and setting three points. Set the first point by left-clicking the mouse where this point is desired. Then drag the cursor to create an adjustable straight line that always extends between the point and the cursor, which can be moved to any position to make a line of any length and angle. When you've moved the cursor to the desired location of the end of the line or second point, press the mouse button to set the second point and create the line. Setting two more points creates the triangle (the fourth point is set at the same position as the first point to close the lines). The points may be set at specific distances apart to create a triangle with precise dimensions.

A perfect ellipse may also be created by selecting the Ellipse tool. After setting the first point to define the center, dragging the cursor away from the first point creates an adjustable circle. Positioning the cursor at the desired location and setting the second point defines the major (long) axis, and dragging the cursor away from the second point creates an adjustable ellipse. Positioning the cursor at the desired location and setting the third point defines the minor (short) axis and fixes the ellipse.

Such shape-creating tools enable you to draw perfectly formed shapes and lines without the drawing skills needed for traditional drawing techniques (pens and rulers). The shape and size of the entities may be edited in a variety of ways, such as those shown in Illustration 3.4.

These functions may not be immediately understandable by looking at static drawings in the example illustrations, but they will be once you are in a program and can see interactively what they do.

## Making a Drawing

Unlike drawing with a pen, rough sketching is not necessary when drawing with a computer, because a digital drawing may be easily edited. Nevertheless, with a 2D program, you must draw lines and shapes by estimating what they should look like, just as you would when drawing by hand with a pen. As an example, the making of a perspective view of a joystick is shown in Illustration 3.5 and explained here:

1. Create the top of the base by selecting the Box tool and drawing a box.
2. Distort the box with the Distort tool. The amount of distortion must be estimated.
3. Rotate the box with the Rotate tool to make it appear as though it is seen in perspective. The amount of rotation must be estimated.
4. Copy (duplicate) the box and paste it below the original to create the bottom.
5. Draw the vertical sides of the base by selecting the Line tool and drawing three lines.
6. Delete the hidden lines of the lower box with the Trim tool.

**Creating a Triangle**

First point

1.  Set first point by clicking the mouse to define first corner.

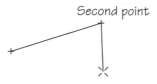

Second point

2.  Set second point to define second corner.

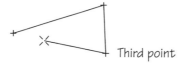

Third point

3.  Set third point to define third corner.

Fourth point

4.  Set fourth point at same position as first point to close lines.

**Creating an Ellipse**

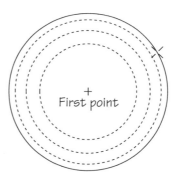

First point

1.  Set first point to define center.

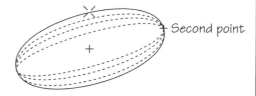

Second point

2.  Set second point to define major (long) axis.

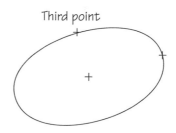

Third point

3.  Set third point to define minor (short) axis.

**Illustration 3.3—Creating an Object**

**Distorting an Object**

**Editing Lines**

1.  Select the object by dragging a "selection box" around it.

1.  Cut part of object with cut off box.

2.  Object is surrounded by a "bounding box" with square "handles."

2.  Object is cut.

3.  Cursor changes shape when positioned on a handle.

3.  Display points on line by using special cursor.

4.  Drag handle to new position.

4.  Drag point to new position.

5.  Object is distorted.

5.  Line is repositioned.

**Illustration 3.4—Editing Objects**

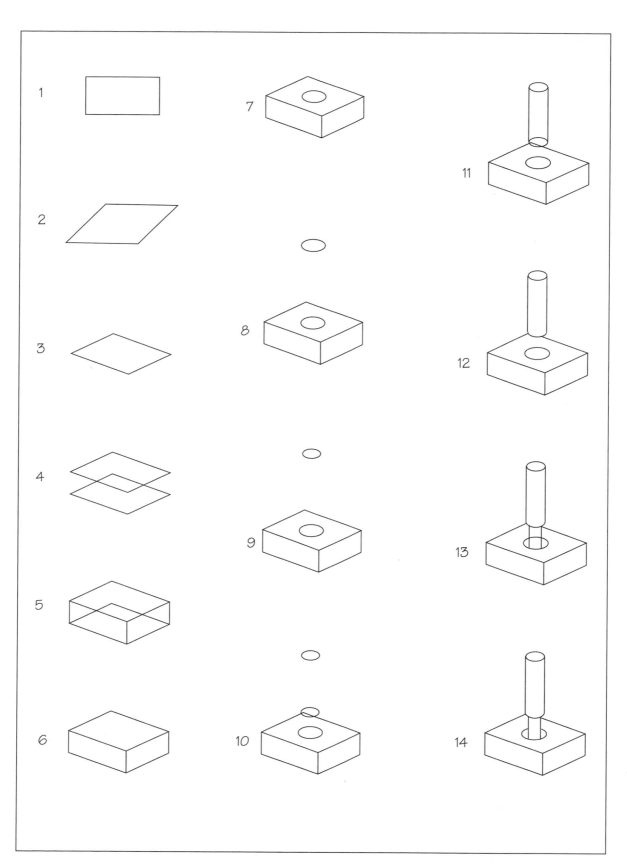

**Illustration 3.5—Drawing With 2D CAD**

7. Draw an ellipse with the Ellipse tool for the hole on top of the box. Refer to Chapter 2 for details on drawing circles in perspective.

8. Copy the ellipse and paste it above the original along the same centerline, to create the top of the handle.

9. Slightly reduce the size of the handle top with the Scale tool.

10. Copy the handle top, and paste it below the original to make the lower end of the handle.

11. Draw the sides of the handle by selecting the Line tool and drawing two lines.

12. Delete the excess portion of the lower end and the portion of the base behind the handle with the Trim tool.

13. Draw the sides of the connecting rod by selecting the Line tool and drawing two lines.

14. Delete the portion of the hole and box behind the connecting rod with the Trim tool.

The joystick was simply drawn until it "looked about right," without regard to dimensions, because it would have been difficult to determine the dimensions of its lines in perspective. Refer to Chapter 2 for a discussion of the appearance of objects in perspective.

## Study Similar Objects for Clues

During or after the creation of a drawing, you can easily edit it to achieve the desired result. If you have trouble making the drawing look right, study an object that is shaped similarly to the one you are drawing, or the portion of the object you are drawing. For example, if you have trouble drawing a box in perspective, find a similar box, position it in the same view angle that you are drawing, and study its lines to get an idea of what they should look like, as shown in Illustration 3.6.

When studying the lines, look for qualities such as their angles relative to the vertical or horizontal axes, angles relative to other lines on the same object, and the relative length of each line with respect to other lines on the same object, and so on. If you are careful in making these observations, you should be able to create satisfactory drawings. However, if you are still having difficulty, you may consider either making a model and tracing it or using a 3D program to create an accurate 3D model (both methods are described below).

Patent drawings are not art, but rather technical illustrations, so they do not have to be artistically perfect or beautiful. However, they do have to be reasonably accurate in depicting the structure of the invention. They must also be reasonably well executed—that is, they must be neat, not sloppy or rough.

## Page Layout

Each figure (drawing) should be big enough to show all of its details clearly. If several different figures are still small enough, they should be placed on the same sheet of paper to avoid using too many sheets of paper. Page layout is easily accomplished by simply selecting and dragging the figures to desired positions on the page, as shown in Illustration 3.7. Although paper is cheap and printing many sheets is easy, using fewer sheets increases paper handling convenience for you and reduces the amount of page flipping the examiner must do. However, if the figures are too large to fit on one sheet comfortably, use as many additional sheets as necessary; do not crowd the figures.

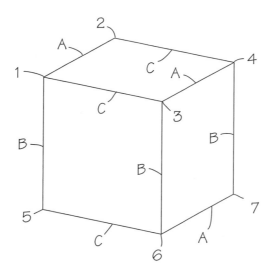

Note that:

Lines A are about 30 degrees above horizontal and parallel to each other.

Lines B are vertical and parallel to each other.

Lines C are about 10 degrees below horizontal and parallel to each other.

Point 1 is positioned about midway between Points 3 and 4 along the vertical direction.

Point 2 is positioned about midway between Points 1 and 3 along the horizontal direction.

Point 4 is positioned about midway between Points 1 and 2 along the vertical direction.

Point 6 is positioned about midway between Points 2 and 4 along the horizontal direction.

**Illustration 3.6—Studying Objects for Clues**

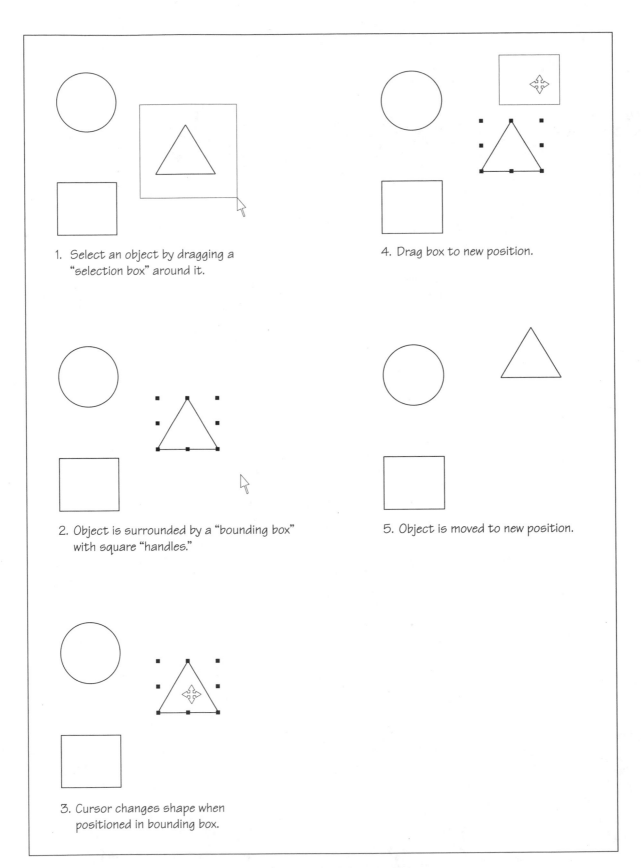

1. Select an object by dragging a "selection box" around it.

2. Object is surrounded by a "bounding box" with square "handles."

3. Cursor changes shape when positioned in bounding box.

4. Drag box to new position.

5. Object is moved to new position.

**Illustration 3.7—Repositioning an Object**

### General Drawing Tips

Keep in mind:

- Use different line widths for different drawing elements. For example, use 0.2 mm or 0.3 mm lines for the object and 0.1 mm or 0.15 mm lines for lead lines and hatching. Refer to Chapters 6 and 7 for more information on line types and widths.

- Use different colors for different line types, so they can be easily distinguished—for example, red for 0.1 mm solid lines, green for 0.2 mm solid lines, yellow for 0.2 mm dashed lines, blue for 0.5 mm solid lines, and cyan for hatching.

- Separate the colors into different layers, so each layer contains lines of the same type and width that can be easily changed by selecting the entire layer and assigning a new type or width to all its lines. After completing the drawing, make all lines black—the PTO does not allow color drawings or black-and-white drawings with lines having different degrees of blackness to be used (unless color is necessary to illustrate the invention properly).

- Select the font (lettering style) before applying the reference numbers. (See Chapter 8 for details on reference numbers.) This is because if you change the font after the numbers are applied, they will shift position and will no longer line up properly with the lead lines. (See Chapter 8 for details on lead lines.) The amount of shifting depends on the fonts used before and after the change.

## Making Drawings by Tracing Photos

A very easy way to make a realistic drawing is to trace a photograph of an actual object, such as the prototype of an invention. (Refer to Chapter 4 for tips on how to take good pictures.) The procedure for tracing a photo with a CAD program is generally as follows:

1. Acquire an image of the object by either taking a picture with a digital camera, or taking a picture with a film camera and scanning a photographic print. Cameras and scanners come with their own software for acquiring and handling images. In either case, the picture is saved as an image file on a computer.

2. Import the image into a 2D CAD program. Not all CAD programs can import images, so be sure to select a program with this function. Each program can load specific types of graphics files, for example, BMP, JPG, and TIFF. Therefore, when you save the file after scanning or taking a picture with a digital camera, you must save it in a format that your CAD program can use.

3. Select the Line tool to trace straight lines, or the Curve tool to trace curves, as shown in Illustration 3.8. Zoom in as necessary to see small details better.

4. When you finish tracing, you can either set the image to be invisible and unprintable, or delete it to save disk space, so that only the tracing is visible and printable.

5. Edit the drawing to fine-tune the positioning of the lines and to clean up extraneous lines.

1. Trace straight lines with line tool.

3. Complete tracing.

2. Trace curved lines with curve tool.

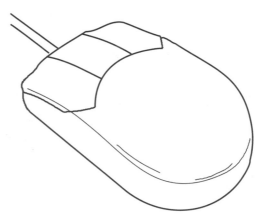

4. Delete image to leave line drawing.

**Illustration 3.8—Tracing a Photograph of an Object**

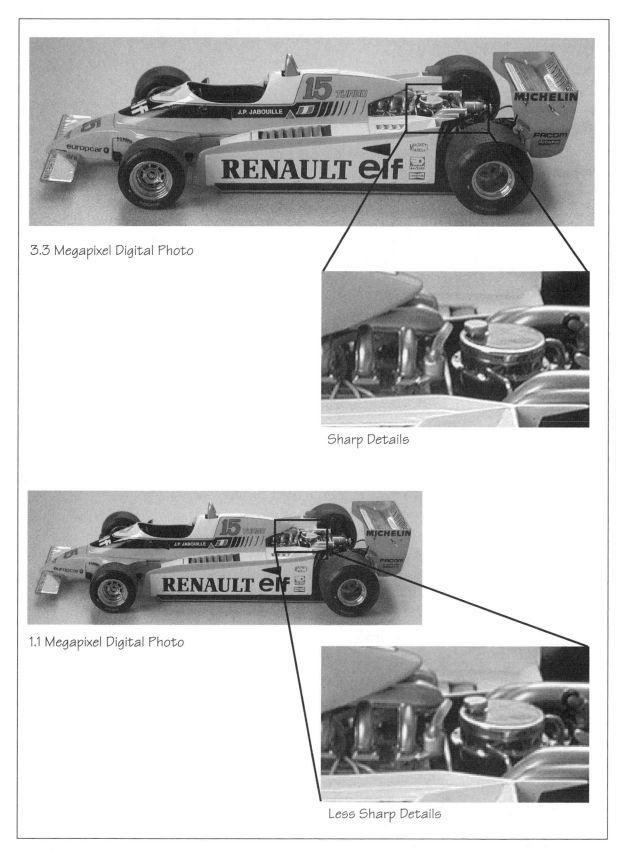

3.3 Megapixel Digital Photo

Sharp Details

1.1 Megapixel Digital Photo

Less Sharp Details

**Illustration 3.9—Difference Between Digital Photos of Different Resolution**

## Tracing Tips

Keep in mind:

- Put the tracing and the image on separate layers to prevent them from interfering with each other. Depending upon the program you use, there may be certain procedures that must be followed to ensure that the tracing stays on top of the image instead of being covered by it.
- Use thick lines, such as 0.2 mm to 0.3 mm, for the outline and major features of the object, and thin lines, such as 0.1 mm, for rounded edges and other curved contours.
- Lines representing rounded edges should be broken, and their ends should not touch the outlines of the object. See Illustration 3.8.

## Digital Camera Images

A digital camera can transfer its images directly to a computer for tracing, so it is much more convenient than a film camera. The current generation of digital cameras has 3 to 8 megapixel resolution. The best digital cameras have the same effective resolution as 35 mm film prints. Higher resolution images have sharper details, which are easier to trace. (See Illustration 3.9.)

## Scanning a Photographic Print

Pictures taken with a film camera must be developed into prints and scanned into a computer with a scanner. A 4" x 6" print should be scanned at 300 to 600 dpi in 24-bit color to produce enough detail for tracing. A 600 dpi scan of the entire 4" x 6" print produces a 9 MB file, which may be too large for some computers to handle with ease. Unless the invention fills the entire print, select only the area to be traced for minimizing the file size and making image processing easier for your computer.

## Drawing With 3D CAD

Three-dimensional (3D) modeling is where CAD really shines. As already discussed above, unlike a 2D drawing, a 3D model is a three-dimensional representation of an object in cyberspace (computer space). Such a model is represented by a wire frame, which defines the edges and surfaces of the object. The model may be rotated and zoomed in or out for viewing from any angle or distance desired. Two-dimensional (2D) "snapshots" may be taken from any angle or distance to create different drawing figures. Therefore, by making just one 3D model, many different 2D drawings may be produced with ease.

## Available Tools and Functions

A typical 3D CAD program includes shape-creating tools, such as Box, Cylinder, Sphere, Cone, Line, and Curve. The entities created by these tools may be modified with editing tools, such as Extrude, Sweep, Drill, Lathe, Slice, Cut Off, Chamfer, and Trim.

For example, as shown in Illustration 3.10, a box may be created by selecting the Box tool. After setting the first point to define one corner, dragging the cursor creates an adjustable 2D box. Moving the cursor to a position behind the first point and setting the second point defines the diagonally opposite corner and creates the 3D box. Likewise, a sphere can be created by selecting the Sphere tool. After setting the first point to define the center, dragging the cursor creates an adjustable rough outline of the sphere. Setting the second point defines the radius and creates the sphere. Although these objects are treated by the program as solids, they are normally shown on screen as see-through wire frames.

Other standard and nonstandard shapes can also be easily created. As shown in Illustration

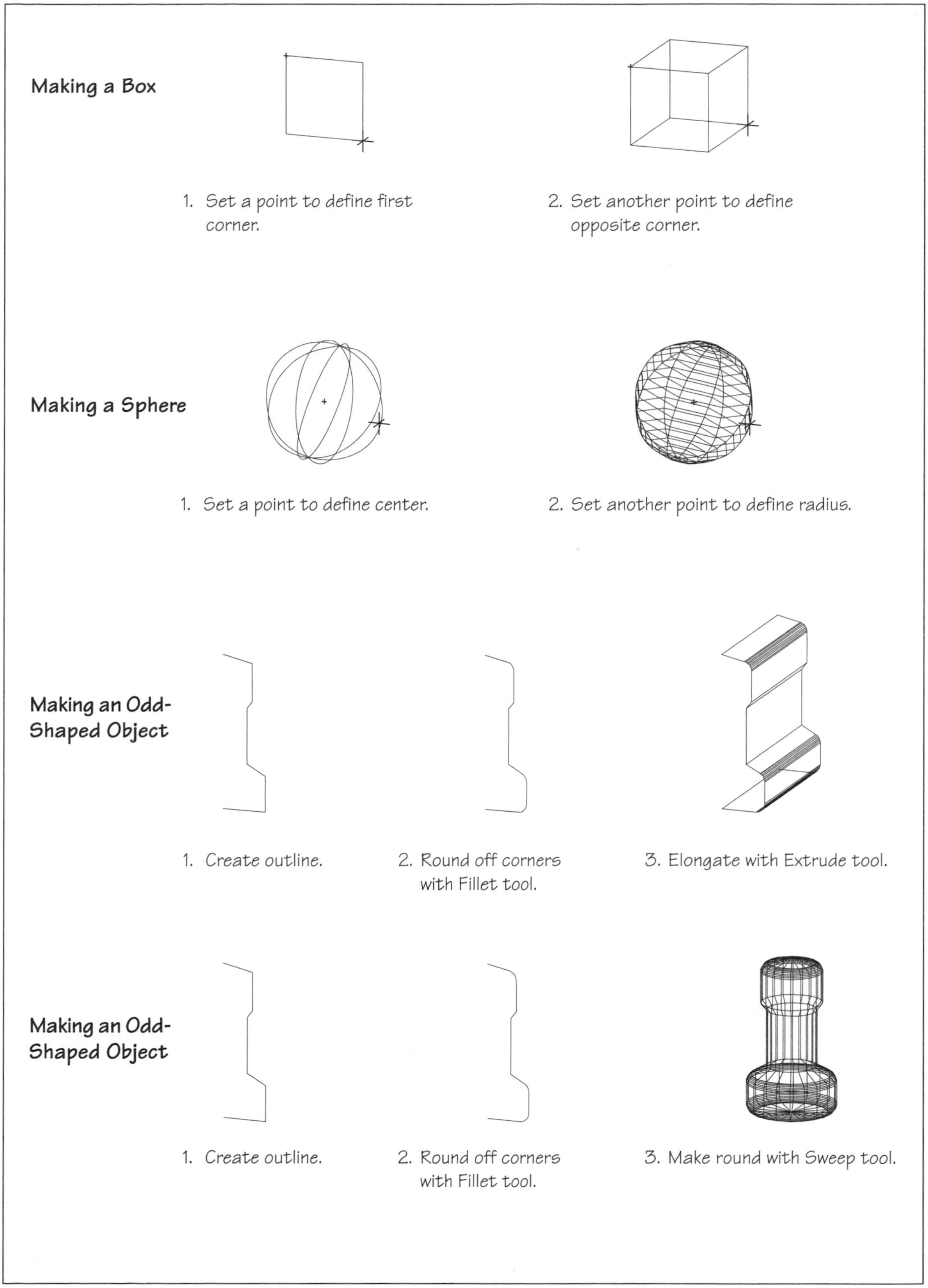

**Making a Box**

1. Set a point to define first corner.

2. Set another point to define opposite corner.

**Making a Sphere**

1. Set a point to define center.

2. Set another point to define radius.

**Making an Odd-Shaped Object**

1. Create outline.

2. Round off corners with Fillet tool.

3. Elongate with Extrude tool.

**Making an Odd-Shaped Object**

1. Create outline.

2. Round off corners with Fillet tool.

3. Make round with Sweep tool.

**Illustration 3.10—Some Tools and Functions**

3.10, one way to create an irregular shape is by drawing a line or curve and modifying it with tools such as Extrude and Sweep. A great variety of 3D models can be created by combining and modifying different shapes and lines. The complexity of the models you can build is limited only by your imagination and the available tools in a program.

When two or more objects are combined to create more complex shapes, they must be accurately positioned relative to each other. This is achieved by watching the coordinate displays (Illustration 3.2) on the screen to ensure that the points are set in the proper positions. Various functions are also available for ensuring accuracy in point setting and object positioning. Some of these functions include Snap Grid, which confines the cursor to movements of a preset distance, such as 1 mm, and Snap To, which causes a selected entity to snap or stick to a selected position on another object.

## Making a Drawing in 3D

Just as there are many different ways to construct an actual object, there are many different ways to make a 3D model, even when using the same program. These construction methods will become apparent after you have studied the program's manual and gone through the exercises in the tutorial. As an example, the joystick, first drawn in 2D, above, is created in 3D in Illustration 3.11 with the following steps:

1. Make the base. Select the Box tool, set one point to define one corner, and set another point a desired distance away to define diagonally opposite corners of the box.

2. Make a cylinder that extends into the base. Select the Cylinder tool, set one point at the center of the box to define the center of the cylinder, set a second point a desired horizontal distance away to define the radius of the cylinder, and set a third point a desired vertical distance away to define the height of the cylinder.

3. Select the Subtract tool, and select the cylinder and the base. The cylinder will be automatically "subtracted" from the base to create a hole.

4. Select the Cylinder tool, set a point at the bottom of the hole to define the center of the rod, and set two more points at desired positions to define the radius and height of the rod.

5. Select the Line tool and draw a line having desired dimensions above the connecting rod to define half the handle's profile.

6. Select the Fillet tool and set points on the corners of the line to round them off.

7. Sweep the line to create the handle.

8. Select the Fillet tool and set points on the edges of the box to round them off.

The model can be easily rotated and zoomed to produce a number of different views from different angles and distances, as shown in Illustration 3.12. These views can be saved as individual 2D drawings without the hidden lines (lines that should not be visible because they are behind solid surfaces).

## View Distance

In addition to view angle, the view distance (zoom factor) is typically adjustable in CAD programs. As shown in Illustration 3.13, when the view distance is large, the object appears only slightly distorted—that is, the perspective lines converge very little. At the other extreme, when the view distance is very short, the perspective lines are highly convergent and the object appears very distorted. The most realistic drawing is produced at a moderate view distance. You can easily experiment with the view distance to see what the best setting is for

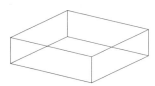

1. Make a box.

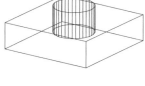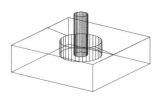

2. Make a cylinder extending into the box.

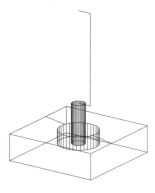

3. Subtract the cylinder from the box to make a hole.

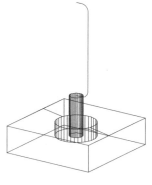

4. Make a cylinder in the hole.

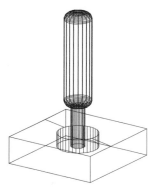

5. Draw a line to define the half profile of the handle.

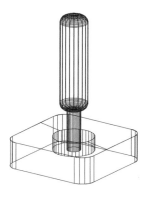

6. Round the corners.

7. Sweep the half profile to make the handle.

8. Round the edges of the box.

**Illustration 3.11—Drawing in 3D**

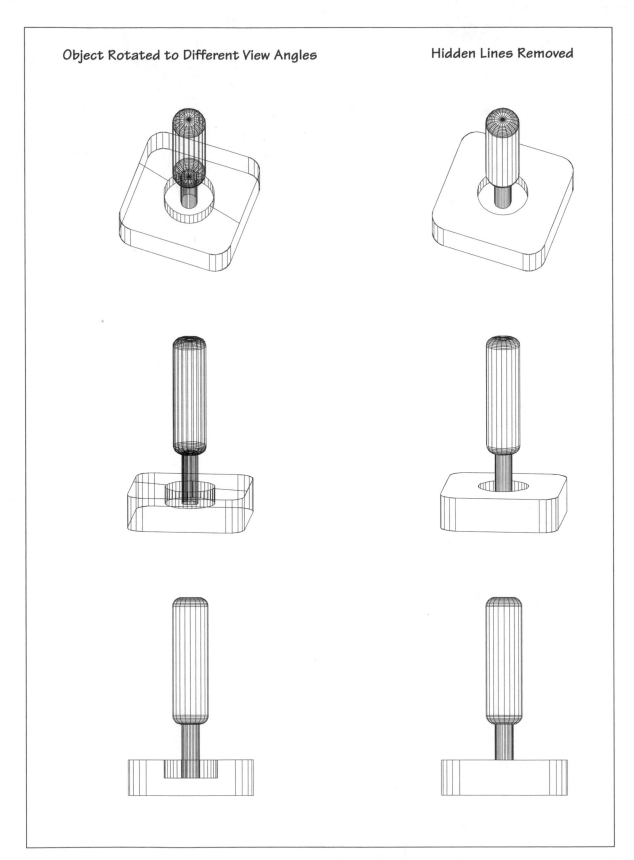

Object Rotated to Different View Angles

Hidden Lines Removed

**Illustration 3.12—Rotating Object to Obtain Different 2D Views**

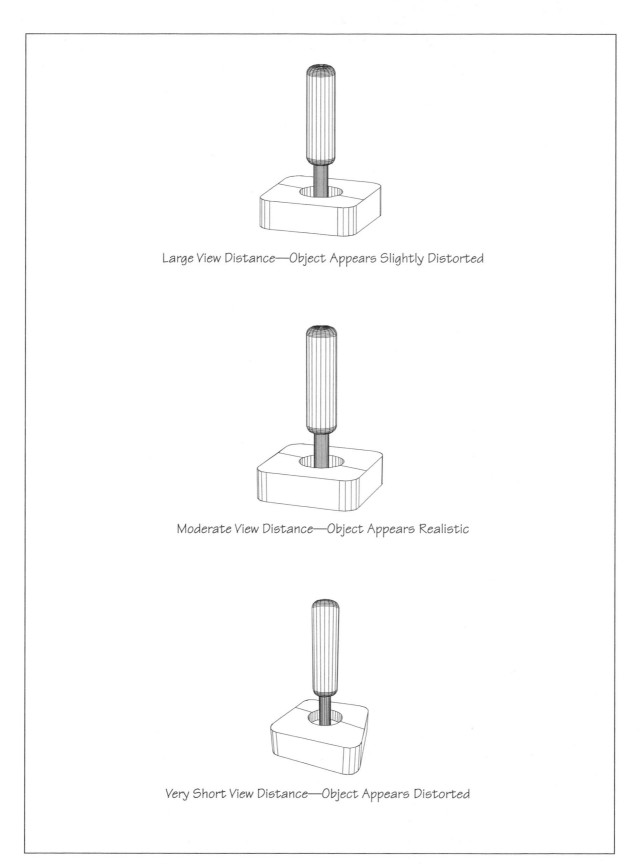

Large View Distance—Object Appears Slightly Distorted

Moderate View Distance—Object Appears Realistic

Very Short View Distance—Object Appears Distorted

**Illustration 3.13—Effect of Zoom on Realism**

each particular drawing. View distance in CAD is equivalent to the technique of foreshortening in traditional drawing techniques.

## Cleanup

The conversion from 3D to 2D is not always without problems; 2D drawings are often produced with missing or unwanted lines. For example, 3D programs represent curved surfaces, such as cylinders and spheres, with many flat facets. Some programs provide the option of eliminating the facet lines when the model is converted into 2D, but other programs do not. In that case, the facet lines must be deleted manually. Unless you use a combined 2D/3D program, you must import (load) the 3D drawing into a separate 2D program for editing.

> **TIP**
>
> **Trace rather than erase.** If a drawing has a large number of facet lines, such as a drawing with many spheres and cylinders, it may be easier to trace the lines you want to keep instead of erasing the unwanted ones. Make the original drawing a single color and put it in one layer. Put the tracing on a separate layer, and make it a different color so you can see your progress. After the tracing is finished, delete the original drawing.

## Great 2D Drawings for Free

Making a 3D model is different from starting in 2D. However, it is no more difficult than making a single 2D drawing, and provides the significant benefit of allowing you to easily create as many 2D drawings from as many view angles as you wish. Each 2D view is visually accurate.

## Shading

A 3D model can be used to produce accurately shaded drawings for a design patent application. See Chapter 7 for a detailed discussion of the technique.

# Drawing Graphical Symbols

Two-dimensional (2D) CAD programs may be used to make drawings of graphical symbols, as used in flowcharts and electronic schematics. Some programs come with a variety of types of ready-made symbols—typically electronic symbols—that can be easily arranged to create a drawing. There are also add-on symbol libraries from a variety of vendors. If the symbols you need are not available, you can easily make them from scratch. You need to make each symbol only once; after it is created, it may be easily duplicated as many times as necessary.

There are many ways to make a drawing using graphical symbols. As an example, one way of making an electronic schematic is as follows:

1. Open the drawings of the symbols you need (symbols are typically stored separately in different files). Copy and paste them into one drawing.

2. Arrange a few symbols next to each other and draw the connections between them, as shown in Illustration 3.14.

3. Arrange more symbols next to the first ones and draw the connections between them. Whenever an identical symbol is needed, simply duplicate one already in the drawing by copying and pasting. The orientation of the symbols may be changed by rotating them with the Rotate tool.

4. Repeat as many times as necessary to gradually build up the drawing.

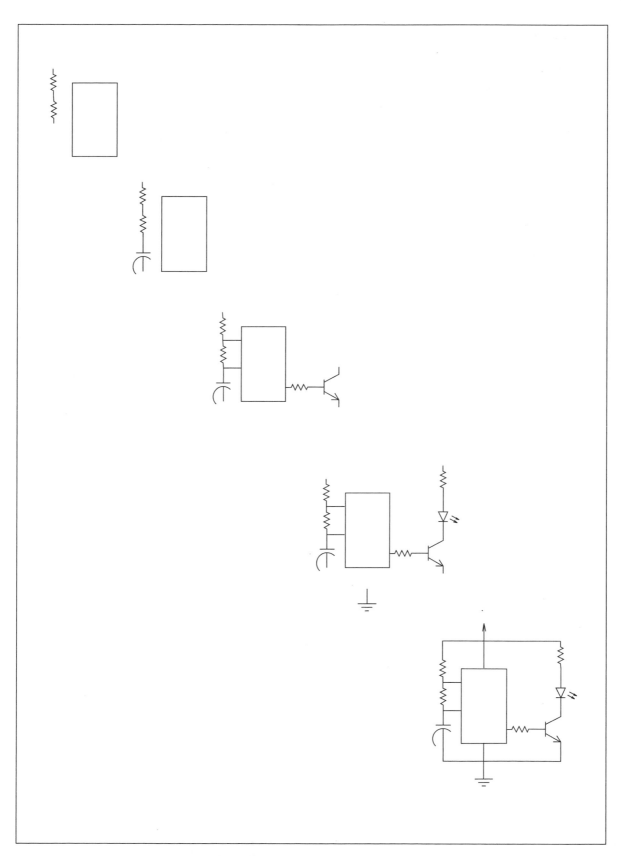

**Illustration 3.14—Drawing Graphic Symbols**

## Retaining Your Drawings

The drawing file should be retained after the application process is finished in case changes to the drawings must be made—for example, if the PTO objects to a drawing, or loses your drawings, or you must make modifications to a drawing, such as correcting a wrong reference numeral. (However, note that you are never permitted to add any "new matter" to a patent drawing.) Also, it is a good idea to back up the file by copying it onto a backup device, so that if you accidentally overwrite or erase it in the computer, it can be restored by copying it back onto the hard drive.

## Summary

Making drawings with a computer is relatively easy and fast. Even the most inexpensive drawing programs will enable you to make great-looking drawings without requiring you to have any traditional drawing skills. If you are skilled in traditional drawing techniques and simply wish to modify your drawings with ease, then a 2D program will suffice. However, 3D programs, or combined 2D/3D programs, are so much more powerful that they are well worth the additional expense and effort to buy and learn them.

The functional advantage of CAD over pens and rulers is similar to that of a word processor over a typewriter, but pens and rulers still hold a cost advantage. If you already have a computer, or are planning on buying one anyway, we strongly suggest that you use CAD. Otherwise, traditional drawing techniques are still perfectly viable. Remember, many professional patent drafters still use traditional (pen and ink) techniques. ●

# Using a Camera

The PTO does not usually accept photographs because they are difficult and expensive to reproduce. However, if an invention cannot be adequately illustrated with black line drawings, black-and-white photographs may be used to illustrate inventions such as cell cultures, histological tissue cross sections, photomicrographs of material details, and animals. Color photographs may be accepted if they are necessary to properly illustrate the invention or design.

No petition is necessary to submit black-and-white photos. If you use color photos, they must be of sufficient quality to enable all the details to be clearly reproducible in black and white in the printed patent and a petition and a petition fee must accompany any color drawings. (See Chapter 8 for details on such petitions.) Keep in mind that color photos are approved only on rare occasions. If your petition is not granted, formal black line drawings must be submitted to replace the color photos when the application is allowed. (See Chapter 7.)

Although the rules severely restrict the submission of photographs, photos are still very useful as the basis for tracing with a computer software drawing or CAD program. This chapter provides instructions on how to take suitable pictures.

## Advantages and Disadvantages

Included in the advantages of photography are that little artistic skill is required, a relatively short time is needed to take a picture, and subtle or certain complex images can be illustrated much better than with line drawings.

The disadvantages include the need for the novice to acquire a new set of skills, the difficulty of photographing very small objects clearly, and the difficulty or impossibility of photographing internal parts without cutting up an invention.

Another significant disadvantage is that when the photographs are eventually published in a patent, they reproduce very poorly on copiers and computer printers—to a degree that much of the detail will become illegible. Succeeding generations of reproductions—that is, copies of copies—will become progressively worse. Finally, still another disadvantage is the difficulty of manually adding figure numbers, reference numbers, and lead lines onto the photographs.

## Inventions Suited for Photography

Photographs or photomicrographs are acceptable as formal drawings in a utility application if they are used to show fine and irregular or natural structures that are not capable of being illustrated with black line drawings—for example, electrophoresis gels, blots, autoradiographs, cell cultures, histological tissue cross sections, animals, plants, in vivo imaging, thin-layer chromatography plates, metallurgical microstructures, textiles, and crystalline structures. Of course, photography cannot be used for illustrating nontangible inventions and graphical representations, such as schematic diagrams, charts, and so on. In design applications, acceptable photographs include those that show subtle ornamental effects.

## Photographs Must Show Invention Clearly

It is vital that the photographs from which line drawings are to be made as well as those which are used to illustrate microscopic details or subtle effects show all the important parts of the invention clearly, without any ambiguity. This is easy to accomplish for very simple inventions or inventions with large parts, but difficult to accomplish for complicated inventions or inventions with tiny parts.

## Equipment

Whether you use photographs as patent drawings or for tracing, they must clearly show all the essential details. The minimum equipment necessary for taking clear pictures includes the following:

- a camera with an optical zoom lens. Digital cameras can take many images without your having to develop prints and transfer them directly into a computer for tracing. (They are superior to film cameras for photographing inventions.) The recommended minimum resolution is 5 megapixels. An optical zoom lens is a must. Avoid cameras with only digital zoom, as well as mobile phone cameras. A 35 mm film camera with a zoom lens can also be used, but a scanner is necessary for transferring the prints into a computer. However, a film camera is not recommended for black-and-white photos because of the scarcity of black-and-white film and the developing services that handle them.
- a tripod for stabilizing the camera for taking sharp pictures, and
- a good inkjet printer and photo-quality inkjet paper for making great photographic prints.

## Taking Pictures

Although artistic photography is a complicated undertaking, patent photography is not, because its only goal is clear, sharp pictures. Aside from reading the manual of your camera, you can take good patent pictures by following the simple rules and tips discussed in this section.

### Choice of Background

A high contrast background should be used. For example, if the object you want to photograph is light colored, the background should be dark colored, and vice versa. The background should also be uniform in appearance and of a solid color, such as a bare tabletop or a large piece of cardboard, so that there will be no confusion as to what is the background and what is part of the object.

### Artificial Lighting

Always shoot (take pictures) in a brightly lit area. If necessary, illuminate the object with two lamps positioned around it, so that all of its details are clearly visible and to avoid dark shadows. Position the lamps to avoid glare reflecting off the object. Objects of dark colors should be lit with very bright lights to make them more visible.

### Flash

Most snapshot cameras will usually flash when shooting indoors, unless the room is very brightly lit. The flash will create shadows if the object is positioned very close to the camera (due to the different lines of sight between the lens and the flash to the object). If the camera flashes, position a lamp, or slave flash unit, or a backlighting umbrella, very close to the side of the object opposite the flash to reduce the shadow, as shown in Illustration 4.1.

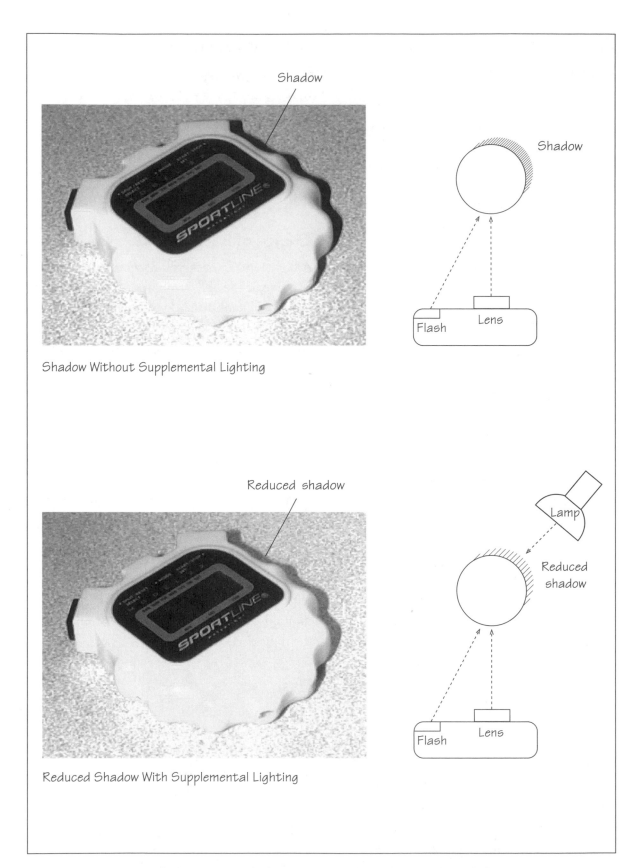

**Illustration 4.1—Shadow Reduction With Supplemental Lighting**

## Sunlight

Avoid putting the object in direct sunlight, which will cast dark shadows that obscure details, as shown in Illustration 4.2. If direct sunlight cannot be avoided, position yourself between the object and the sun, so that you will photograph the side of the object that is most evenly lit. Also position the object to minimize shadows. If at any time there are dark shadows on the object, use the flash to reduce them. Most snapshot cameras have a Day Flash setting that makes the camera flash even in bright light.

## Maximize Object Size

Make the object fill the viewfinder frame—that is, make it appear as large as possible—so that all of its details are as clear as possible. This is particularly important when there are small details. See Illustration 4.3. If an object or a detail is very small, you must use a zoom of high enough power or a macro lens to make it appear large enough.

## Zoom In to Reduce Distortion and Preserve Focus

If you are not using a zoom lens, any object that you photograph close-up will appear distorted, as shown in Illustration 4.4. For this reason, we recommend using a zoom lens. Use the maximum zoom and stand far enough away from the object so that the object fills the frame. This will substantially reduce the distortion, as shown in the second half of Illustration 4.4. The distance from camera to object depends upon the size of the object; the larger the object, the farther away you must stand.

Zooming in is essential when photographing a small object. Without a zoom, you must stand so close to the object that most cameras will not focus. (The normal minimum focus distance is between 1.5 to 3 feet.) Many cameras have focus indicators in the viewfinders that typically flash when the camera cannot focus on the object. Many cameras have a macro setting (extreme close-up) that allows you to take pictures at less than the normal focus distance.

## Depth of Field

If you use a camera with manually adjustable aperture (F-number or F-stop) and exposure (shutter speed), set the aperture to F-16 or higher to make both the front and back of the object in focus—that is, to increase the "depth of field." Set the exposure or shutter speed control on "A" (automatic). Keep in mind that the higher the F-number, the longer the exposure, and the steadier the camera must be to take sharp pictures. Therefore, a tripod is a must. The use of a high F-number is necessary, particularly when the shooting distance is small relative to the size of the object. For example, when shooting a telephone from just 60 cm (2 feet) away, or shooting a car from 2 meters (6 feet) away, the aperture should be set to a high F-number. Snapshot cameras typically have fully automatic aperture and exposure that are not user adjustable.

## Use a Tripod

To ensure sharp pictures, use a tripod to steady the camera, and press the button slowly (or use a cable shutter release or remote control) so as not to move or jar the camera.

## Take Many Pictures

Photography requires guesswork. Therefore, take pictures from different sides, angles, and under different lighting conditions to increase the likelihood of obtaining usable images. Keep track of the settings for each shot, so the best settings may be used again, if necessary. Remember—the resulting drawings must show every feature of the invention recited in the claims.

**Dark Shadows**

Bright sun without flash

**Reduced Shadows**

Bright sun with flash

**Illustration 4.2—Shadow Reduction in Bright Sun**

 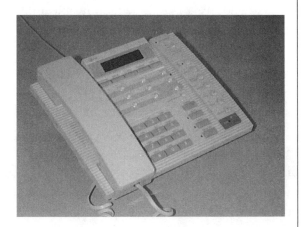

DON'T make the object appear
small in the frame.

DO make the object fill the frame.

**Illustration 4.3—Maximize Object Size in Frame**

**Distorted**

Photographed up close without zooming in

**Not Distorted**

Photographed farther away and zoomed in

**Illustration 4.4—Zooming in to Reduce Distortion**

Digital cameras have LCD color monitors for instant review of captured images. If an image is not good enough, you can take another picture immediately with a different setting or lighting condition. Take many pictures and choose the best after transferring the images to the computer.

## Paper Size

If permitted, photographs submitted as patent drawings must meet the same paper size and margin requirements as line drawings. (See Chapter 8 for paper, margin, and other formal requirements.) Computer printouts of digital photographic images should be made on regulation letter or A4 size paper with borders that meet the margin requirements. The images should be properly positioned on the paper prior to printing. Some CAD programs, particularly *DesignCAD*, can also print images and even line drawings overlaid on images. Images from film must be developed on photographic paper that meets the size requirements of line drawings. These photographs must also be printed with white borders that meet the same margin requirements as line drawings.

## Summary

The PTO will accept photographs as patent drawings in rare situations only. Black-and-white photos can be used for patent drawings where fine detail must be illustrated and color photos or drawings can be used if color is an essential feature of an invention, but a petition and a fee are required for color submissions. However, regardless of whether you can submit them as patent drawings, photographs are useful as a source for tracing line drawings. The resulting drawings will usually be much better than those done from scratch. It's best to use a digital camera to take photos for tracing, and for the actual patent drawings, when photos are permitted. ●

# Patent Drawings in General

The patent laws and rules require most patent applications to be filed with drawings. However, there are some situations in which patent drawings are not necessary. This chapter discusses the drawing requirement, when you can get away with not submitting a drawing, and the three types of patent drawings required by the PTO for the various types of patent applications.

## The Drawing Requirement

Title 35 of United States Code, Section 113 (35 U.S.C. § 113), which is part of the patent laws, states the requirement for patent drawings this way: "The applicant shall furnish a drawing where necessary for the understanding of the subject matter to be patented." Since the vast majority of inventions cannot be clearly conveyed by words alone, drawings are necessarily in almost all patent applications.

### When Drawings Are Not Required

Drawings may not be required in applications for inventions that can be clearly conveyed by words alone, without any ambiguity. There are very few instances when this can be done, but the following types of inventions are specifically exempt:

- a process, such as a heat-treating process for hardening metal
- a composition, such as a road surfacing material, a chemical, or a drug
- coated articles or products, such as paper or cloth coated with a water-repellent material
- articles made from a particular material or composition, such as nonslip floor tiles made from recycled tires
- laminated structures, such as plywood, and

- inventions in which the distinguishing feature is the presence of a particular material, such as a hydraulic system distinguished solely by the use of a particular hydraulic fluid.

It is impossible to draw some inventions, such as a heat-treating process, articles made from a particular material (the material being the only novelty), and compositions. However, if it is possible to illustrate an invention with a drawing, even though it is adequately conveyed by words alone, your examiner may require you to provide one. For example, coated articles and laminated structures are specifically exempt, but since it is possible to illustrate them with drawings that show the different layers of the invention, the examiner may require you to provide drawings.

Even if your invention is exempt from the drawing requirement, we strongly recommend that you submit drawings whenever possible for the following reasons:

- Examiners like every patent to contain a drawing, if possible, because it makes the invention much easier to understand.
- Drawings please and interest an examiner and show him or her that you, the applicant, are making an effort to present the invention as clearly as possible.
- When you get a patent, the drawing will make it easier to recognize as a relevant patent when others do patent searches, so it will be more effective in warning potential infringers and in preventing others from getting patents on improvements of your invention.
- It communicates your invention better to any company to which you offer your invention for sale or license, and any judge or jury who may ultimately rule on its validity and infringement if you ever have to go to court.

## If No Drawing Is Submitted With a Patent Application

A patent application is checked for completeness when it is first received at the PTO. If it is filed without a drawing, and the PTO determines that a drawing is necessary for the understanding of the invention, the application will not be given a filing date because it will be considered incomplete. It will also be considered incomplete and not be given a filing date if it mentions a drawing, but none is submitted. In either case, the PTO will notify you to furnish the drawing. When the drawing is received in the PTO, the application will be given a filing date as of the date of the drawing's receipt.

If you have not furnished a drawing because you felt it wasn't necessary for the understanding of the invention, but the examiner requires you to submit one because it is possible to illustrate or explain the invention better with one, then your application will not be denied a filing date. There is no need to explain why you have not filed a drawing, because the examiner will make a decision based solely on the specification (written description of the invention).

**EXAMPLE:**

LeRoy files a patent application on a heat-treating process for making softballs that involves specific temperatures and steps. LeRoy explains the process clearly and completely in the specification. His application will be assigned a filing date, because no drawing is necessary for the understanding of the invention. However, months after filing, when the application is taken up for examination, the examiner requires LeRoy to furnish a flowchart-type drawing for illustrating his heat-treating steps, so that his patent will be an easier-to-understand search reference. LeRoy must provide the drawing in the time period set by the examiner—usually three months—otherwise his application will go abandoned. LeRoy's application will retain its original filing date.

## Three Types of Patent Drawings

If your invention is not exempt from the drawing requirement, as discussed above, you must provide a drawing. Different types of drawings are required for different types of patents. Refer to *Patent It Yourself* for additional details and help in choosing the proper type of patent to seek for your invention. Let's briefly look at the specific drawings that must accompany each of the types of patents.

### Utility Patent Drawings

Utility patents cover useful inventions, including:

- machines, such as tools, devices, engines, equipment, electronic circuits, and so forth
- articles of manufacture, such as paper clips, pencils, and other simple devices
- methods, such as manufacturing processes, software, and surgical procedures
- compositions, such as chemicals, drugs, and biological material, and
- new uses of old devices, such as using aspirin to speed the growth of swine.

Each utility patent application must include as many drawings as necessary to show every essential feature of the invention, so that its structure and operation can be fully understood. The important elements are labeled with reference numbers, which are referred to in the written description portion of the application. Illustration 5.1 shows a typical utility patent drawing, which happens to be of a geared, rotary scalpel.

Although the example shows a tangible device, utility patent drawings can comprise graphical representations, such as flowcharts and electronic schematics, to illustrate abstract concepts. Photographs may be submitted instead of line drawings under certain rare conditions. (See Chapters 4 and 8.) Utility patent drawings are discussed in detail in Chapter 6.

## Design Patent Drawings

Design patents cover inventions with unique or ornamental qualities, for example, a light fixture design, a shoe design, a camera housing design, or a sofa design. A design patent covers only the aesthetic or ornamental aspect (styling) of an invention.

An invention may be covered by both utility and design patents—the utility patent may cover its utilitarian aspects, while the design patent may cover its styling.

Illustration 5.2 shows a typical design patent drawing, which happens to be of a floppy disc clock. Each design patent application must include several figures to show the invention from all possible viewpoints, so that its appearance can be clearly understood. No reference numbers should be used, because a design patent does not include an extended description of the invention. The drawings must include adequate shading—that is, lines or marks that depict surface contour.

Photographs may be submitted instead of line drawings under certain conditions. (See Chapters 4 and 8.) Design patent drawings are discussed in detail in Chapter 7.

## Plant Patent Drawings

Plant patents cover asexually reproducible plants—that is, those that are reproducible by grafting and cutting, such as flowers. Plants with practical uses, such as medicinal herbs, may also be covered by utility patents. Plants that are novel only in appearance, such as ornamental flowers, cannot be covered by utility patents.

Each plant patent application must include as many drawings as necessary to artistically show every distinguishing characteristic of the plant, from as many viewpoints as necessary. If color is a distinguishing characteristic, then color drawings or photographs must be (and usually are) used. (See Chapters 4 and 8 for details on photography.) No reference numerals may be used, because a plant patent does not include a description of the plant, other than a descriptive title. Plant patents are extremely rare, so no drawing sample is provided here.

## Number of Copies to File

Only one copy of the drawing(s) need be filed in utility, design, and plant applications where a black-and-white line drawing or photograph is used. However, if color drawings are used, three copies must be filed in utility and design applications and two copies in plant applications.

# Formal and Informal Drawings

The PTO requires drawings to conform to a set of strict standards, discussed in detail in Chapter 8. Drawings that are determined by the PTO's Drafting Branch to comply with the standards are considered to be "formal" drawings, whereas those that do not are

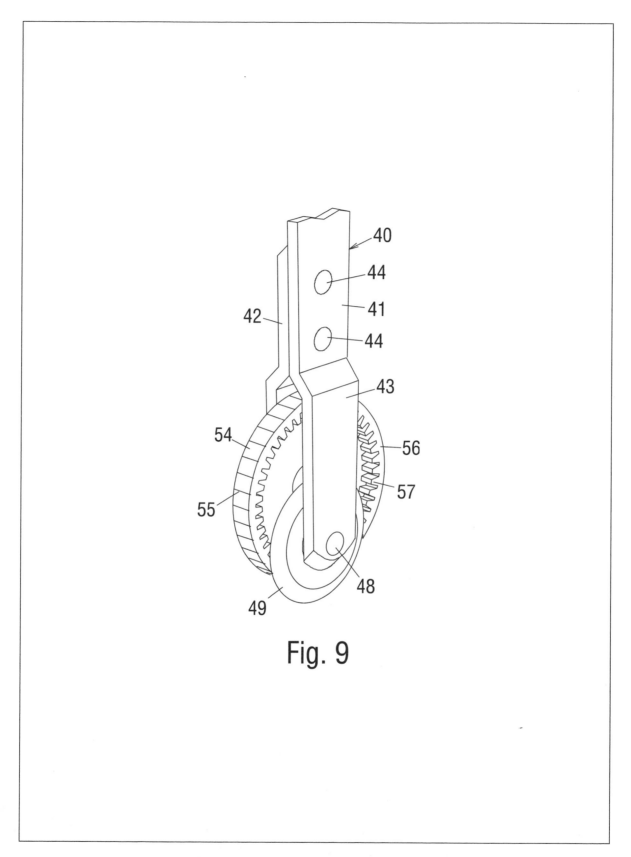

# Fig. 9

**Illustration 5.1—Typical Utility Patent Drawing**

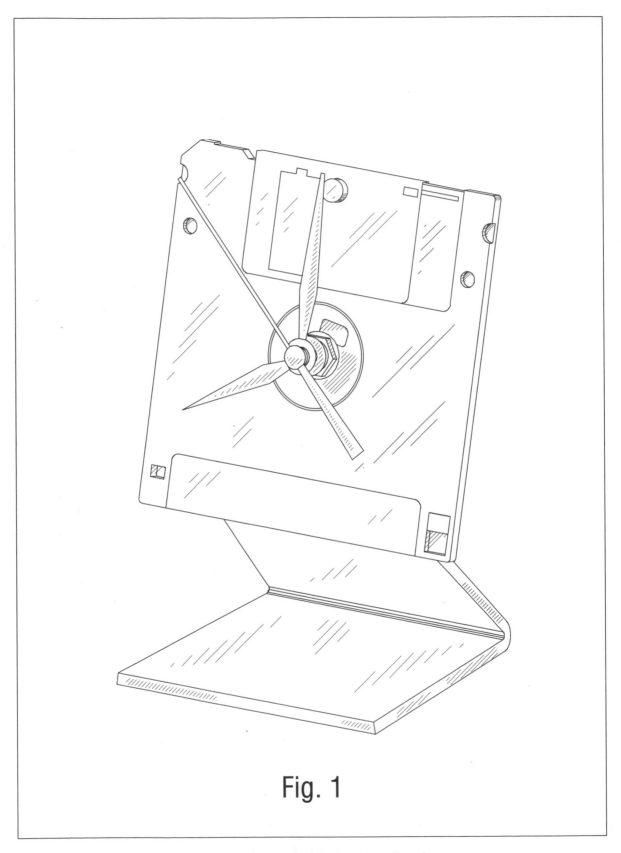

Fig. 1

**Illustration 5.2—Typical Design Patent Drawing**

considered to be "informal" drawings. Freehand sketches are considered as informal drawings. An application filed with informal drawings will be given a filing date, but formal drawings must be submitted before the application will be examined. Therefore, formal drawings should be submitted with the application to avoid delays.

## Even Informal Drawings Must Be Clear and Detailed

If freehand sketches are submitted as informal drawings when you file your application, these sketches should be detailed and clear enough to fully convey your invention. Keep in mind that the formal drawings (required before examination can take place) must show the same information as in the informal drawings.

PTO rules prohibit the addition of new matter to the same application. New matter is any technical information not in the application as originally filed. New matter can be added by filing a continuation-in-part application, but the new information won't get the benefit of the original filing date. Therefore, if an examiner objects to a sketch because it does not show a certain part clearly enough to make it understandable, you cannot make it more distinctive in the formal drawings; new information (new matter) would have to be provided to make the part understandable.

Consider the difference between blurry and sharp photographs of a newspaper. The text on the newspaper cannot be read in a blurry photograph but it can be easily read in a sharp photograph. The sharp photograph has more "information" than the blurry one. Therefore, informal drawings should be carefully executed and should clearly show the essential details.

## Photographs

You can submit photographs, whether black-and-white or color, as informal drawings for your utility or design patent application. Black-and-white photographs are not accepted as formal drawings unless they are photomicrographs. (See Chapter 4.) The PTO discourages color photographs (and color drawings) because they are difficult and expensive to reproduce. Color photographs may be used only if color is necessary to properly illustrate the invention or design. (See Chapter 4.) You must send a petition and petition fee when submitting color photos (and drawings). (See Chapter 8 for details on such petitions.) If the petition is not granted, formal black line drawings must be submitted to replace the color photo or drawings. Keep in mind that color photos (or color drawings) are approved only on rare occasions.

## Overview

The following table summarizes the types of drawings or photos that are accepted as informal drawings, formal utility drawings, or formal design drawings.

| | Informal Utility or Design Drawing | Formal Utility Drawing | Formal Design Drawing |
|---|:---:|:---:|:---:|
| Sketches | ✔ | | |
| Black line drawing that does not comply with all PTO rules (see Chapter 8 for rules) | ✔ | | |
| Black line drawing that complies with all rules (see Chapter 8 for rules) | | ✔ | ✔ |
| Black-and-white photo | ✔ | | |
| Black-and-white photo when line drawings cannot adequately illustrate invention (no petition required) | | ✔ | ✔ |
| Color photo or color drawing | ✔ | | |
| Color photo or color drawing with granted petition (petition fee required) | | ✔ | ✔ |

## Engineering Drawings Are Not Suitable

Inventors who finance the manufacturing and marketing of their inventions usually have a set of engineering drawings or blueprints made. Engineering drawings are created according to engineering standards, which are very different from patent drawing standards. However, they may be submitted as informal drawings, provided they clearly show the invention, and reference numerals are added to label the parts. As discussed above, if such drawings do not show the invention clearly, they cannot be clarified later, so make sure that they are clear and understandable even if they are filed as informal drawings.

If you have computerized engineering drawings, commonly known as CAD (computer-aided drafting) drawings, you may be able to modify them into formal patent drawings. See Chapter 3 for details on CAD drawings. ●

# Utility Patent Drawings

This chapter details the specific requirements of formal utility patent drawings; refer to Chapter 5 for a discussion of formal and informal drawings. Also refer to Chapter 5 and *Patent It Yourself*, our companion volume, for additional details on utility patents, including the types of inventions that qualify for them and how to prepare the written portion of the patent application.

It is very important to plan the drawings carefully before starting to draw, such as the number of views from different angles, the specific angle of each view, whether to use sectional or exploded views, and how to show the movement of movable parts. The more complicated the invention, the more planning is necessary. There are many issues that must be worked out first. This chapter will help you accomplish that. Therefore, you should understand this chapter before planning the drawings.

## Amount of Detail Required

The two most important requirements regarding utility patent drawings are:

- The drawings and the written description (collectively known as the "disclosure") must be detailed and clear enough to enable a person skilled in the pertinent field to make and use your invention. That is, the disclosure must be "enabling." For example, if your invention is a medical laser, your drawings and description must be detailed enough to show a medical laser engineer how to make and use your invention. While your drawings do not have to be detailed enough for everyone to understand the invention, you should try to make

them understandable to a layperson since your examiner (and any judge who may subsequently rule on your patent) may not have a technical background in the field of your invention.

- The drawings must show all the parts or elements mentioned in the specification, including the description of the invention (technical description) and claims (legal description). For example, if the description and claims mention Parts A, B, and C, the drawings must show all three parts.

## Some Details May Be Left Out

Satisfying the above requirements doesn't mean that the drawings must show every tiny detail. As mentioned, they have to show only enough to enable "a person skilled in the pertinent field to make and use your invention." Therefore, details that such a skilled person would know to provide may be left out. Generally, implicitly required elements, such as screws that attach parts together, need not be shown or described. If your invention is electromechanical (a mechanical device with electrical parts), you do not have to show the wires if you provide a separate electrical diagram. Some conventional elements may be illustrated with symbolic representations if their detailed illustration is not essential for an understanding of the invention. For example, if a conventional, off-the-shelf steam generator is used in a new steam cleaner, the steam generator may be simply represented by a box labeled "Steam Generator."

Also, a conventional element may be mentioned in the description but not shown in the drawings if it is not essential for an understanding of the invention. Such an element should be followed by the note "(not shown)."

EXAMPLE 1:

The invention in Illustration 6.1 includes an electrically driven roller 23 that drives a belt 21r around passive rollers 5 and 6. Instead of showing a detailed drawing of a motor connected to the driven roller, a circle is used to represent it. A simple electrical circuit (the lines and symbols connected to the right of roller 23) shows that the roller is electrically driven by a battery, which need not be numbered or mentioned in the description because it is readily understood by anyone skilled in the field. Note that the rollers are not shown to be connected to any supporting structure, which is acceptable as long as this fact is mentioned in the description. For example, you may write, "The elements shown in Fig. 1 are mounted in a suitable housing and the rollers are journaled in suitable bearings (not shown)," because the housing will also be readily apparent to anyone skilled in the field.

EXAMPLE 2:

The motor vehicle gear position indicator in Illustration 6.2 includes a housing 10 positioned above a steering column 12. Housing 10 need not be shown mounted to any supporting structure, if such structure is conventional, and the description mentions such structure. For example, "Housing 10 is mounted in a conventional instrument panel (not shown)."

## Better to Include Too Much Rather Than Too Little Detail

There is no precise way to determine exactly how detailed the drawing must be. When in doubt, you should err on the side of providing more detail, because while too much detail would not hurt, too little detail definitely will since the PTO will not allow you to add any new technical matter to the disclosure after your application is filed.

## Dimensioning Is Usually Unnecessary

Do not include the dimensions or angles of the parts in the drawing unless they are crucial to the understanding of the invention, or if they are important in distinguishing your invention from the prior art (similar but older devices). However, if you do include dimensions or angles, the PTO prefers metric units (millimeters, centimeters, and meters) over English units (inches and feet). If you prefer to include English units, you should use both metric and English—for example, "level 5 is 10 cm (2.5 inches) long."

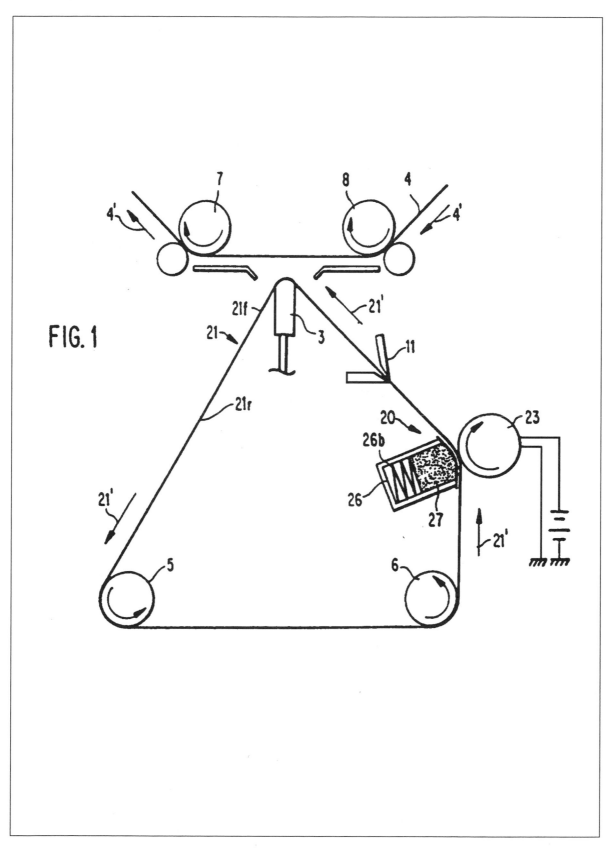

**FIG. 1**

**Illustration 6.1—Leaving Out Some Detail**

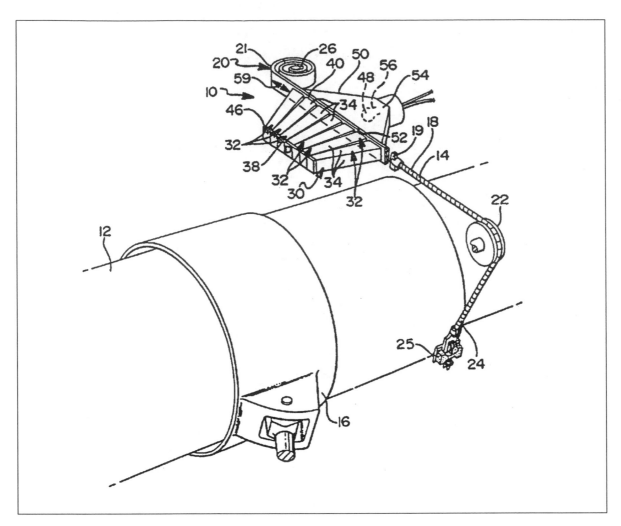

**Illustration 6.2—Leaving Out Some Detail**

## Idealized Parts

You can apply for a patent even if you have not made a model. If you have a rough model or prototype of your invention, you do not have to show an exact representation of it in the drawings; you can show it in an idealized form if you wish. For example, if the model has a part that was fabricated by attaching two or more elements together, it can be shown as a single, integral part, such as in Illustration 6.3. Joints between parts that are not meant to be separable—that is, they are permanently connected—can be left out. Also, a detail can be eliminated if it is not necessary for a complete understanding of an invention, and you do not care to claim it.

**EXAMPLE:**

You invented a portable table with a new folding mechanism. When you built your prototype, you used a height-adjustable leg that you happened to find in your workshop. You can show the leg in a simplified, nonadjustable form, if:

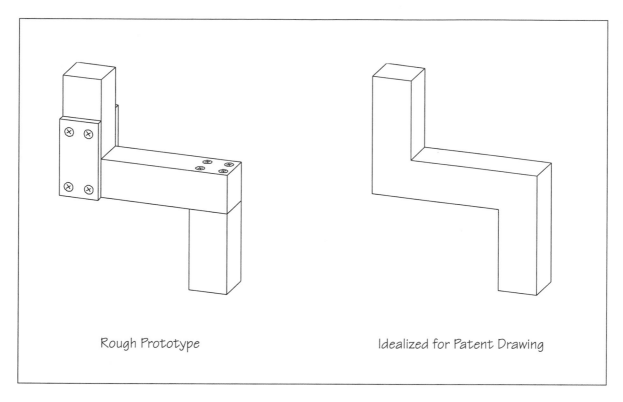

**Illustration 6.3—Idealized Parts**

- You feel that the adjustability of the leg is not an important part of your invention.
- You do not describe the leg as being adjustable in the description.
- You do not recite the leg as being adjustable in the claims.

## Invention Part of Larger Machine

An invention that forms part of a larger conventional machine, such as a transmission for a motor vehicle, can be shown with just a small portion of the larger machine to illustrate its role. Illustration 6.4 shows a transmission controller that includes a control box 30 and an actuator 28. The dashboard is partially presented to show where the control box is installed, and a "disembodied" transmission 16 is presented to show where the actuator is attached. Such a drawing is perfectly acceptable.

## Number All Parts

All parts or elements in a utility patent drawing mentioned in the description and claims must be designated with reference numerals or characters. See Chapter 8 for details on reference numerals.

## Make as Many Drawings as Necessary

Most inventions cannot be clearly understood with one figure. You must make as many figures as necessary, so that the structure and operation of your invention may be easily understood. Later in this chapter, we detail the different types of figures or views that may be used.

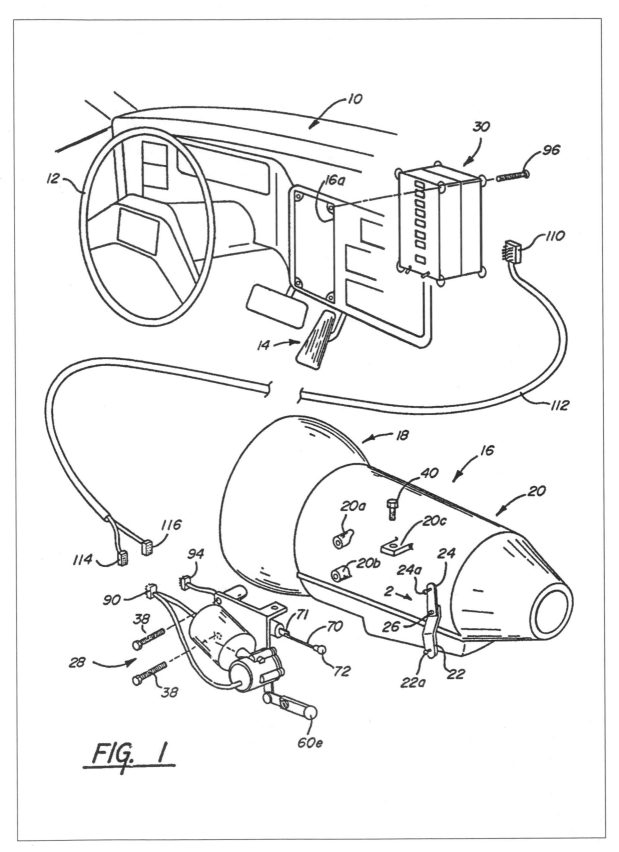

**FIG. 1**

Illustration 6.4—Invention Part of Larger Machine

## No Changes Are Permitted After Filing

As stated, no "new matter"—that is, technical information not shown or described in the original drawings or description—can be added after the application is filed. For example, the drawings cannot be changed to incorporate substitute parts, new features, or improvements. Therefore, submitting a drawing that does not clearly illustrate the invention is an error that cannot be fixed, because new parts would have to be added to the drawing to improve understandability. Such parts will most likely be considered to be new matter and, therefore, will not be accepted by the PTO.

The determination of whether a drawing adequately conveys an invention is made when the application is first seen by an examiner. This usually happens many months to over a year after the filing date. (See Chapter 13 of *Patent It Yourself*.) If the application is rejected because the drawings are not clear enough, the only ways to overcome the objection are to try to convince the examiner to reverse position (a difficult task) or to change the drawings and file them with a second application, known as a continuation-in-part application (CIP), which requires a new filing fee. (See Chapter 9 for details on how to overcome rejections.) The new matter filed with a CIP will not get the benefit of the original filing date. (See Chapter 14 of *Patent It Yourself* for more information on CIPs.) Therefore, the drawing is just as important to the whole application as the written portion and must be clear and adequately detailed.

---

### How to Check for Adequacy

Having created an invention, the inventor is so familiar with it that he or she sometimes takes its structure and operation for granted and omits small but vital details in the drawing. One way to avoid falling into this trap is to show the drawing and description in confidence to others (preferably those who are skilled in the same field) and ask them if your documents are clearly understandable. At the very least, carefully consider if they are understandable to someone skilled in the field, but who has never seen your invention before.

---

# Types of Views

A complete understanding of an invention often requires multiple figures or views that show it from different view angles, sliced open to reveal internal parts, or disassembled. A single sheet of paper may contain several figures. The figures must not touch each other, and must be far enough apart so that they are clearly separated.

## Orthogonal and Perspective Views

Orthogonal (engineering) and perspective figures are the most commonly used figures. (See Chapter 1 for details.) Perspective figures are easier to understand than orthogonal figures, but they are also more difficult to draw. To save work, you may illustrate your invention solely with orthogonal figures, unless they are too difficult to understand, in which case you should add one or more perspective figures.

**TIP**

**Choose a view angle carefully.** The angle of a perspective figure should be chosen carefully, so that as many of your invention's features as possible are clearly visible. If one perspective figure cannot show all the important features, additional perspective figures should be used. It is best to make the first drawing in an application a perspective figure to provide the reader—for example, the patent examiner, a judge, or a potential licensee—with a general understanding of the invention.

## Exploded Views

The comprehension of some inventions may be enhanced by an exploded view (figure), which shows the device disassembled. The constituent parts are separated as far as necessary to show the essential details of each one. Each part is preferably moved out along a predetermined axis, but an individual part may be oriented in any position necessary to show its essential details, so long as projection lines are added to show how the part was moved out. An exploded view should always be accompanied by another figure showing the parts assembled, as shown in Illustration 6.5. Exploded views are generally unnecessary, because internal parts are usually better illustrated with sectional views (discussed below). If you wish to use exploded views, note the following about brackets and projection lines.

**Brackets.** As shown in Illustration 6.6, unconnected parts must be "enclosed" by a bracket to show that they belong to the same figure. The bracket can be oriented in any position. The parts in Illustration 6.7 are purposely positioned so that they are all touching to eliminate the need for a bracket, but such positioning is not as clear as that of Illustration 6.6. No bracket is needed for an exploded view, even if the parts are unconnected, if it is the only figure on a

sheet. Note that the exploded pipe fittings of Illustration 6.6 and Illustration 6.7 are positioned along a straight line because they share a common axis.

**Projection lines.** The parts in Illustration 6.8 do not lie along a single axis, so each part is separated as if it is pulled in a straight line from its assembled position or moved out. Projection lines (the dot-dashed lines) are provided to show how the parts fit together. As shown in Illustration 6.9, when space constraints prevent the parts from being positioned in straight lines from their assembled positions, zigzagged projection lines can be used. No brackets are necessary in Illustration 6.8 and Illustration 6.9 because the projection lines connect all the parts. Projection lines should always be provided when parts are not separated linearly, so as to make their assembly clear.

## Partial Views

A very long object that cannot fit onto a single sheet without making the details too small can be broken up, so that each piece can be shown larger than it could have been if the object is shown whole, as long as there is no loss in comprehension. There are several ways to do this:

- Break it into two or more pieces to fit them onto a single sheet, such as in Illustration 6.10. A simple, long bar is used to illustrate the point. The pieces should be connected by projection lines to show how they fit together. If no projection lines are used, a bracket should be used. See above for details on the use of brackets.

- Shorten it by removing a section, as shown in Illustration 6.11, but no important details should be removed. Again, a simple, long bar is used to illustrate the point. It is broken in three places to show the three conventional ways for representing a shortened object. The left break is the

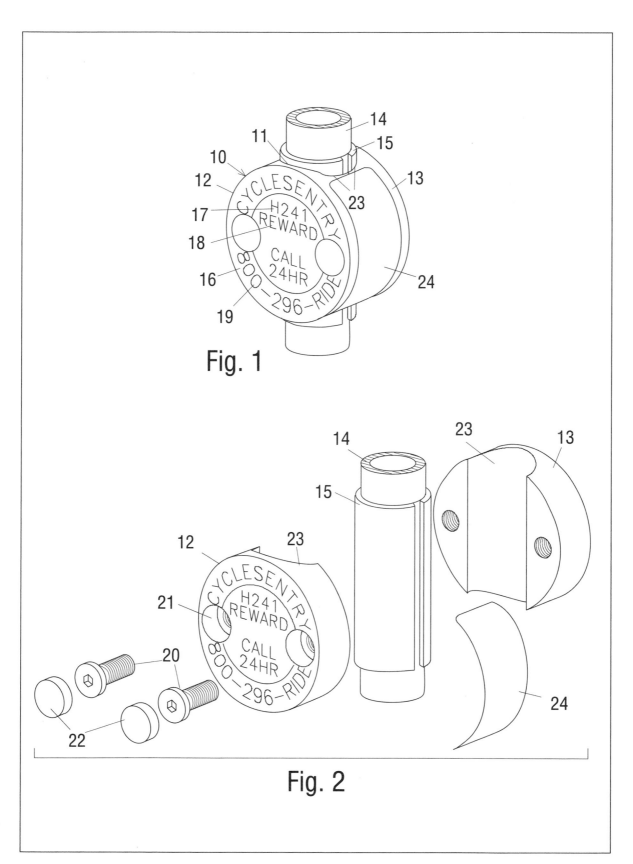

**Illustration 6.5—Exploded View Accompanied by Assembled View**

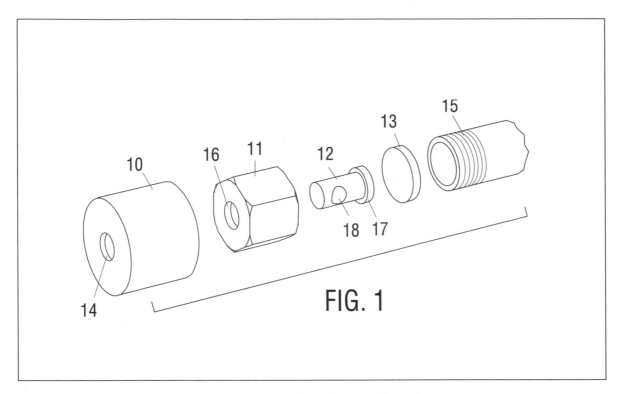

**Illustration 6.6—Exploded View With Bracket**

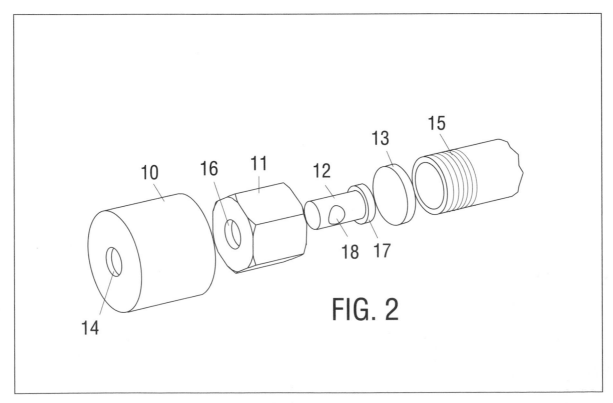

**Illustration 6.7—Exploded View Without Bracket**

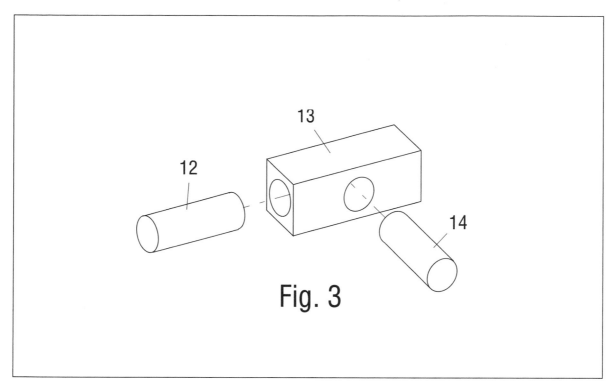

**Illustration 6.8—Exploded View With Projection Lines**

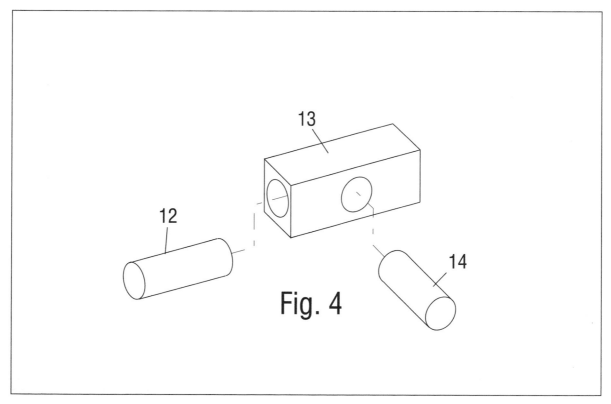

**Illustration 6.9—Exploded View With Zigzagged Projection Lines**

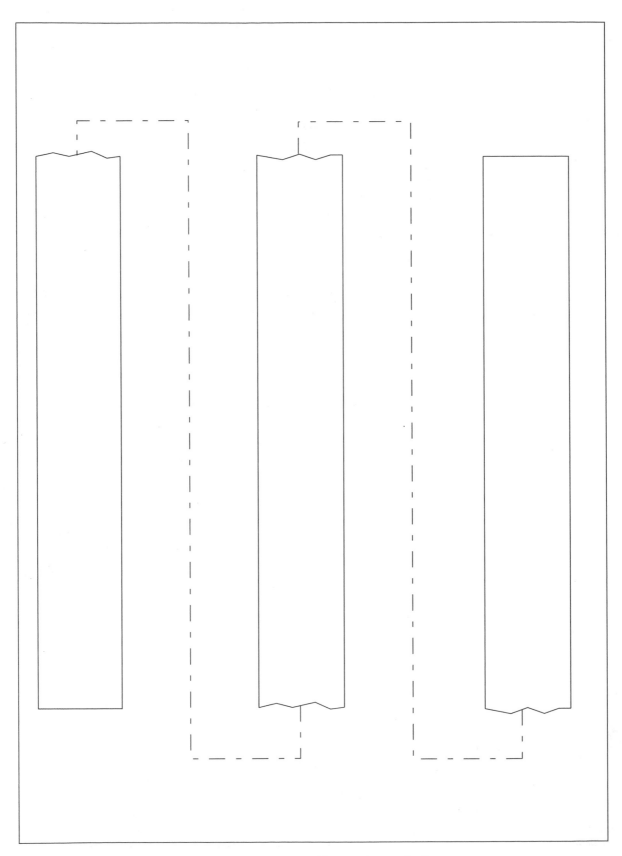

**Illustration 6.10—Long Object Broken to Fit Sheet**

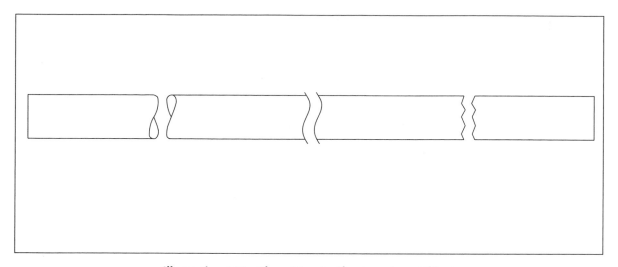

**Illustration 6.11—Three Ways to Shorten a Long Object**

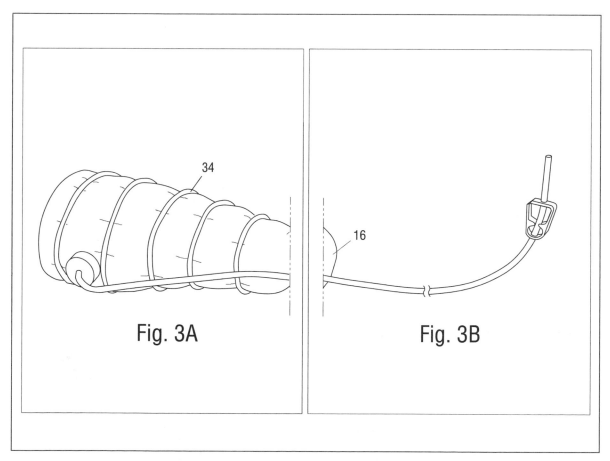

**Illustration 6.12—Spreading a Large Figure Onto Multiple Sheets**

type typically used for a cylindrical object, whereas the other two types can be used for anything.

- Spread it across two or more sheets, such as the drinking bag in Illustration 6.12. The views must be arranged on each sheet so that the sheets can be tiled (positioned like bathroom tiles) next to each other to assemble the complete figure. A dot-dot-dash (phantom) line should be provided to denote the broken edge of each partial view. Any arrangement of the sheets can be used, for example, side-to-side, top-to-bottom, and rectangular array, as long as the sheets can be assembled without ambiguity or blocking the drawings on each other. Each partial view should be labeled with a figure number having a letter suffix, for example, Fig. 3A and Fig. 3B.

Also, an invention can have a part broken off and omitted if comprehension is not affected. The broken edge is customarily made jagged to indicate its nature, such as the portions of element 14 below its horizontal surface in Illustration 6.13.

## Sectional Views

If a device has hidden parts or internal features that should be shown, one or more sectional (cutaway) views may be used. Illustration 6.14 shows a general view of a box, Fig. 1, and a sectional view, Fig. 2, of the hollow interior of the box. Whenever a sectional view is used, section lines (a broken line with perpendicular end arrows) should be placed on a general view, such as in Fig. 1. The broken line between the arrows defines the sectioning plane, that is, where the object is sliced. The arrows indicate the view direction. Numbers corresponding to the figure number of the sectional view must be placed next to the arrows, and sized about 5 mm or ⅕" high. If the general view

is orthogonal, such as in Illustration 6.14, the position of the sectioning plane is assumed to be perpendicular to the drawing sheet (the sheet of paper the drawing is on).

For example, the broken line in Fig. 1 indicates that the object is sliced at about its midpoint. The arrows indicate that, to see the sliced section as it appears in Fig. 2, a person must be standing to the right of the object and looking toward its left end. The number "2" is placed at the tip of each arrow, to indicate that the sectional view is Fig. 2. The broken line may be referred to in the specification (description portion of the application) as section "line 2—2." For example, Fig. 2 shows a sectional view of the box of Fig. 1 taken at the sectioning plane and in the direction indicated by section lines 2—2.

## Perspective General View

Instead of an orthogonal general view, such as in Illustration 6.14, you can use a perspective general view, which is easier to understand. However, in a perspective general view, the sectioning plane may be positioned at any angle to the drawing sheet, so greater care should be taken to make its orientation clear. Illustration 6.15 shows how the broken line and arrows are drawn in a perspective general view:

1. "Slice" the object with an imaginary, rectangular sectioning plane. The dashed lines are only for illustrating the plane and where it meets the object; they should not appear in a patent drawing.

2. Draw the broken line on the sectioning plane. Imagine threading a string through the object; the broken line is the part of the string that remains visible.

3. Position the arrows at the ends of the broken line, so that they are perpendicular to the imaginary plane and pointed in the direction of the view.

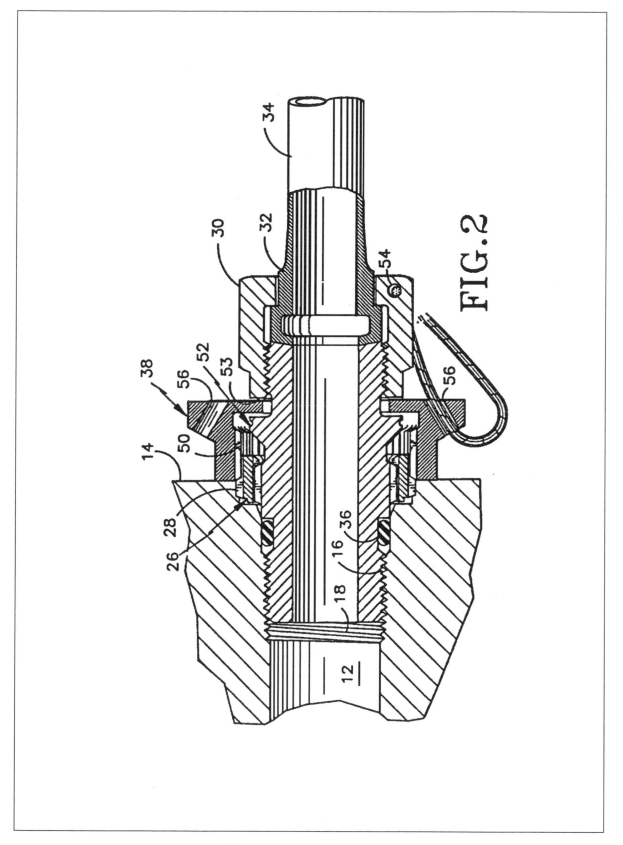

FIG.2

**Illustration 6.13—Broken View**

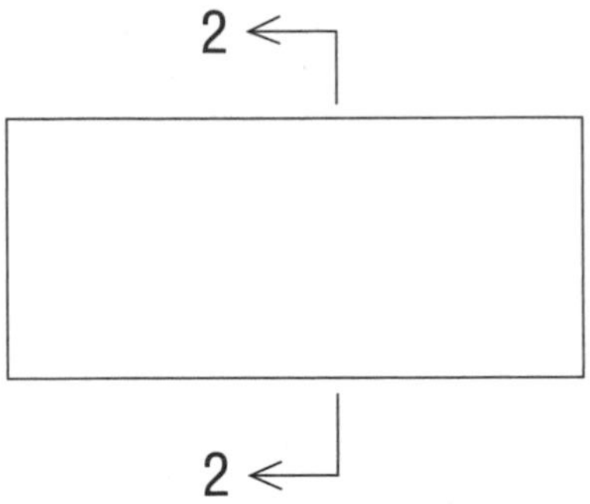

Fig. 1

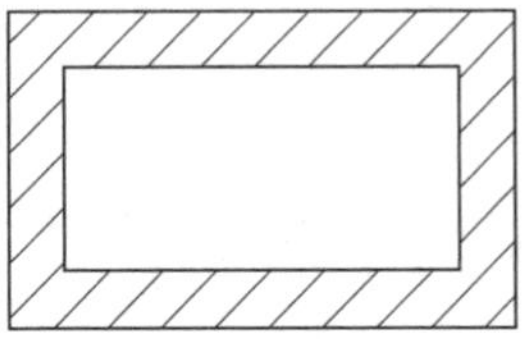

Fig. 2

**Illustration 6.14—Sectional View**

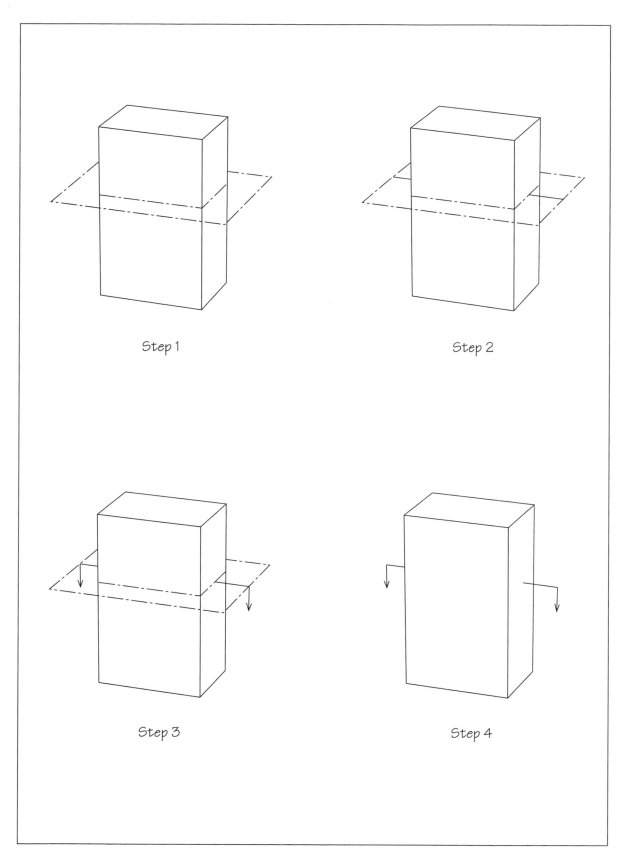

Step 1

Step 2

Step 3

Step 4

**Illustration 6.15—Positioning Broken Lines and Arrows in Perspective General View**

4. The finished broken line with arrows appears in the patent drawing, without the imaginary plane.

The sectioning plane in the illustration shown is horizontal with respect to the object, but a sectioning plane may be arranged in any orientation desired.

## Partial Sectional View

In contrast to Illustration 6.14 of an object completely sliced in half, Illustration 6.16 is a partial sectional view, in which a motor or generator is shown with a portion cut away. The delineation between the sectional and general views is preferably jagged to clearly show that it is a sectional cut. The nonsectioned portion of the motor or generator provides a built-in general view, so that no broken line and arrows are needed. Partial sectional views may be used when it is not necessary to show all of an object's interior.

## Orthogonal Versus Perspective Sectional Views

The easiest type of sectional view to make is the orthogonal sectional view, such as those shown in Illustrations 6.14 and 6.16, in which the viewer is looking at the exposed surface at a right angle, or head-on. However, just as with other orthogonal views, orthogonal sectional views tend to be difficult to understand, particularly if the object depicted is complicated. A much clearer type of sectional view is the perspective sectional, such as Fig. 3 in Illustration 6.17. The general view for a perspective sectional should also be a perspective of the same angle, which in this illustration is Fig. 2. A broken line with arrows is not necessary in this case, because the orientation of the sectioned object, and where the section is taken, are clear when the two views are compared.

## Line Types and Hatching

The "exposed surfaces" of a sectioned part must be covered by hatching, which are oblique parallel lines. Crisscross hatch lines, such as a weave pattern, cannot be used. Also double line hatching (lines arranged in pairs) is forbidden. The angle of hatching is ideally 45 degrees from horizontal. The hatching in adjacent parts should be at opposite angles to clearly show that they represent different parts. If there are more than two adjacent parts, their hatch styles and angles can be varied to distinguish them, as shown in Illustration 6.18. Different areas of a continuous part, such as the two ends of the sectioned ring in Illustration 6.19, should have the same hatch style, spacing, and angle.

The hatch lines should be thinner than the edge lines (lines representing the outline and edges of the object) to avoid confusion. In Illustration 6.20, the figure with thinner hatch lines is clearly easier to understand than the one with identical line widths throughout.

In addition to the continuous lines shown in Figs 18 to 20, the PTO recognizes three types of discontinuous lines, as follows: (1) Hidden lines (even dashes) to indicate (a) an area which is shown enlarged in a different figure (Fig 6-21) or (b) a hidden part (Fig 8-21), (2) Phantom lines (long dash followed by two short dashes, repeated) for components that are not part of the invention (Fig 8-21), and (3) Projection lines (long dash followed by a single short dash, repeated) for showing how separated parts fit together (Fig 8-21).

## Enlarged Views

A portion of a device may be enlarged in a separate figure to show details. Dashed circles are used to surround the enlarged portion in the general view and the enlarged view, as shown in Illustration 6.21. A reference number in the

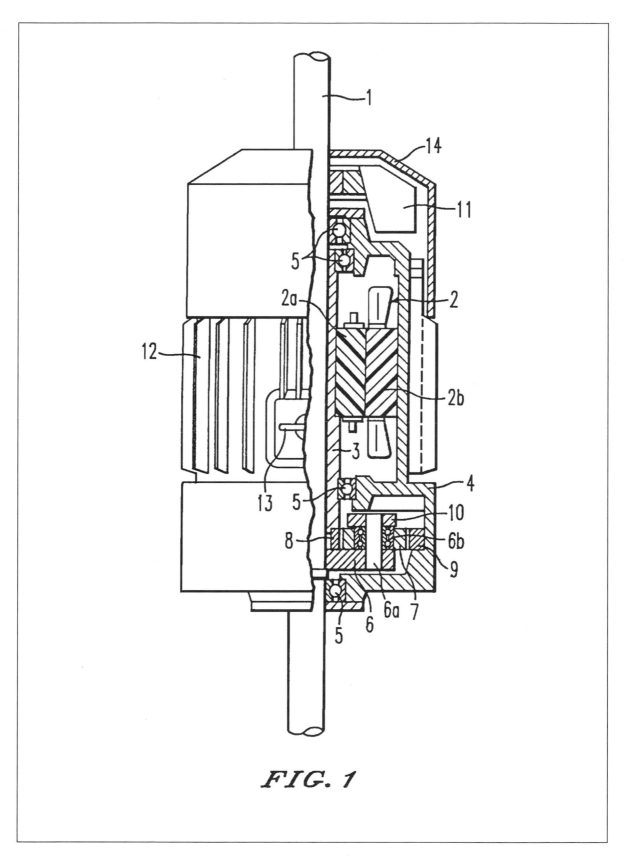

**FIG. 1**

**Illustration 6.16—Partial Sectional View**

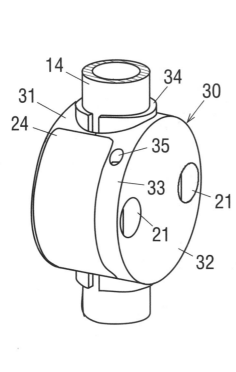

## FIG. 2

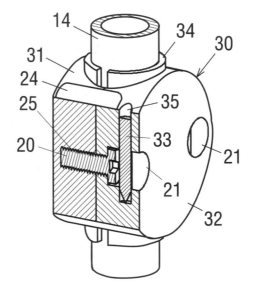

## FIG. 3

**Illustration 6.17—Perspective Sectional View**

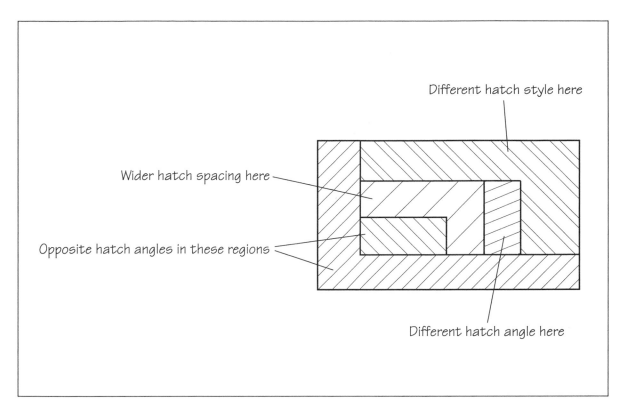

**Illustration 6.18—Vary Hatching to Distinguish Adjacent Regions**

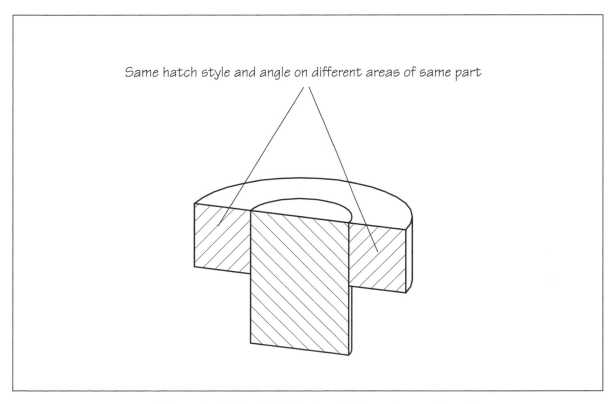

**Illustration 6.19—Hatch Angle on Different Areas of Same Part**

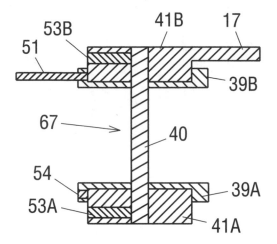

Thick hatch lines make a drawing confusing.

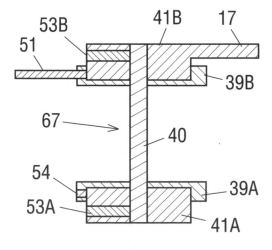

Thin hatch lines make a drawing clearer.

**Illustration 6.20—Thin Versus Thick Hatch Lines**

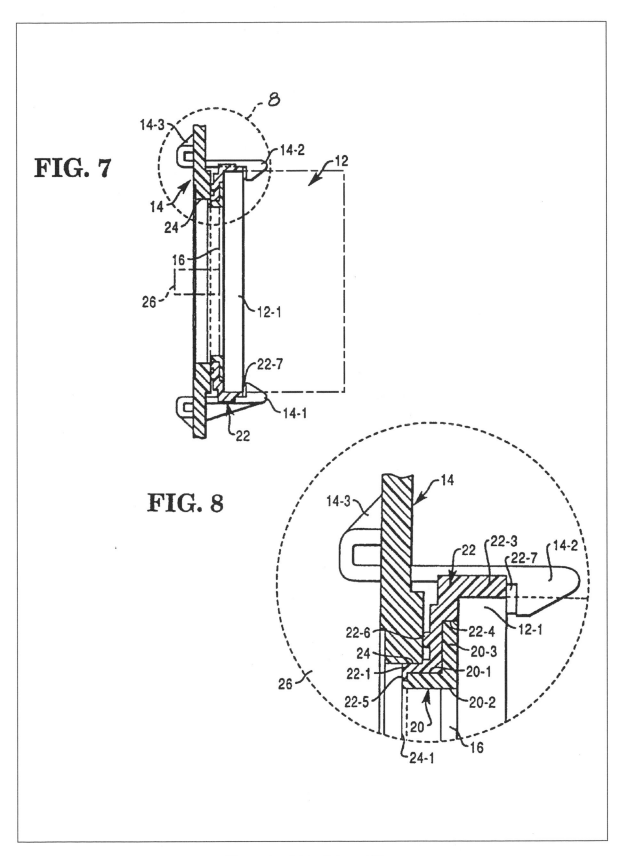

FIG. 7

FIG. 8

**Illustration 6.21—Enlarged View**

general view, which is "8" in this illustration, is applied to the dashed circle to indicate the figure number of the enlarged view, which is Fig. 8 in this illustration.

## Inventions With Moving Parts

An invention with moving parts should be shown with the parts positioned in an initial or at-rest condition. Movement of the parts may be shown in several different ways.

**Arrow.** If the movement of a part is simple, it may simply be indicated by an arrow, such as the rotation of the hinged arm in Illustration 6.22.

**Moved part.** If it is necessary for comprehension, a part may be drawn in solid lines to show it in its initial position and drawn in phantom lines (dot-dot-dash lines) in the same figure

to show it in a moved position. This should be done only if there is no risk of confusion. Illustration 6.23 shows both the original and moved positions of a sleeve on a rod.

**Separate figures.** The initial position of a part may be shown in solid lines in one figure, and its moved position in solid lines in a separate figure, such as the sleeve and rod in Illustration 6.24. The movement of the part may be indicated by an optional arrow. Separate figures should not be connected.

**Long sequence.** A complicated invention should be illustrated with a sequence of figures to clearly show the movements and interactions of all the parts in as many distinct steps as necessary. Illustrations 6.25 through 6.32 show the different figures for illustrating a fairly complicated invention—a dual-cycle toilet flusher that provides selectable small- and big-capacity flushes.

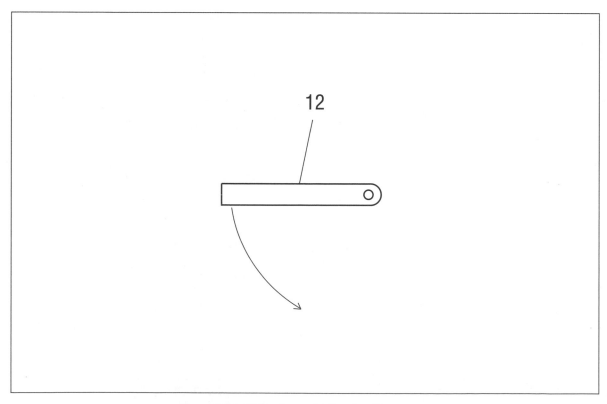

**Illustration 6.22—Arrow Indicating Movement**

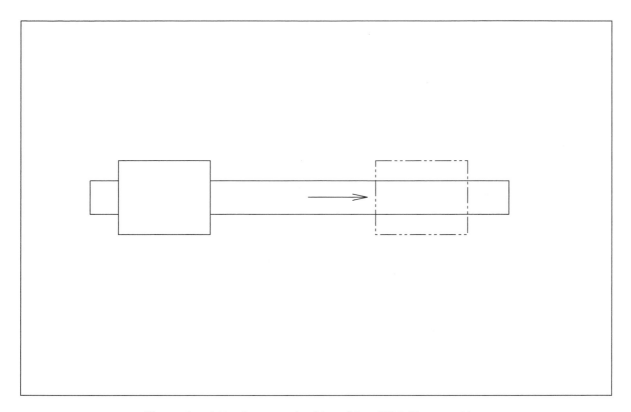

**Illustration 6.23—Representing Moved Part With Phantom Lines**

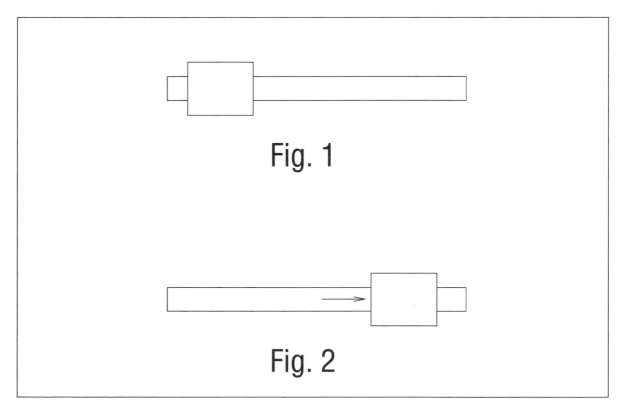

**Illustration 6.24—Representing Moved Part With Separate Figures**

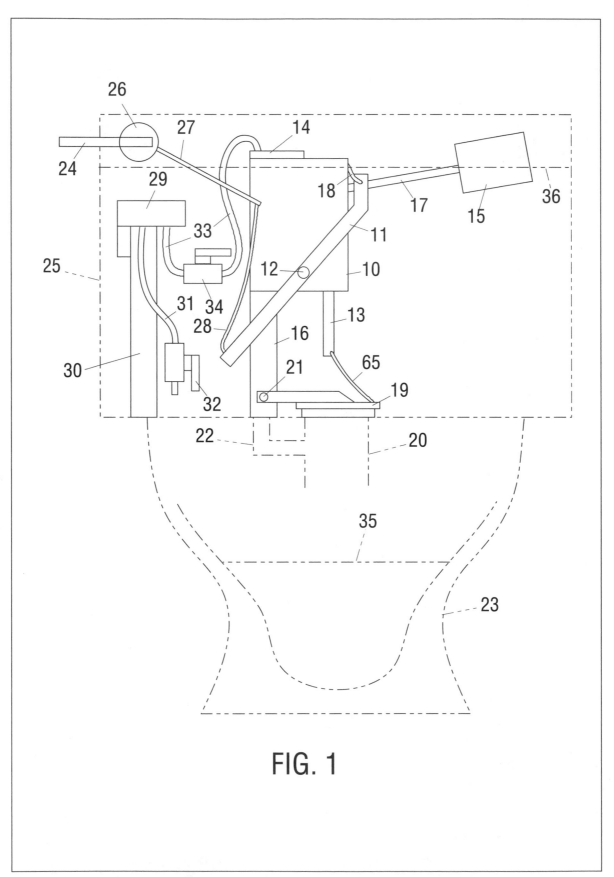

# FIG. 1

**Illustration 6.25—Illustration of Structure and Operation of Complicated Invention**

Fig. 1 of Illustration 6.25 is a general view that shows the device installed in a conventional water tank. Note that the toilet bowl and the water tank, which are not part of the invention, are shown in phantom (dot-dot-dash) lines. Elements that are not part of the invention may be, but are not required to be, shown in phantom lines. Because the flushing mechanism is inside the tank, using phantom lines for the tank enables the flushing mechanism to be shown in solid lines. On the other hand, if the tank is shown in solid lines, the flushing mechanism would have to be shown in hidden (dashed) lines, which would make it harder to draw and much harder to read.

Another alternative is to show the flushing mechanism in solid lines, and the tank cut away to expose the flushing mechanism. However, this would have required a separate, non-cutaway general view with a broken line and arrows to indicate the sectioning plane and view direction (see above, on sectional views). Therefore, in this case, showing the tank and toilet bowl in phantom lines saves work and makes the invention easier to understand.

Fig. 2A of Illustration 6.26 is a detailed general view of the flushing mechanism alone in an initial or at-rest condition. It is provided in addition to Fig. 1, because the flushing mechanism in Fig. 1 is too small to show all of its details. Showing the flushing mechanism alone in a separate figure allows it to be drawn big enough to occupy the entire sheet, so that all the details can be clearly seen. Note that Fig. 2A is an easy-to-understand perspective view. Also note that water level 36 is shown as a phantom line. Fig. 2B is a top sectional view of a cam assembly 67, which includes nested, rotating elements on both sides of the flushing mechanism. Showing cam assembly 67 in a top sectional view allows both sides, as well as the relationship of all the nested elements, to be

clearly shown. Without the top sectional view, several additional perspective views, which are more difficult to draw, would have to be used to convey the same information. Note broken line 2B—2B with arrows indicates the sectioning plane and view direction.

Figs. 3A and 3B of Illustration 6.27 show the flushing mechanism after the flush lever (not shown) has been pressed for a small flush—that is, after the first distinct step in the operation of the mechanism. The device is shown in Fig. 3A with some outer parts omitted to show the position of the inner parts. The description part of the application should note that specific parts are omitted for clarity. For this invention, the statement could be: "In Fig. 3A, housing 10, trigger 43A, cam 39A, and disc 41A (shown in Fig. 2A) are omitted to clearly show the inner mechanisms they would otherwise obscure." The back sides of cam assemblies 67 and 68 are shown, in a separate rear view in Fig. 3B, in positions that correspond to those shown in Fig. 3A. Note that it would not have been possible to clearly show the operation of the mechanism with an orthogonal side view or side sectional view, because of the many layers of parts. Note that drain hole 20 is unconnected to the rest of the device, so a bracket is used to "enclose" them and indicate that all parts belong to the same figure; the bracket is not needed if drain hole 20 touches the rest of the figure.

Illustrations 6.28 through 6.32 show subsequent steps in the operation of the flushing mechanism. Additional outer parts are omitted to show the movement of deeply buried inner parts. The omitted parts can be omitted only if they have been shown in previous figures and are not essential for the understanding of the current figure. Note that Fig. 5 is taken from the opposite side—that is, a rear view to show the operation of the parts on that side. The written description (specification) should state

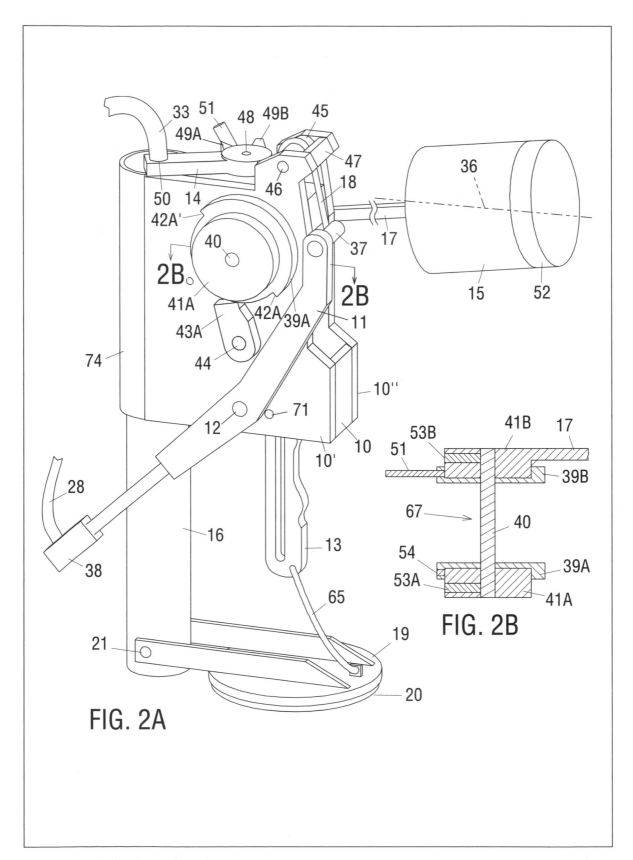

FIG. 2A

FIG. 2B

**Illustration 6.26—Illustration of Structure and Operation of Complicated Invention**

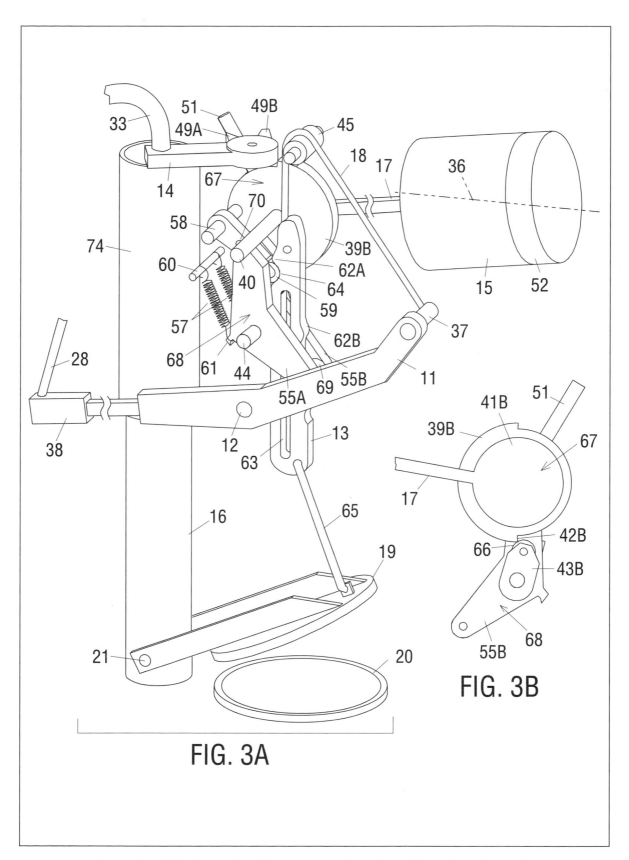

**FIG. 3A**

**FIG. 3B**

**Illustration 6.27—Illustration of Structure and Operation of Complicated Invention**

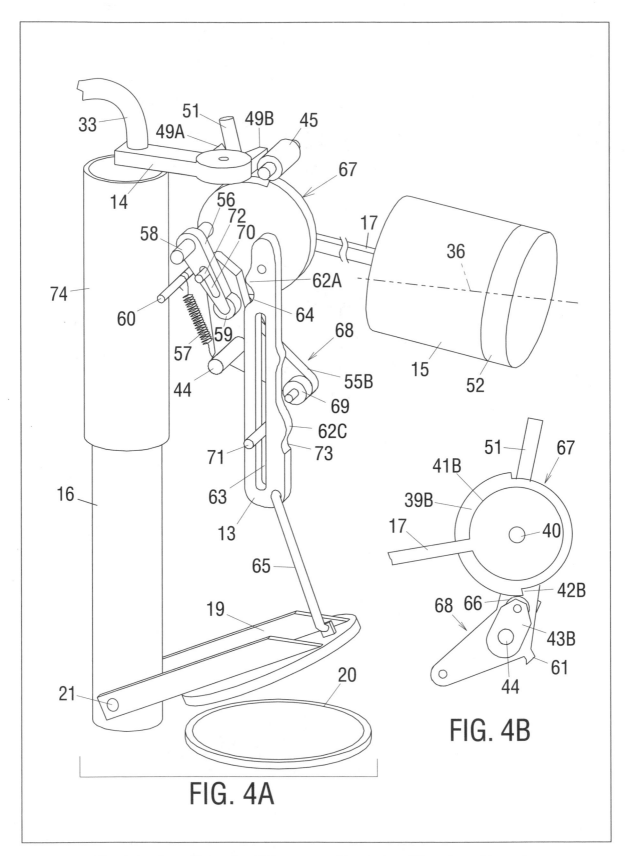

FIG. 4A

FIG. 4B

**Illustration 6.28—Illustration of Structure and Operation of Complicated Invention**

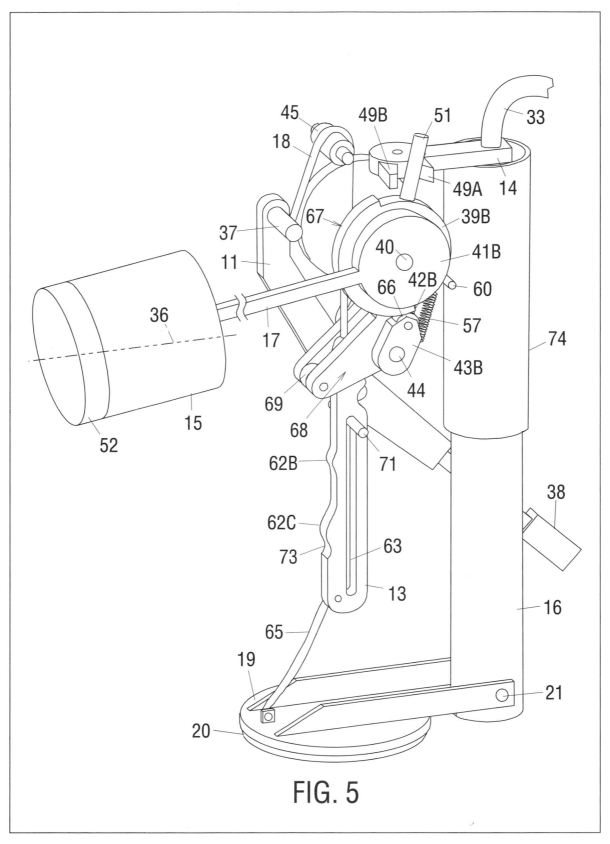

## FIG. 5

**Illustration 6.29—Illustration of Structure and Operation of Complicated Invention**

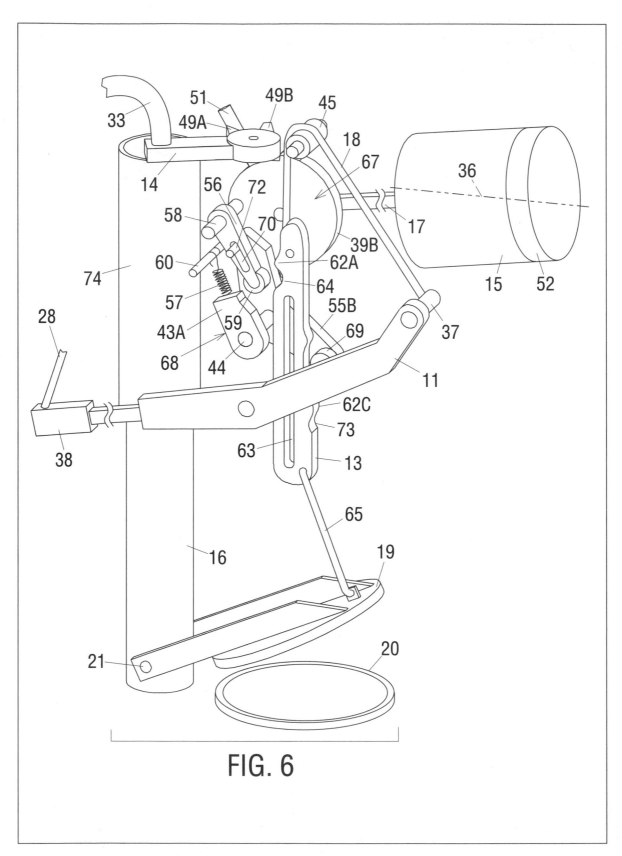

# FIG. 6

**Illustration 6.30—Illustration of Structure and Operation of Complicated Invention**

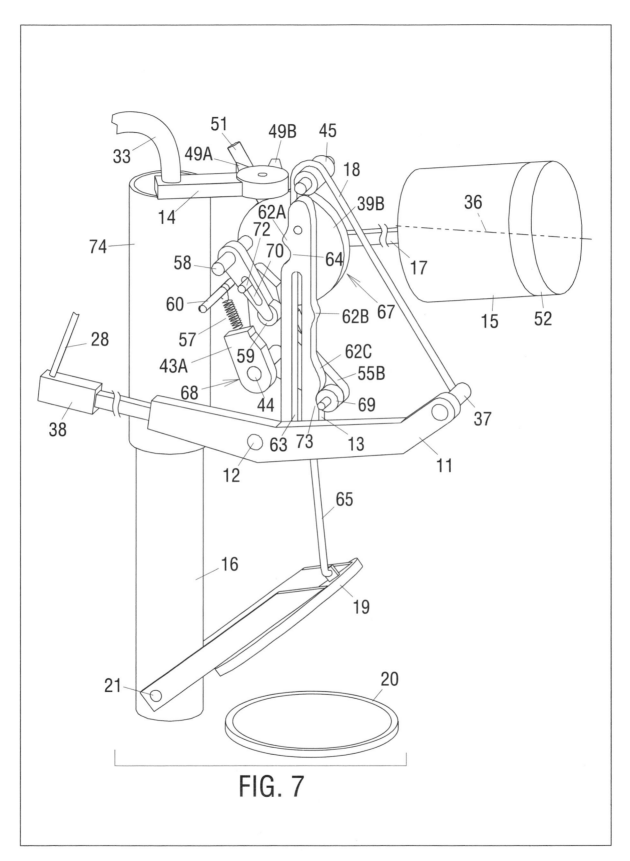

# FIG. 7

**Illustration 6.31—Illustration of Structure and Operation of Complicated Invention**

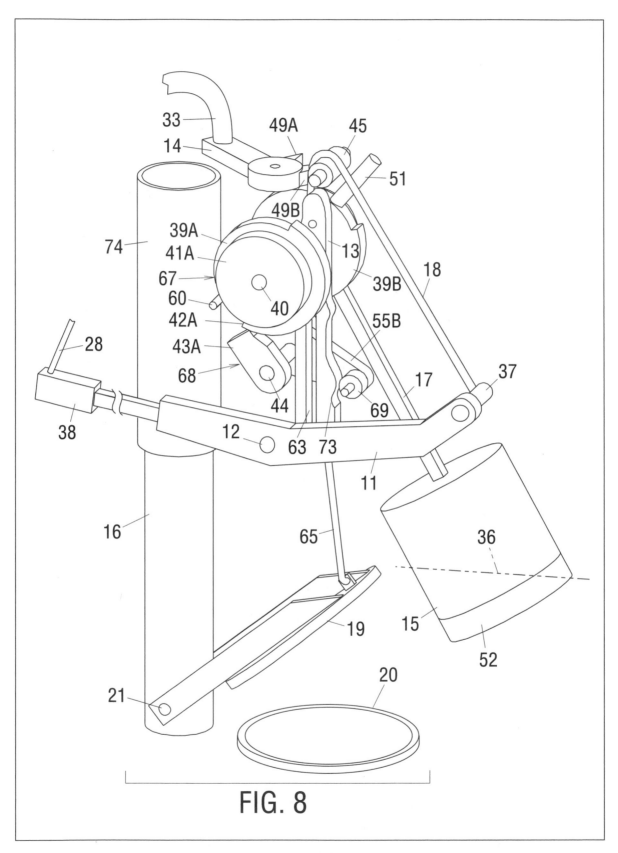

# FIG. 8

**Illustration 6.32—Illustration of Structure and Operation of Complicated Invention**

clearly the side from which a view is taken, and mention that parts are omitted to show others. The sequential figures thus cooperate to clearly show the physical structure and every distinct step in the operation of the flushing mechanism.

## Shading

Shading is the representation of shadows on an object to depict surface contour. It is distinguished from hatching, which is applied to sectioned portions of an object.

Shading is not required in utility patent drawings, but it can improve comprehension of figures in some situations. Consider the unshaded cylinder in Illustration 6.33. Is the top open or closed? The shaded versions make it clear. Flat parts may also be lightly shaded, such as the closed top of the cylinder on the lower right. The object should be shaded as if it is illuminated by a light source on the upper left. Refer to Chapter 7 for details on shading techniques.

## Graphical Symbols

There are standard symbols for many fields of technology, including electronics, fluid power (hydraulics), computer logic, plumbing, and process flow. Symbols are also considered drawings, so they are subject to the basic drawing requirements discussed in Chapter 8.

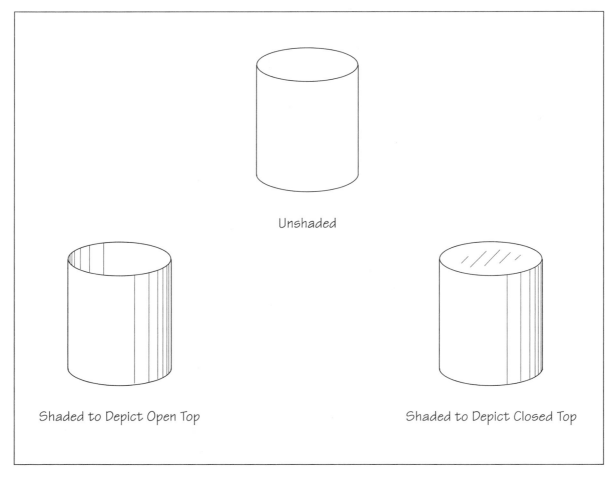

Unshaded

Shaded to Depict Open Top

Shaded to Depict Closed Top

**Illustration 6.33—Shading Improves Comprehension**

There are too many types of symbols to cover here comprehensively, but some common classes are discussed below.

## Electronic Schematics

A simple electrical circuit incorporated into a mechanical device, such as the timer shown in Illustration 6.34, may be drawn as actual parts and wires if the connections are simple enough. Alternatively, a separate schematic or electrical diagram may be used, such as the lamp controller circuit in Illustration 6.35. More complex electronic circuitry should always be illustrated with a separate schematic. Also, a figure may show a combination of actual parts and electronic symbols, such as the pill dispenser in Illustration 6.36.

Any element, including electrical components, mentioned in the description must be designated with a reference numeral using a lead line, as shown in Illustration 6.35. Customary letter-and-numeral designations for electronic parts may also be used, such as D3, R12, L3, Q23, IC5, C21, and T1. ("D" means diode, "R" means resistor, "L" means inductor, "Q" means transistor, "IC" means integrated circuit, "C" means capacitor, and "T" means transformer.) If the value of a component—such as the resistance of a resistor—is important, it should be included in the description or the drawing. Parts not mentioned in the description need not be designated with reference numbers, but they may be labeled with values in the drawing. A subcircuit, such as that indicated by reference numeral 260 in Illustration 6.35, may be enclosed by a box in dashed line. If an electrical connection or line is mentioned in the description, it must also be designated with a reference numeral, for example, "input line 125 of A/D converter 230…." The line terminations—whether inputs or outputs—may be labeled, such as in Illustration 6.35. If a circuit is too large to fit on one sheet, it may be extended across several sheets. (See above, on partial views, for details.) Although electronic schematics are used in these illustrations, the same rules and principles also apply to other types of schematics.

## Block Diagrams

An electronic circuit may be represented by a block diagram, such as in Illustration 6.37, instead of a detailed schematic, if the blocks represent conventional circuits. (If any block repeats a nonconventional circuit, the details of the current should be drawn on a separate figure and explained in the specification.) Generally, block diagrams are used to show very complex circuitry that would otherwise require huge schematics. The blocks must be designated with reference numerals and lead lines and should be labeled with short names or descriptions positioned within the blocks. The lines connecting the blocks must be designated with reference numerals if they are specifically mentioned in the description, although it is not usually necessary to mention the lines. If the lines are not specifically mentioned, they do not have to be designated with reference numerals. Note the arrows on the interconnection lines to show the direction of signal flow. A block diagram too large for one sheet may be spread across several sheets. (See above, on partial views, for details.)

Note that whenever a labeled block is used to represent a component, including a circuit, the component represented by the block must be already known to a PHOSITA (person having ordinary skill in the art); otherwise the patent application must specifically show and describe the component.

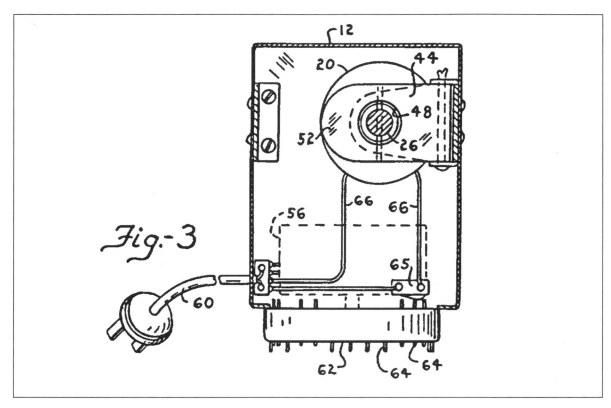

**Illustration 6.34—Electrical Circuit Drawn as Actual Parts**

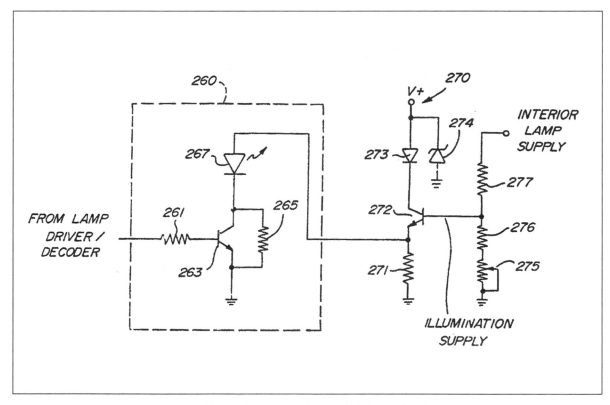

**Illustration 6.35—Electronic Schematic**

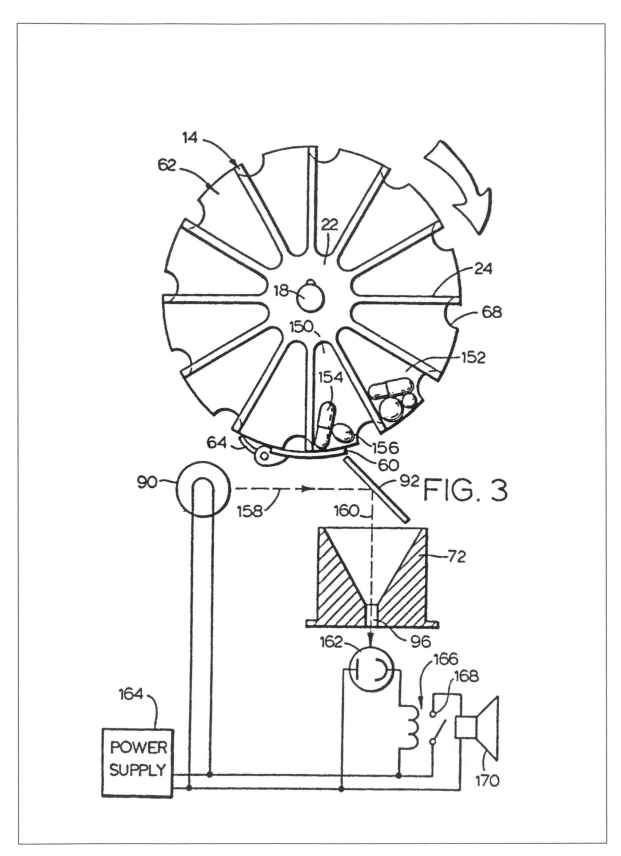

**Illustration 6.36—Actual Parts Combined With Symbols**

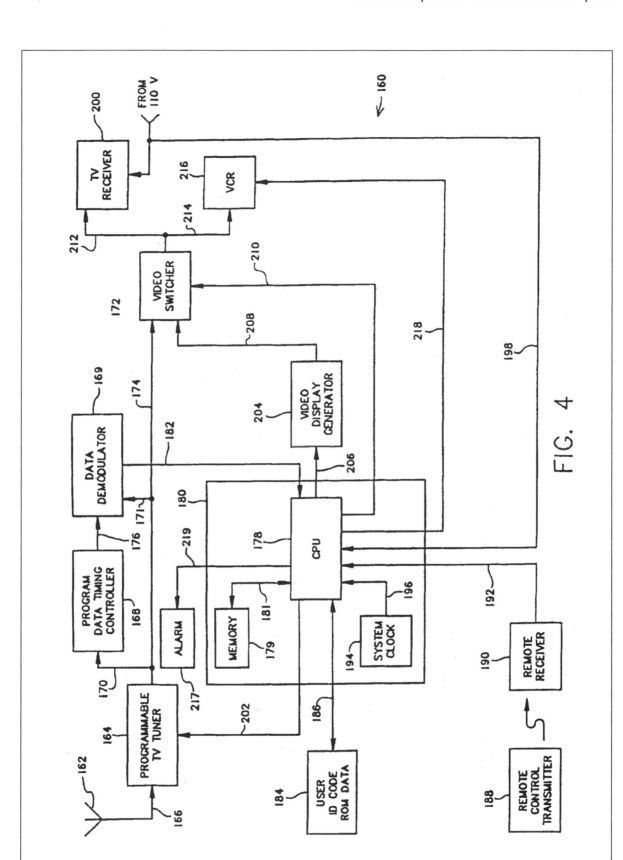

FIG. 4

**Illustration 6.37—Block Diagram**

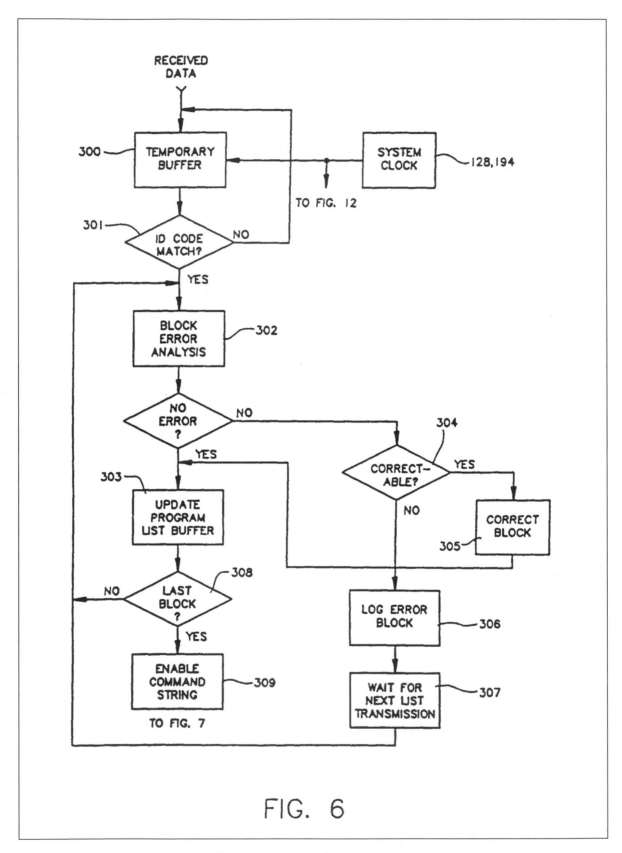

FIG. 6

**Illustration 6.38—Software Flowchart**

# FIG. 4a

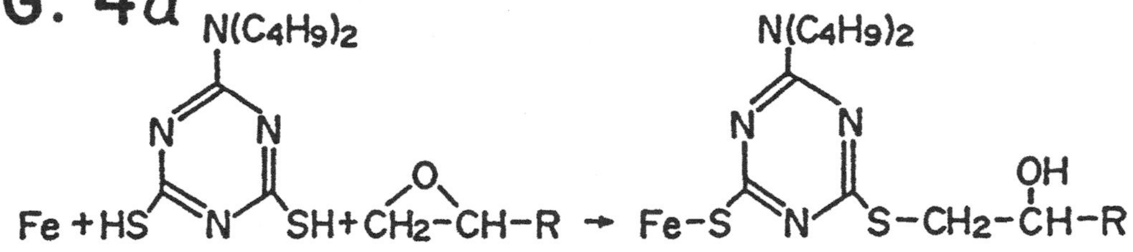

$$N(C_4H_9)_2$$

$$Fe + HS-\!\!\!\!\text{(triazine)}\!\!\!\!-SH + CH_2-CH-R \rightarrow Fe-S-\!\!\!\!\text{(triazine)}\!\!\!\!-S-CH_2-CH-R$$

# FIG. 4b

$$Fe + 3R-\!\!\!\!\text{(ring)}\!\!\!\!\begin{matrix}OH\\OH\\OH\end{matrix} \rightarrow \text{Fe complex}$$

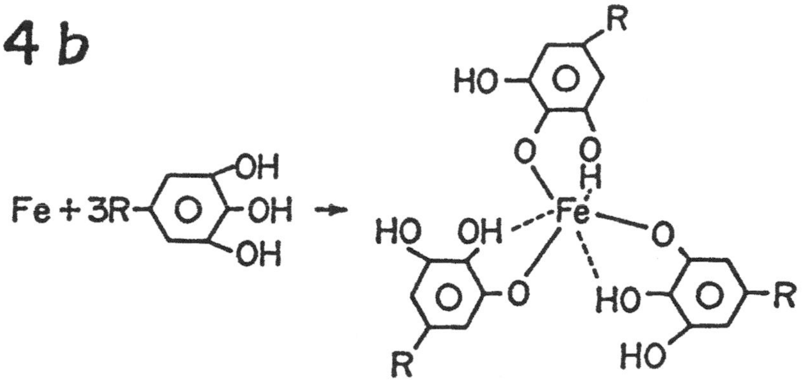

# FIG. 4c

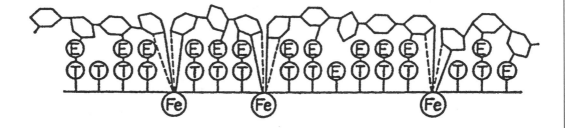

T: Triazine dithiol
E: Epoxy compound

**Illustration 6.39—Chemical Formulas**

## Flowcharts

Processes such as manufacturing methods and computer programs are typically illustrated with flowcharts. The shapes of the boxes used in computer flowcharts should conform to standard practice: rounded box = connector; rectangles = process; diamond = decision; parallelogram = input/output; and so on. A typical software flowchart is shown in Illustration 6.38, and includes boxes connected by arrows. Each box includes a short description. All the boxes should be designated with reference numerals and lead lines. Again, if a flowchart is too large for a single sheet, it may be spread across several sheets. (See above, on partial views for details.)

## Formulas and Tables

Chemical formulas, mathematical formulas, and tables are substantially textual information, so they may either be submitted as drawings or incorporated into the description. Tables and formulas may be included in the claims (legal description).

If presented as drawings, each formula and table must be labeled as a separate figure. Technically, the individual symbols and characters in a formula are not connected. However, no bracket, such as that required for exploded views, is usually required. If a formula is so complex that it may be confused as separate figures, then a bracket must be used. Typical chemical

# FIG. 7

| OVERALL GEAR RATIO | MAIN GEAR UNIT GEAR RATIO | AUXILIARY GEAR UNIT RATIO |
|---|---|---|
| FIRST | FIRST | REDUCTION |
| SECOND | SECOND | REDUCTION |
| THIRD | THIRD | REDUCTION |
| FOURTH | THIRD | DIRECT |
| FIFTH | FOURTH | DIRECT |

**Illustration 6.40—A Typical Table**

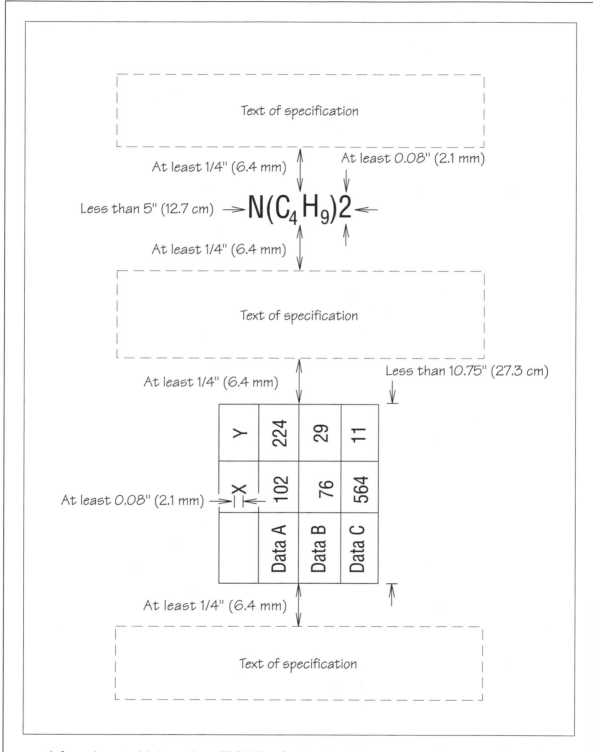

A formula or table less than 5" (12.7 cm) wide should be positioned horizontally, and a formula or table more than 5" wide but less than 10.75" (27.3 cm) wide should be positioned vertically.

**Illustration 6.41—Formulas and Tables in Specifications**

formulas are shown in Illustration 6.39, and a typical table is shown in Illustration 6.40.

If incorporated into the specification, characters used in formulas and tables must be of a block (nonscript) type font or lettering style, as shown in Illustration 6.41. Capital letters must be at least 0.08" or 2.1 mm high (about 10 points), although smaller lower caps may be used. A space of at least 0.25" or 6.4 mm should be provided between complex formulas and tables and the text of the description. Lines and columns of data in tables should be closely positioned to conserve space. The width of a formula or table should be limited to 5" or 12.7 cm, so that it may appear within a single column in the printed patent. If it is not possible to limit the width of a formula or table to such size, it may be placed vertically, and have a maximum height of 10.75" or 27.3 cm.

## Waveforms and Plots

Electrical waveforms and plots of other numerical relationships must be presented as drawings. A group of waveforms that illustrates events related in time must be presented as a single figure with a common vertical axis and extend in a horizontal direction, as shown in Illustration 6.42. The horizontal direction represents time, so therefore the waveforms must be drawn to the same scale, so that signals that occur simultaneously line up properly. Alternatively, waveforms may be presented as separate figures, as shown in Illustration 6.43. Electrical waveforms, whether presented as a single or separate figures, may be connected with optional dashed lines to show relative timing relationships between them. This is the only exception to the rule that prohibits separate figures from being connected. (See Chapter 8 for details on drawing rules.)

Each waveform must be designated with reference letters or descriptive text. The designation of each waveform may be placed anywhere next to the vertical axis, such as to the left in Illustrations 6.42 through 6.44. Different portions of interest in each waveform may be designated with reference numerals, such as in Illustration 6.44, and/or labeled with descriptive text, such as in Illustrations 6.42 through 6.44.

Short waveforms may (and should) be presented in electronic schematics. For example, a cycle of a sine wave can be provided adjacent to the input of a rectifier and a DC pulse can be provided adjacent to the output.

Typical plots are shown in Illustration 6.45. Each plot must be shown as a separate figure and provided with a descriptive label.

## Nonstandard Symbols

Standard symbols should be used whenever possible, but nonstandard symbols may be used if they are not likely to be confused with standard symbols. Nonstandard symbols are subject to the approval of the PTO. If you are unfamiliar with standard symbology for the field of your invention, and your invention is a very simple device, you can probably use nonstandard symbols. For example, a widget with just a few electronic parts connected in a simple way can be illustrated by drawing the actual parts, or labeled rectangles to represent the parts, such as in Illustration 6.46. However, this technique cannot be used for anything but extremely simple devices, because much of the information conveyed by standard symbols cannot be conveyed by labeled rectangles.

## Character Size

Any numeral or letter used with graphical symbols in drawings, including lowercase letters in the labels, must meet the size requirement for reference characters, which is a minimum of ⅛" or 3.2 mm high (about 12 points; see Chapter 8 for details on character size requirements).

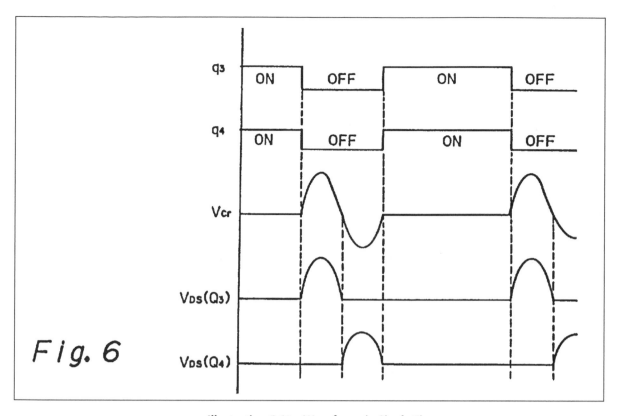

*Fig. 6*

Illustration 6.42—Waveforms in Single Figure

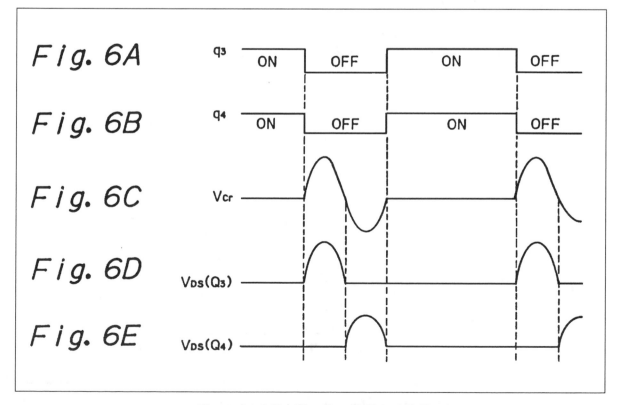

*Fig. 6A*

*Fig. 6B*

*Fig. 6C*

*Fig. 6D*

*Fig. 6E*

Illustration 6.43—Waveforms in Separate Figures

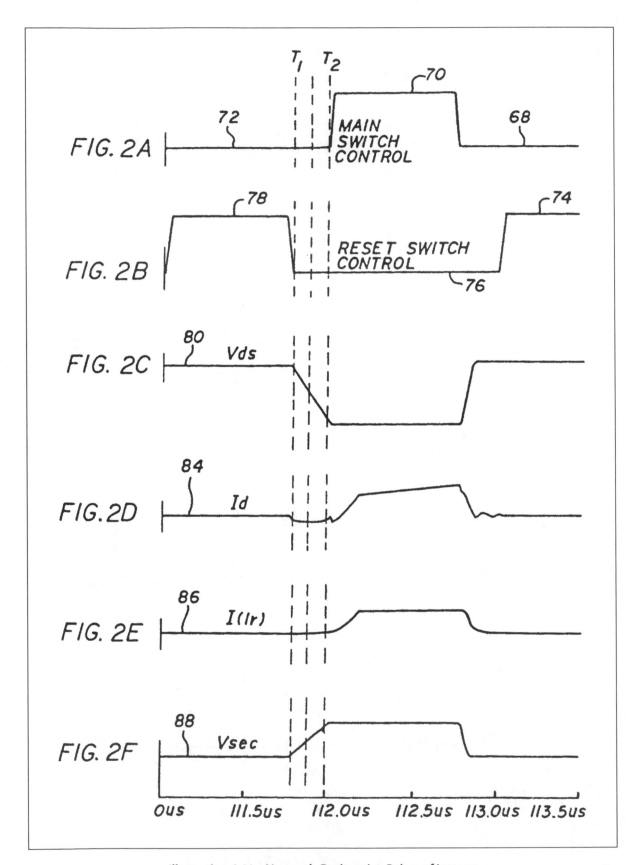

**Illustration 6.44—Numerals Designating Points of Interest**

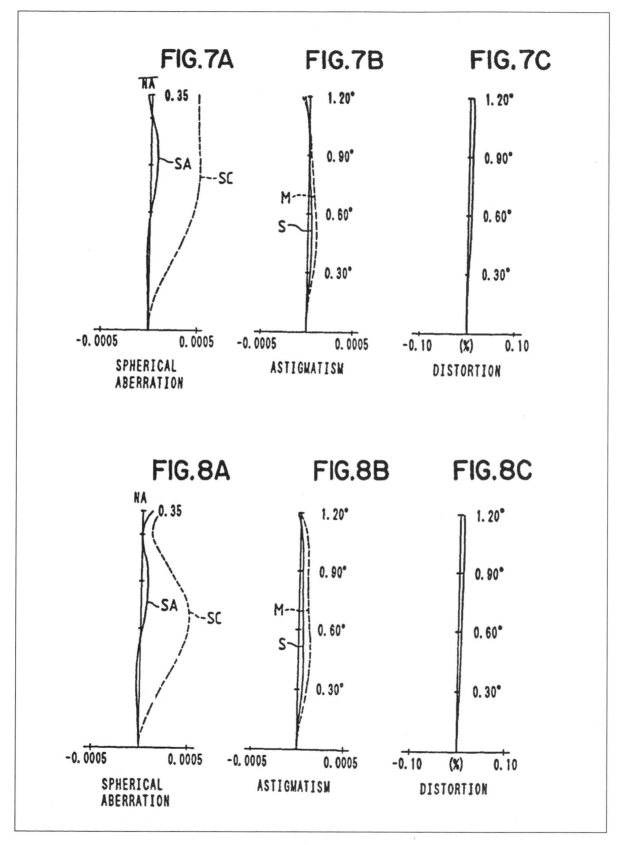

**Illustration 6.45—Plots**

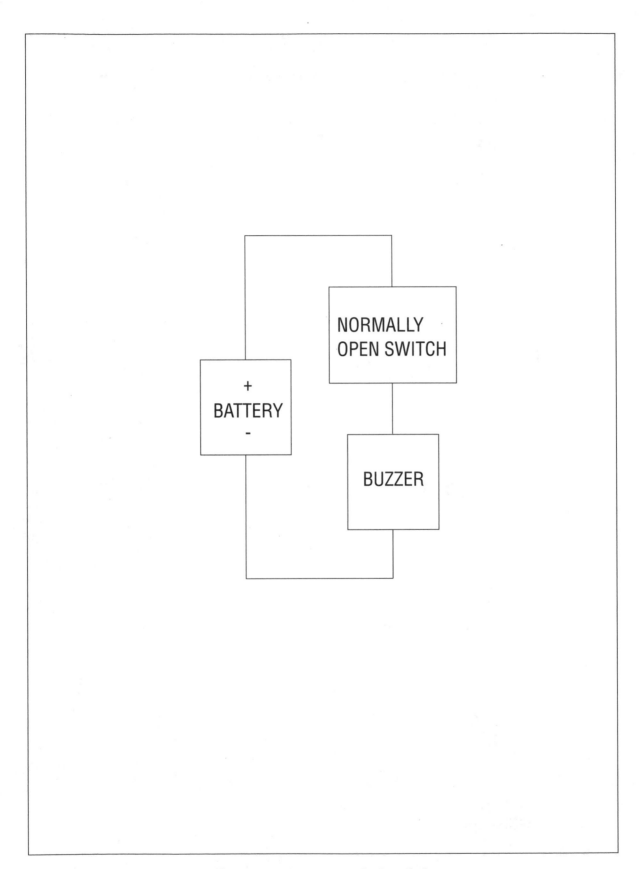

**Illustration 6.46—Nonstandard Symbols**

It is best to use all caps, because if a mix of upper- and lowercase letters is used, and the lowercase letters are 3.2 mm high, the caps will be too large. An exception to the size rule allows superscripts (for example, the "3" in $2^3$) and subscripts (for example, the "2" in $H_2O$) to be smaller than 3.2 mm.

## Descriptive Text

Descriptive text is usually not allowed in patent drawings, except in blocks such as block diagrams, flowcharts, and tables. However, descriptive text should be used, and may be required, where the part is unusual or the figure is not easily understandable.

## Multiple Embodiments

Multiple embodiments (versions) of an invention may be included in a patent application. The different embodiments must be presented as separate figures. For example, if one embodiment of a telephone has a particular handset, and you wish to show an alternative handset, you cannot show it in the same figure as the first handset, even if you use dashed lines. The alternative handset must be shown in a separate figure, although the rest of the telephone does not have to be shown again.

We recommend using a common figure number with distinguishing letter suffixes for each embodiment. For example:

Embodiment 1:

    Fig. 1A (front view)

    Fig. 1B (side view)

    etc. (See Illustration 6.47.)

Embodiment 2:

    Fig. 2A (front view)

    Fig. 2B (side view)

    etc. (See Illustration 6.48.)

If an examiner determines that the claimed embodiments are sufficiently different, he or she will require you to restrict the application to a single invention—that is, to elect (choose) the claims to one embodiment and cancel the claims that show the other embodiment. You may argue that the variations are not great enough to warrant treating the embodiments as separate inventions, or you may accept the requirement. If you accept the requirement, you may either file a divisional (separate) application for the canceled embodiment, or drop it. (See "divisional applications" in *Patent It Yourself,* Chapter 14, for details.)

## Line Types and Width

Typical line types and widths for utility patent drawings are shown in Illustration 6.49:

- Edge lines (lines that represent edges and corners of an object) should be continuous lines about 0.2 mm thick.

- Hidden lines (lines that represent parts or edges that are hidden behind other parts) should be dashed lines about 0.2 mm thick. Hidden parts should be shown only when necessary so as to avoid cluttering the figure.

- Phantom lines (lines that represent components that are not part of an invention, or a moved position of a component that is part of the invention) should be dot-dot-dash lines about 0.2 mm thick. Components that are not part of the invention may also be shown in continuous lines, which are actually preferable because they are clearer.

- Shading lines (lines that represent shadows or surface contour) should be continuous or irregularly broken lines about 0.1 mm thick. Their thinness distinguishes them from edge lines to avoid confusion.

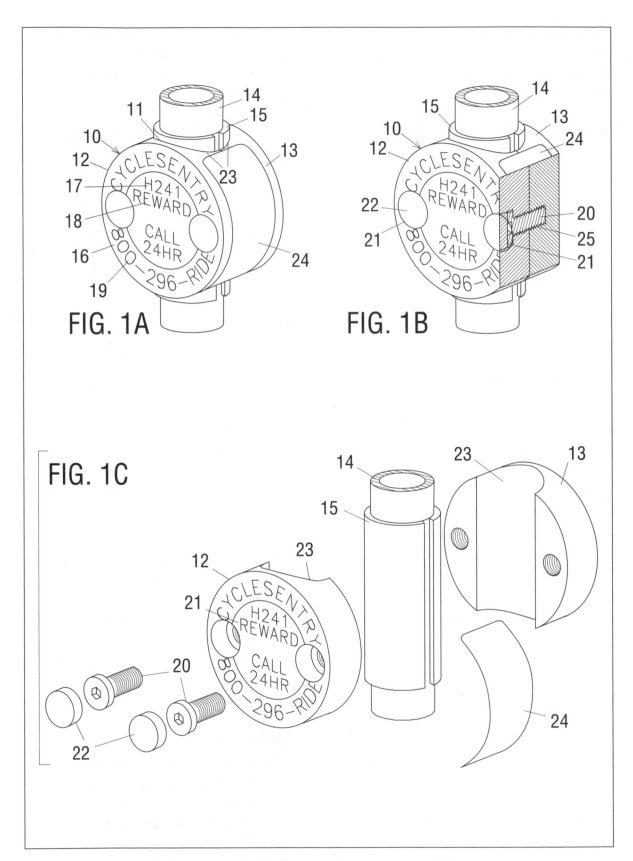

**Illustration 6.47—Distinguishing Multiple Embodiments**

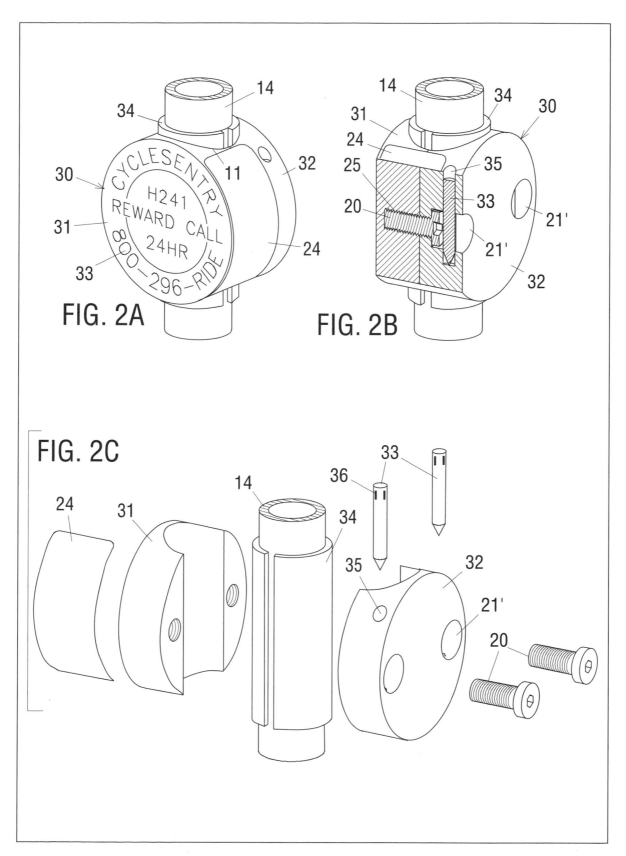

**Illustration 6.48—Distinguishing Multiple Embodiments**

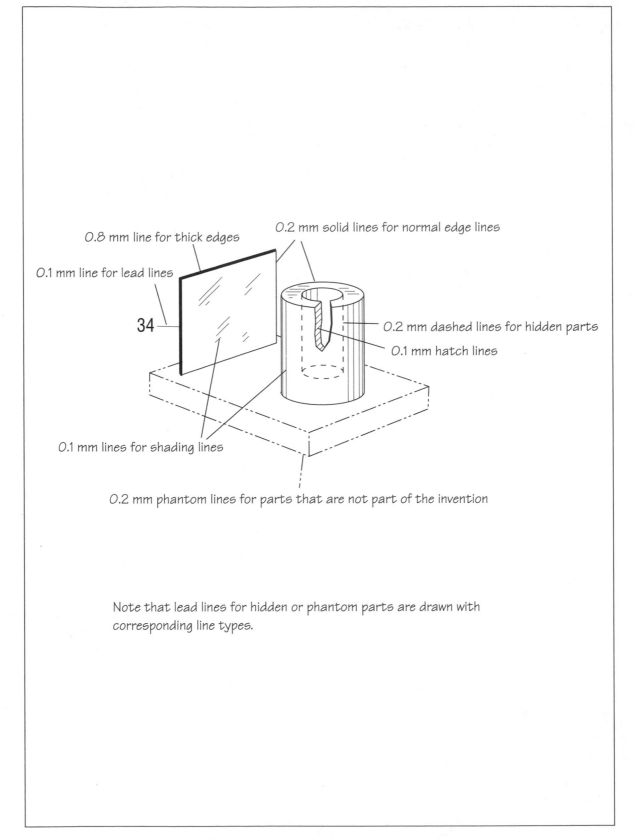

0.8 mm line for thick edges

0.2 mm solid lines for normal edge lines

0.1 mm line for lead lines

34

0.2 mm dashed lines for hidden parts

0.1 mm hatch lines

0.1 mm lines for shading lines

0.2 mm phantom lines for parts that are not part of the invention

Note that lead lines for hidden or phantom parts are drawn with corresponding line types.

**Illustration 6.49—Line Types and Widths**

- Thick edge lines (lines representing thick sheets or cords) should be about 0.5 to 0.8 mm thick.
- Hatch lines (oblique parallel lines that represent sectioned parts) must be continuous lines, and should be about 0.1 mm thick. Their thinness distinguishes them from edge lines to avoid confusion.
- Lead lines should be no more than 0.1 to 0.2 mm thick. A lead line may optionally be of a type that corresponds to the part it is touching, for example, a continue lead line for a part in continuous lines, a dashed lead line for a part in dashed line, and so on.

## Some Additional Points to Keep in Mind

In addition to the guidelines discussed above, here are some other pointers.

**Not too thick.** Edge, hidden, and phantom lines should not be much thicker than 0.2 mm, because thicker lines tend to obscure small details. For example, if the lines are made too thick, the gap between two closely spaced parallel lines would get too small or even disappear.

**When thicker is okay.** In a sectional view, edge lines may be about 0.3 mm thick, instead of the normal 0.2 mm, to more clearly distinguish them from the 0.1 mm hatch lines. Cords, cables, thick edges of sheets, or anything that is too thick to be represented by 0.2 mm lines, but not thick enough to be represented by a pair of parallel lines, may be represented by a single thick line of about 0.5 to 0.8 mm.

**Graphical symbols.** Graphical symbols—including schematics, flowcharts, and waveforms—should be made with continuous or dashed lines as necessary and be about 0.2 to 0.3 mm thick.

# Design Patent Drawings

This chapter details the specific requirements of formal design patent drawings. Refer to Chapter 5 for a discussion of formal and informal drawings and design patent drawings. Also refer to *Patent It Yourself*, Chapter 1, for details on design patents, including the types of inventions that qualify for them, and Chapter 10 for how to prepare the written portion of a design patent application.

## Amount of Detail Required

Unlike a utility patent, which covers the structure or composition of useful devices or useful processes, a design patent covers the specific ornamental appearance of an object, which is solely defined by the drawings. Therefore, design patent drawings must accurately illustrate the object's shape, proportions, surface contours, and any special material properties or textures. The drawings must show every feature of the object that is visible during normal use, so that no part of it is left to conjecture. They must be shaded to depict surface contour or characteristics, such as transparency, and to distinguish between open and solid areas. If the drawings depict the object inaccurately—for example, if they show incorrect proportions, contours, or other details—the resulting patent may end up protecting the wrong shape. Therefore, it is extremely important that the drawings be accurate in depicting the shape you wish to monopolize.

### Show Idealized Form

If you have made a rough mock-up of your design that is not visually identical to the design you wish to patent, you should show the object in its idealized form in the patent drawings. You can apply for a patent on a design even if you have not made a model. Therefore, even if you have made a model, the drawings may be idealized as much as you wish, without regard to the appearance of the model. The important thing is to show the object accurately in its ideal form.

**CAUTION**

**Drawings cannot be changed after filing.** Because of the proscription against adding new matter to any patent application, the appearance of a design invention cannot be changed after filing, not even slightly. Therefore, features cannot be added to or removed from design drawings. However, if a feature was described in the original application as not being part of the invention, or if the feature was shown in dashed lines (which are used to illustrate features that are not part of the invention; see below) in the original drawings, it may be removed if desired. See Chapter 9 for details on the rules regarding changing drawings.

## Views Required

A design patent application must provide a complete set of views from all sides. This is usually accomplished with the six standard views, including orthogonal front, back, right, left, top, and bottom views (this requirement does not apply to utility patent drawings).

The entire design must be shown in each of these views. One or more perspective views, perhaps one front and one back, should also be included if the orthogonal views do not clearly illustrate the invention. The angle of the perspective view should be carefully selected to maximize comprehension. Note that there are no reference numbers like those typically used in utility patent drawings, because reference numbers are not allowed in design patent drawings. (See Chapter 1 for details on orthogonal and perspective views.)

As shown in the drawings of a computer mouse in Illustrations 7.1 and 7.1a, Fig. 1 is a rear perspective view, Fig. 2 is a top orthogonal view, Fig. 3 is a rear orthogonal view, Fig. 4 is a left side orthogonal view, Fig. 5 is a front orthogonal view, Fig. 6 is a right side orthogonal view, Fig. 7 is a bottom orthogonal view, Fig. 8 is a front perspective view, and Fig. 9 is a left perspective view. Although several perspective views are used in this illustration, one is usually enough for simple designs, such as the mouse. However, designs that are very complicated or difficult to understand should have as many perspective views as necessary.

## Exceptions to the Rule

There are a few exceptions to the use of six standard views:

- Any view that is duplicative of another need not be shown. For example, if a design has identical or symmetrical right and left sides, then only one side need be shown. The description of the figures in the specification should note such fact. For example, "Fig. 3 is a right side view of the wheel; the left side view is a mirror image of the right side."

- A view of any side of a design that is plain and unornamented, such as the flat bottom of a lamp base, may be omitted. The description of the figures in the specification should note such fact. For example, "The lamp includes a plain and unornamented bottom, which is not shown."

- A thin and flat object, such as fabric or embossed designs, would require only front and rear views. Again, the description should note such fact. For example, "The design is a thin and flat sheet; therefore only front and rear views are shown."

## Consistency of Views

The appearance of the design must be consistent throughout the different views. That is, there must be no discrepancies between the views in the appearance of any element in the design. For example, a design for a computer housing must not be shown with a round button in one view and a square button in another view. All details must match.

## Drawings Must Show All Features

Design patent drawings must show every part of the design that is visible during normal use; the only exceptions are listed above. If a design includes novel aesthetic features that are visible during normal use, but which cannot be illustrated by the standard views discussed above—for example, interior surfaces—the following views may be used in addition to the standard views.

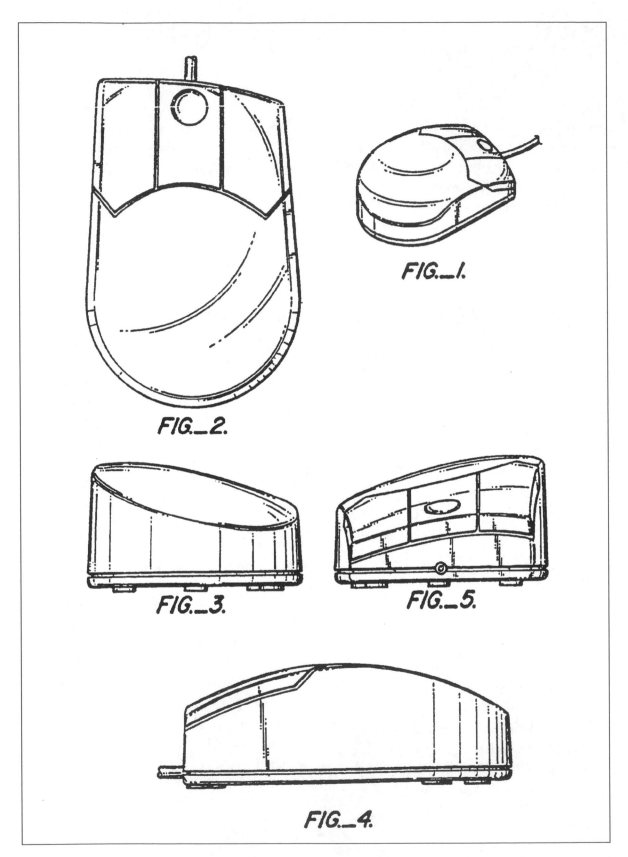

FIG.__1.

FIG.__2.

FIG.__3.

FIG.__5.

FIG.__4.

**Illustration 7.1—Views Required**

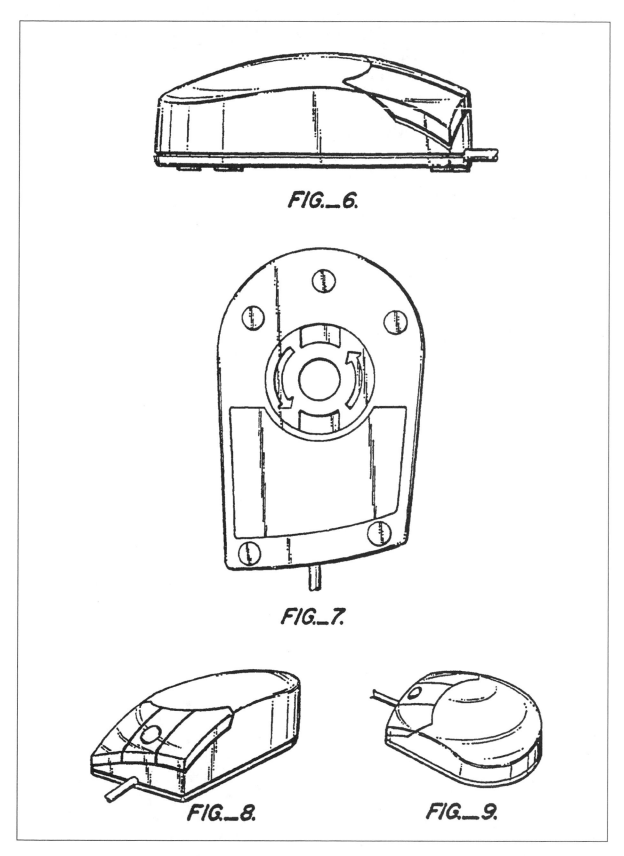

FIG._6.

FIG._7.

FIG._8.　　　　FIG._9.

**Illustration 7.1(a)—Views Required (continued)**

## Sectional View

As shown in Illustration 7.2, in addition to the standard views (only two shown here), a glass cover is shown in Fig. 3 in a sectional view sliced in half to illustrate its ornamental internal contour. The sectional view is necessary in this case, because the internal contour of the cover would not be clear from a bottom view, which is also required, but not shown here. A broken line with arrows must be placed on a general view (a suitable nonsectional view), such as Fig. 2 in Illustration 7.2, to indicate the sectioning plane and view direction. The number of the figure that shows the sectional view should be placed adjacent to the arrows, as shown in Fig 2. See Chapter 6 for details on sectional views.

## Exploded View

A design object with parts that are separable during normal use may have such parts shown separated, and independently positioned as necessary to show their internal design features, such as Fig. 2 in Illustration 7.3. In such an exploded view, a bracket must be used to "enclose" or connect the parts that belong to the same figure. Projection lines (dashed lines connecting separated parts) should not be used in design drawings. Again, in addition to the exploded view, the object must also be shown assembled in the standard views, such as Fig. 1. (Other standard views, as discussed above, are also required, but they are not shown in Illustration 7.3.)

## Parts Shown Separately

Normally separable parts may also be illustrated in separate figures to show their interior design features. In Illustration 7.4, the dish and lid are shown assembled together in Fig. 1, and the dish is shown alone in Fig. 2 to illustrate its contour that is normally covered by the lid. The description of the figures should state the fact that a part is shown separately. For example, "Fig. 1 is a front perspective view of a dish with lid showing my new design. Fig. 2 is a front perspective view of the dish, shown without the lid to illustrate interior ornamental features." Again, as discussed above, the entire object must also be shown assembled in the other normally required views (not shown here).

### Caution About Purely Functional Parts

In design patent drawings, sectional or exploded views cannot be used to show purely functional internal features that are without any aesthetic value, such as working mechanisms. Of course, if an internal functional part has an ornamental shape—for example, a stylized engine in an automobile—it may properly be shown.

## Parts Behind Transparent Surfaces

Any part that is visible behind a transparent surface should be shown in solid (rather than hidden or dashed) lines, just as it would be seen in real life. The lines representing such parts should be thinner than the other lines, to distinguish them, such as in Illustration 7.5.

## Movable Parts

Movable parts cannot be shown in alternate positions in design patent drawings in the same figures, but they can be shown in separate figures. If a design object has normally separable parts, use sectional or exploded views, as discussed above.

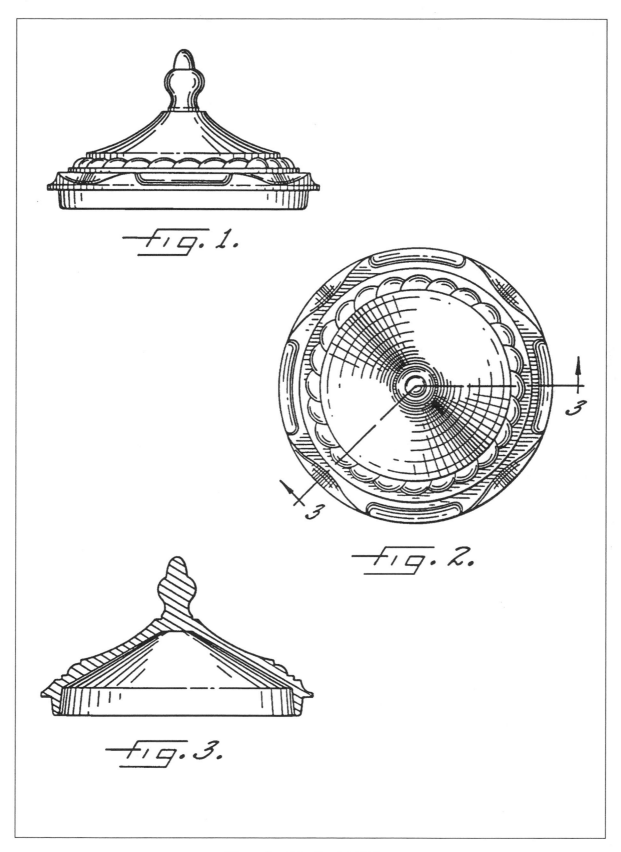

Illustration 7.2—Sectional View

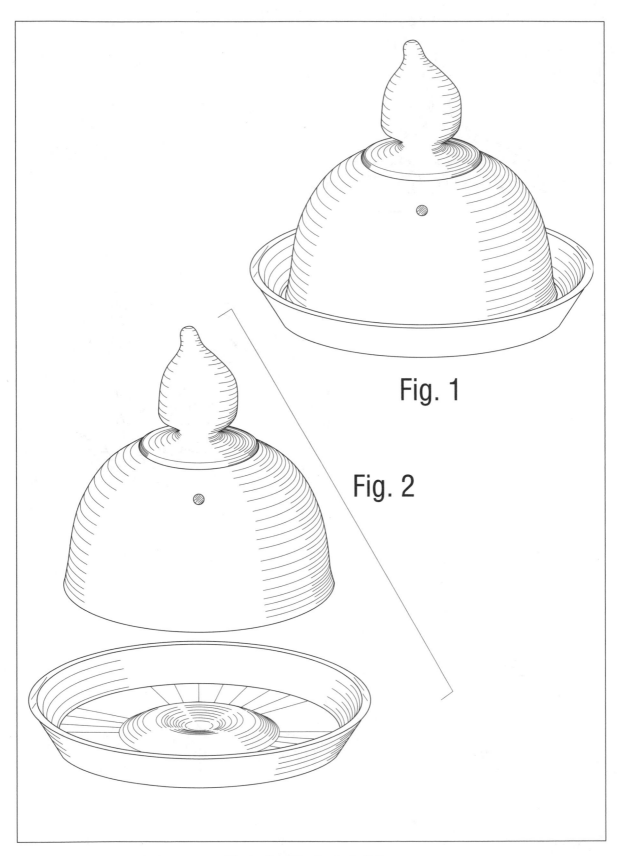

Fig. 1

Fig. 2

**Illustration 7.3—Exploded View**

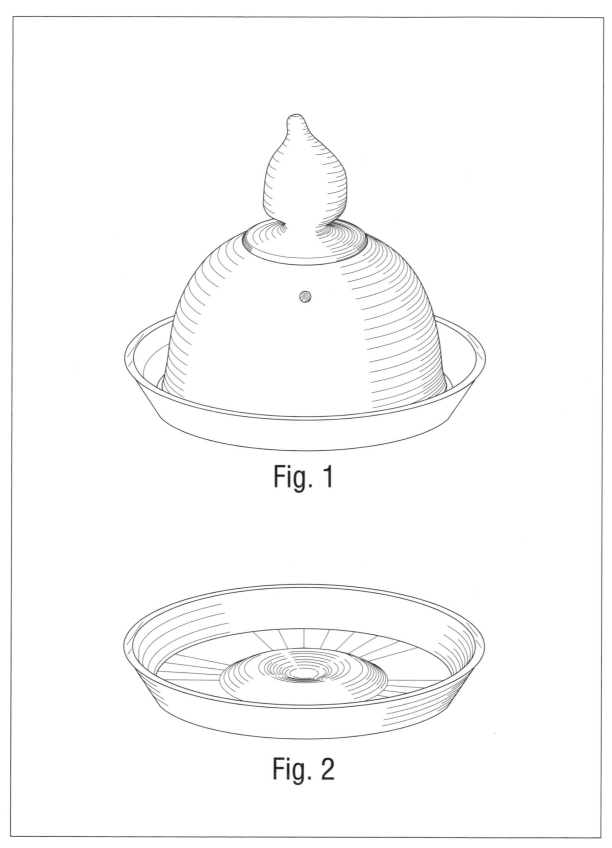

Fig. 1

Fig. 2

**Illustration 7.4—Separable Parts Shown Separately**

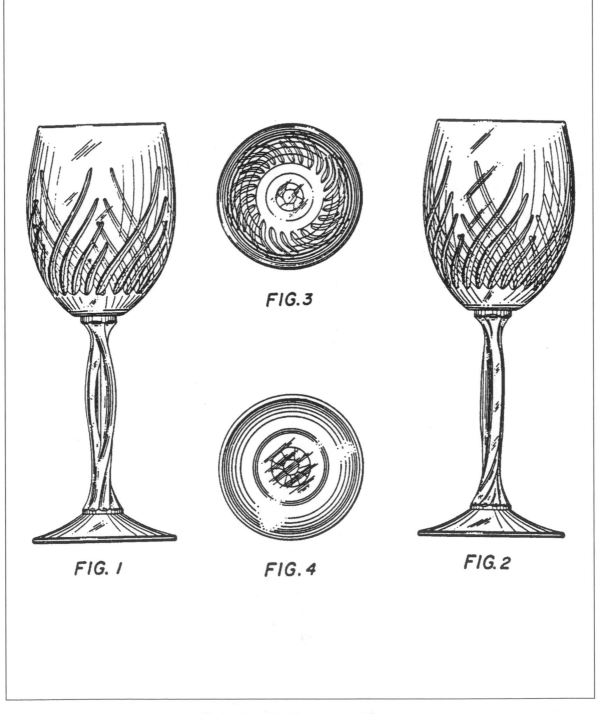

FIG. 3

FIG. 4

FIG. 1

FIG. 2

**Illustration 7.5—Transparent Objects**

## Surface Markings

Surface markings, such as labels and logos, may be shown in continuous lines in the drawings. As discussed above, anything shown in continuous lines will be considered part of the invention. Therefore, you must consider whether such markings are an integral part of your invention before they are included. If a marking is simply one of different possible variations, such as the time displayed on a digital clock, then such marking should be shown in dashed lines. (See Chapter 8 for details on dashed lines.) If a marking is intended to be merely an example, it should be noted in the description of the figures. For example, "The marking shown in Fig. 1 is merely exemplary." You may simply omit a marking if it is not an important part of your design.

## Unclaimed Matter

Any element shown in continuous lines is considered as part of an invention, whereas any element shown in dashed or phantom lines (see Chapter 8 for details on dashed and phantom lines) is not considered to be part of the invention. Therefore, do not use dashed or phantom lines unless they represent elements that you do not wish the patent to cover (unclaimed matter)—for example, a background setting or person using the design.

In the telephone design shown in Illustration 7.6, the base unit is shown in continuous lines and the handset is shown in dashed lines. The base unit is covered by the patent, but the handset is not. The handset is shown merely to convey the design more clearly, but is actually unnecessary, because the base unit is clearly recognizable as such without it. Elements in dashed or phantom lines should be shown only when they are absolutely necessary to clearly convey the design.

## Shading Techniques

Shading is the representation of surface contour and texture, and is a very important part of design patent drawings. If a drawing is filed without shading, or with inadequate shading, the examiner will object to the drawings and require you to provide new, corrected drawings. The PTO will accept new drawings that correct minor shading problems, as long as such problems do not cause significant ambiguity in the appearance of the invention. See Illustration 6.33 in Chapter 6 for an example of ambiguity caused by the lack of shading.

If shading, or its absence, causes enough ambiguity, the examiner may reject the design application as being based on inaccurate drawings. (See Chapter 9 for details on rejections by the PTO.) Such a rejection usually cannot be overcome, because it is not permissible to add any new matter (information) to an application after filing, including shading that substantially affects the shape of the design. Therefore, you must make sure that the drawings as filed clearly depict every feature of your design, including any surface contour or texture that must be illustrated by shading. Other than on the design object, shading must not be applied to anything else on the drawing, such as the background.

### Linear and Stippled Shading

The shading should be applied as if the light source is to the upper left of the drawing, so that the shadows are on the right and bottom sides. The two conventionally accepted types of shading are linear and stippled. Linear shading uses parallel lines—either continuous or broken—as shown in Illustration 7.7 and Illustration 7.8, whereas stippled shading uses tiny dots, as shown in Illustration 7.9. Either type of shading is acceptable to the PTO, so

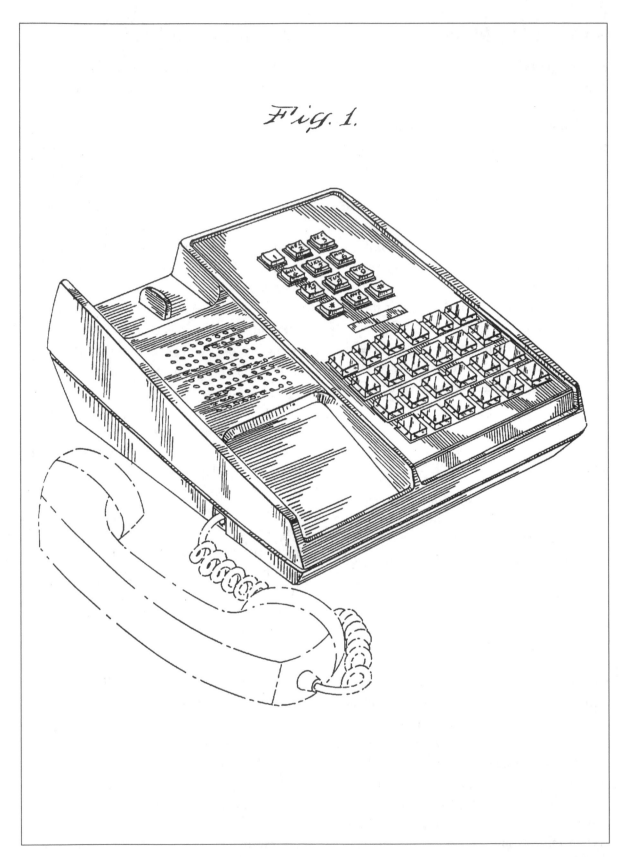

*Fig. 1.*

**Illustration 7.6—Unclaimed Matter**

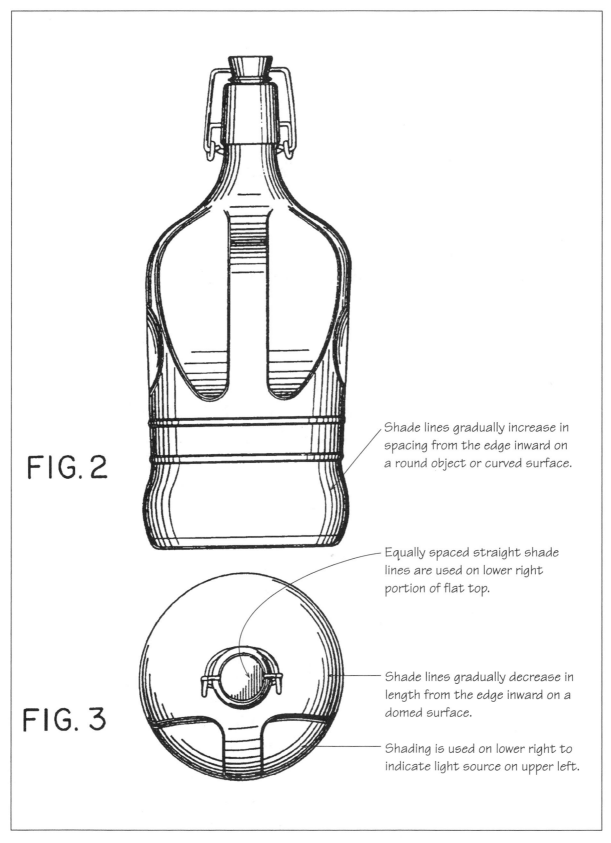

FIG. 2

FIG. 3

Shade lines gradually increase in spacing from the edge inward on a round object or curved surface.

Equally spaced straight shade lines are used on lower right portion of flat top.

Shade lines gradually decrease in length from the edge inward on a domed surface.

Shading is used on lower right to indicate light source on upper left.

**Illustration 7.7—Linear Shading**

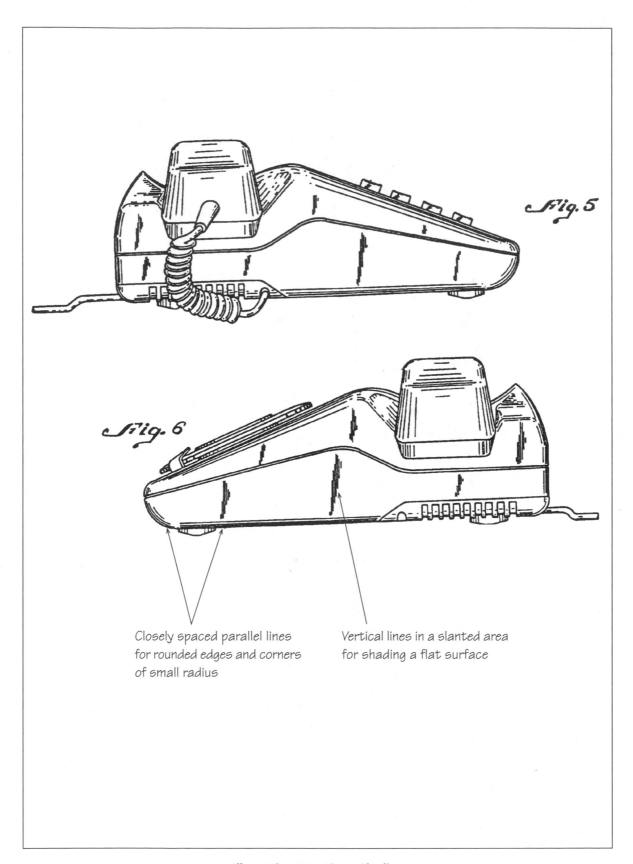

*Fig. 5*

*Fig. 6*

Closely spaced parallel lines
for rounded edges and corners
of small radius

Vertical lines in a slanted area
for shading a flat surface

**Illustration 7.8—Linear Shading**

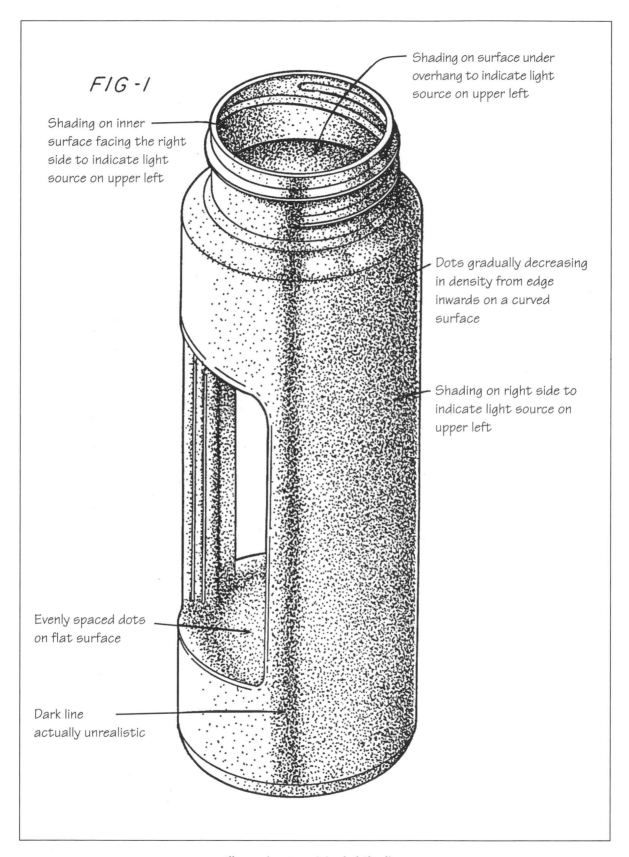

**Illustration 7.9—Stippled Shading**

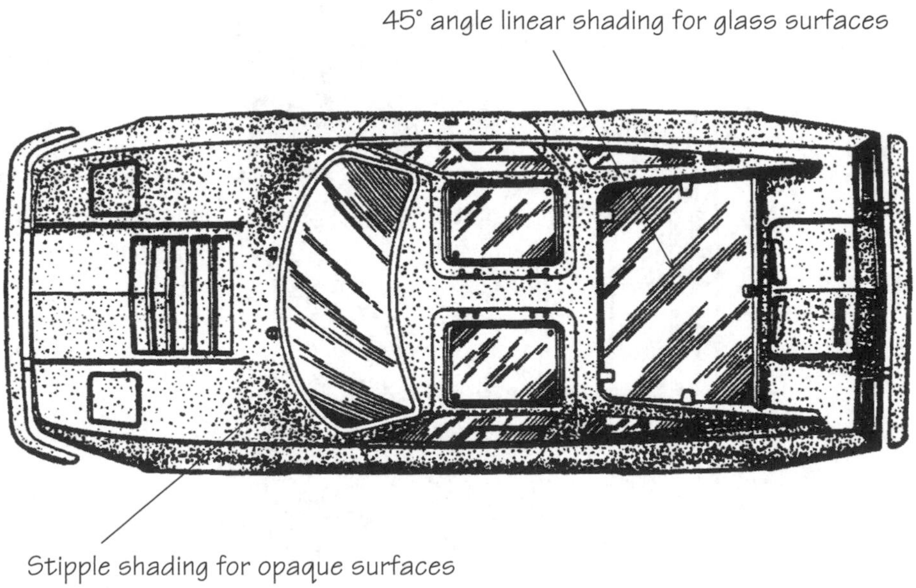

45° angle linear shading for glass surfaces

Stipple shading for opaque surfaces

**Illustration 7.10—Combined Stippled and Linear Shading**

choose the one you prefer. The techniques for applying shading in specific situations are discussed in the illustrations.

Stipple shading is normally used for representing shadows—that is, surface contour—but it may also be used for representing rough textures, such as foam, coarse fabric, or concrete. Linear shading is preferably used for depicting transparent or shiny surfaces, such as glass or polished metal. Linear and stippled shading can be combined in a drawing and used wherever suitable. For example, the body of a car can be stipple shaded, and its glass can be linear shaded, such as in Illustration 7.10. Solid black shading is not allowed, except to depict a solid black color when color is an important design feature, such as on a paint scheme of a racing car. (See below for details on the representation of color.)

## Computer-Generated Shading

An illustration of a wire frame model created by a 3D CAD (computer-aided drafting) program is shown in Illustration 7.11. Most 3D CAD programs automatically apply graduated shading to a wire frame model to make it appear solid, as shown in Illustration 7.12 (2D CAD programs do not automatically apply shading). The model can be rotated to different angles and shaded again. Lines can be overlaid on the shaded illustration, as shown in Illustration 7.13. The shaded renderings can be filed as informal drawings for a design application to show the contours of the invention. Formal drawings with linear or stippled shading (see Illustrations 7.8 and 7.9) have to be filed when an application is approved. Currently no computer program can automatically apply linear or stippled shading.

# Representation of Color and Material

If the novel features of your design include colors, materials, or ornamental effects that cannot be illustrated by black line drawings, color drawings or photographs may be filed with a petition and a petition fee. If the petition is not granted, they must be replaced with black line drawings. See Chapter 8 for details on such petitions. If you must resubmit drawings, it is possible that some features may change when you convert from color to black and white. If the result is new matter, the examiner will object to the line drawings. Such an objection can be avoided by filing black line drawings and color with the original application to represent colors and materials whenever possible. The standard hatch patterns shown in Illustration 7.14 can be used to represent simple solid colors.

Illustration 7.15 shows a unique color scheme on a truck; the colors are represented by hatch patterns. The patterns are applied without regard to the object's surface contour, such as in Illustration 7.16, where the lines of the patterns are drawn straight even on a curved object. The patterns representing materials are applied in a similar way. This may seem to be a very inefficient way to represent colors, but it is necessary, because patents are printed only in black ink to minimize cost, and a color drawing or photograph converted into black and white by a photocopier usually becomes very difficult to understand.

When such patterns are used, the description of the drawings must state such fact. For example, "The drawings include standard drafting symbol patterns for representing color." If the particular colors indicated in the drawings are merely exemplary, the description of the figures should state such fact. For

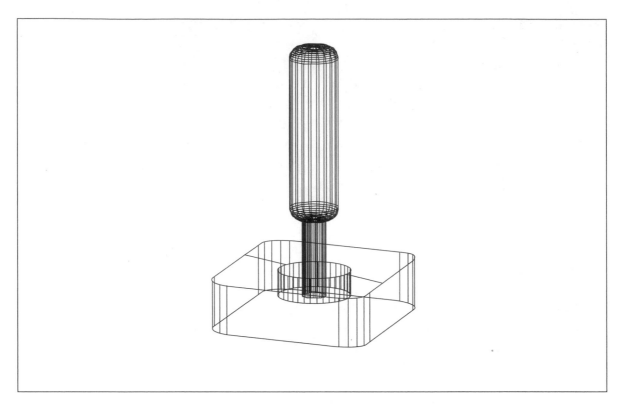

**Illustration 7.11—Wire Frame 3D Model**

**Illustration 7.12—Shaded 3D Model**

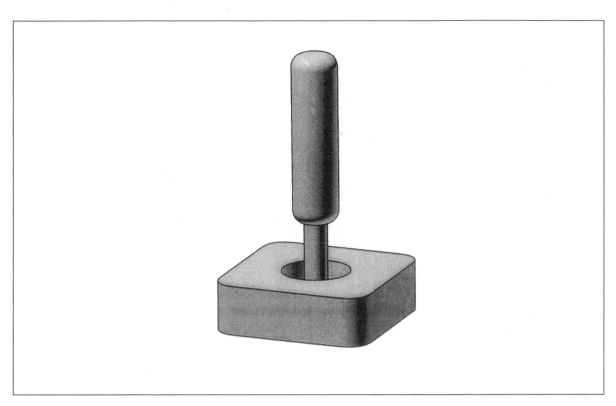

**Illustration 7.13—Shaded 3D Model Overlaid With Lines**

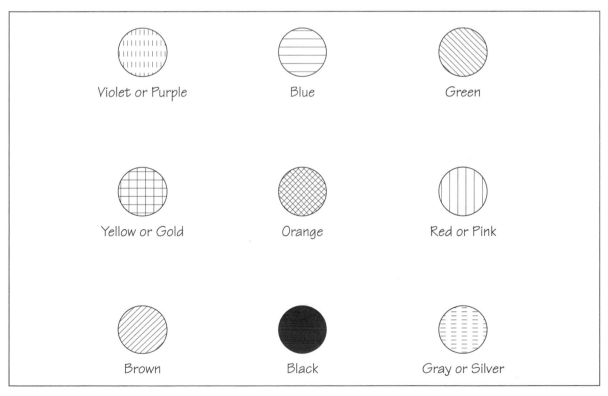

**Illustration 7.14—Patterns for Representing Color**

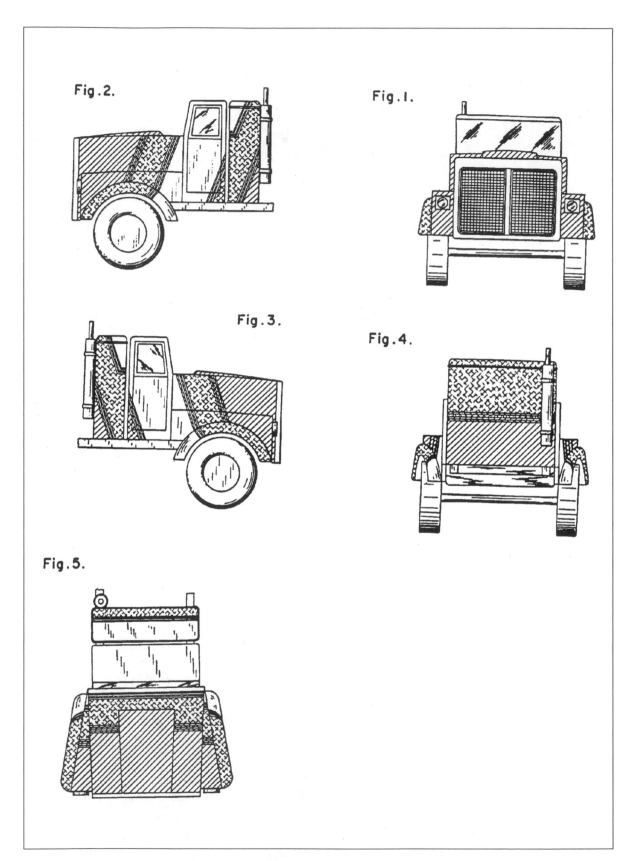

Fig.2.

Fig.1.

Fig.3.

Fig.4.

Fig.5.

**Illustration 7.15—Hatch Patterns Representing Color Scheme**

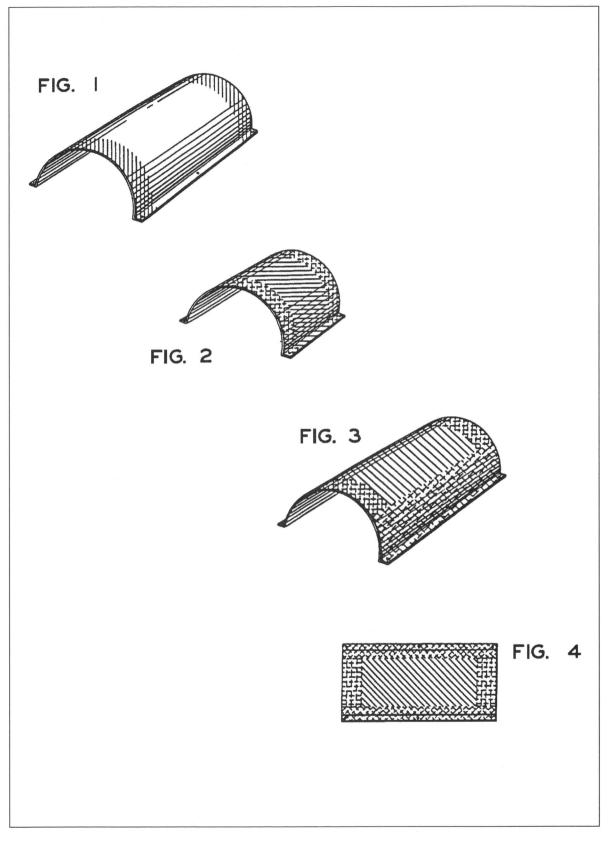

**Illustration 7.16—Hatch Patterns Representing Color Scheme**

example, "The colors on the wheel are not limited to those specifically indicated in the drawings." Note that these special patterns are not necessary if the colors or materials of your design are unimportant.

## Line Types

For design drawings done in black lines, such as in Illustration 7.17, suitable line types and widths are as follows:

- Edge lines (lines representing edges) of an invention must be continuous lines. They should be about 0.2 to 0.3 mm thick. Use 0.3 mm lines for edge lines in sectional views. Never use dashed or phantom lines for the design.

- Environmental structures and exemplary surface markings must be dashed or phantom lines. They should be no thicker than the lines representing the design.

- Shading for opaque surfaces should be parallel continuous lines, broken lines, or dots. They should be about 0.1 to 0.2 mm thick, and thinner than the edge lines. They should be oriented vertically or horizontally with respect to the object. In computer-generated shading, as described above, the dot sizes are not directly controllable.

- Shading for transparent or translucent surfaces should be parallel continuous or broken lines. They should be about 0.1 to 0.2 mm thick, and thinner than the edge lines. They should be oriented obliquely (slanted) with respect to the object.

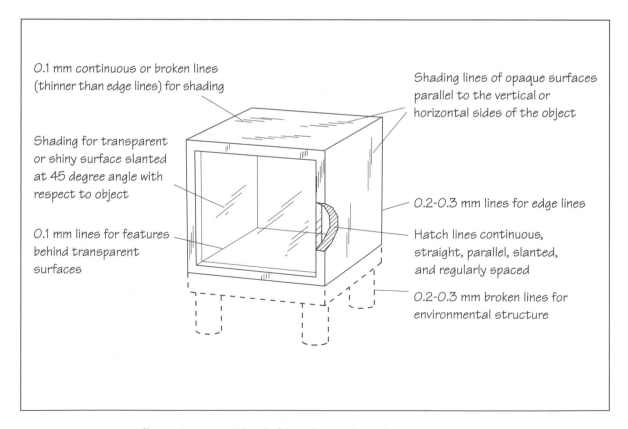

**Illustration 7.17—Line Styles and Types in Design Patent Drawings**

- Hatch lines in sectional views should be straight, continuous, parallel, slanted lines about 0.1 mm thick. (See Chapter 6 for details on hatching.)

# Photographs

Photographs, whether black-and-white or color, can be submitted as informal drawings in design patent applications. Black-and-white photographs are accepted as formal drawings in design patent applications only if the invention cannot be adequately illustrated with black line drawings—for example, on the rare occasions when there is no better means of showing subtle ornamental effects. Similarly, color photos are accepted as formal drawings in design patent applications only if they are the sole practical medium for illustrating the invention. A petition and a petition fee must accompany color drawings; no petition or fee is needed for black-and-white photos. (See Chapter 8 for details on such petitions.) If the petition is not granted, formal black line drawings must be submitted to replace the color photos when the application is allowed. Like black-and-white photos, color photographs are approved only on rare occasions. The PTO discourages photographs because they are difficult and expensive to reproduce. See Chapter 4 for details on patent photography, including its advantages and disadvantages.

## Background

All photographs must have a plain background, without anything that is not part of the object. In other words, whatever the photographs show would be considered to be part of the invention. (See Chapter 4 for details on taking photographs of inventions.)

## Views Required

The views required in photographs are the same as those required in black line drawings.

## Size and Margins

The size and margin requirements for photographs are the same as those for line drawings. (See Chapter 8 for details on size and margins.) Therefore, if a photograph is mounted on cardboard, the cardboard must be one of the acceptable sizes—that is, 8½" × 11" (letter size) or 21 cm × 29.7 cm (A4 size). The photograph must be small enough to leave an acceptable border between itself and the paper, but large enough to show the invention clearly. If a photograph is submitted without the cardboard, the photograph itself must be one of the standard aforementioned sheet sizes.

## Figure Numbers

Photographs must be labeled with consecutive figure numbers, such as Fig. 1 and Fig. 2. Photographs not mounted on cardboard must have the figure numbers applied directly on them, which may be difficult, so it is better to mount them on cardboard and have the figure numbers applied on the cardboard. (See Chapter 8 for details on numbering figures.)

# Multiple Embodiments

Where multiple embodiments (versions) of a design object are permitted, they may be shown in the same design patent application. Separate figures must be used for each view that shows a different design. For example, assume that the first embodiment of a desk is shown in top perspective, front, back, top, bottom, left, and right side views. The second embodiment of the desk consists entirely of a unique inlaid pattern on the top; otherwise it is the same in other respects. The second embodiment can thus be shown with just two additional views—a top perspective view and a top view—because the other views would merely be duplicative. The description of the figures showing the second embodiment should state, for example, "Fig. 8 is a top perspective view of a second embodiment of the desk showing an alternative design of the top. Fig. 9 is a top view of the second embodiment of the desk; the other views are duplicative of the views of the first embodiment."

Multiple embodiments of a design object are permitted in one application only if the embodiments have minor variations and the novel and unobvious feature(s) of the design are present in all embodiments. That is, a common inventive concept must be present in every embodiment. If the embodiments have more than just minor variations, the examiner will likely require you to restrict the application to a single invention—that is, to choose one embodiment, and cancel the figures that show the other embodiment. You may argue that the variations are not great enough, or you may accept the requirement. If you accept the requirement, you may either file a divisional (separate) application for the canceled embodiment, or drop it. If you want to file a divisional application you must make it copending with the present application— that is, you must file the divisional before the present application issues or becomes abandoned. (See divisional applications in *Patent It Yourself*, Chapter 14, for details.) ●

# General Standards

This chapter discusses the general PTO standards for formal patent drawings for utility and design patent applications. Provisional patent applications, which are not examined by the PTO, can be submitted with informal drawings. See *Patent It Yourself* for details on provisional and regular patent applications, and Chapter 5 of this book for details on formal and informal drawings.

Although the drawings in existing patents are good examples of what proper drawings should look like, they cannot be entirely relied upon, because the drawing rules change from time to time, and improper drawings are sometimes allowed and printed due to oversights of the PTO. Therefore, inconsistencies between drawings in existing patents and the illustrations and rules in this book may be due to rule changes or the drawings in question being improperly allowed.

# Paper, Margins, and Sheet Numbering

Paper used for black line drawings must be flexible, strong, white, smooth, not shiny, and durable. Only one side of the paper may be used.

## Paper for Laser Output

For laser printer output from a CAD program (see Chapter 3 for details on CAD), use a good quality, white, smooth-surfaced laser printer paper of at least 20 lb., but preferably 24 lb. (Pound, or "lb.," is a measure of paper thickness; an equivalent measure is called "sub," or substance. The higher the number, the thicker the paper.) A smooth-surfaced paper will provide the sharpest lines. Such paper

is available at most stationery stores or large computer retailers. Avoid "computer paper"—the type with holes along the sides for dot matrix printers—and the lowest quality copier papers (less than 20 lb.), which are rough and thin.

## Paper for Inkjet Output

For inkjet output, do not use laser printer paper, or even cheap "inkjet paper" (usually identified by the fact that it comes in 500 sheet reams) because these papers allow the ink to feather (spread out between the fibers of the paper). Specialty ink-jet papers must be used, such as the Epson line of high quality papers—the Photo Quality Inkjet Paper, Matte Paper Heavyweight or the Archival Matte. Avoid shiny paper. The PTO prefers paper that is not shiny.

## Paper for Ink Drawings

For pen and ink drawings, Mylar film or vellum is preferable, but bristol board can be used. All of these provide a smooth finish that prevents feathering and are tough enough to withstand repeated erasing without damage. Such paper is generally available only at art supply stores.

> **CAUTION**
>
> **Beware of translucent paper.** Ink drawings made on vellum or Mylar film must be photocopied onto white paper, because vellum and Mylar film are translucent (semitransparent) and do not meet PTO standards, which require white, opaque paper. Use a copier in good condition and, if possible, clean its platen (glass), corona wires, and fuser rollers and vacuum its inside to ensure that the copies will be clean and free of specks.

## Paper Size and Margins

All drawing sheets in an application must be the same size. Each sheet of paper must include an imaginary margin, free of any marks. Acceptable paper sizes and margins are shown in Illustration 8.1. The margin must be invisible; it cannot be framed by a rectangle. The dashed rectangles in the illustrations are there only for showing the imaginary margins; they must not appear in actual drawings. The usable portion of a sheet within the margins is known as the "sight." Crosshairs, as shown in Illustration 8.2, should be placed at opposite corners of the sight to indicate its boundaries. The centers of the crosshairs should be centered on the corners, so that the outer arms of the crosshairs lie in the margins. The crosshairs can be placed on either the lower-left and upper-right or upper-left and lower-right corners, and should be about 2 cm (¾") long.

> **TIP**
>
> **Make sure the figures are positioned at least a few millimeters away from the margins,** because the PTO sometimes complains of margin intrusions, even when the figures are clearly inside them. Keeping the figures well clear of the margins will avoid such a problem. (See Chapter 9 for additional details.)

## Paper Orientation

A sheet of paper positioned so that it is taller than it is wide, such as those shown in Illustration 8.1, is said to be in "portrait" orientation. This is the preferred position. A sheet of paper positioned so that it is wider than it is tall, such as those shown in Illustration 8.3, is said to be in "landscape" orientation. Landscape orientation should be used only for long horizontal figures that cannot fit onto a sheet in portrait orientation without appearing too small. When

a sheet is oriented in the landscape mode, the sheet number should be on the right side and oriented as if the sheet were in the portrait mode. All other lettering and numbers on the sheet should be in the landscape mode, however. The top of a sheet in the landscape mode is the long side with the wider margin; see Illustration 8.3.

> **CAUTION**
>
> **Avoid landscape orientation whenever possible.** Do not use landscape orientation—that is, paper positioned so that it is wider than it is tall—unless it is absolutely necessary. This is because, at the PTO, the drawings are converted to computer files and associated with the same computer folder that also contains the written description (specification) of the invention, which is printed in portrait orientation. Therefore, drawings in landscape orientation force the examiner to turn his or her head or rotate the drawing images to view them upright, which can be irritating. And of course, you don't want to irritate the examiner if you can avoid it!

## Sheet Numbering

Your sheets of drawing paper must be numbered in consecutive Arabic numerals (the symbols 1, 2, 3, and 4), starting with 1. The required format is "sheet number/total number of sheets." For example, if there are a total of four sheets, they should be numbered 1/4, 2/4, 3/4, and 4/4. No other marking—such as inventor name and title—may accompany the sheet numbers. However, the title of the invention, the inventors' name(s), and a serial number, if it is a replacement drawing and already filed may be placed in the top margin, centered. As shown in Illustration 8.4, the sheet numbers must be placed on the top center of each sheet, below the imaginary top margin—that is, within the sight. If a drawing figure on

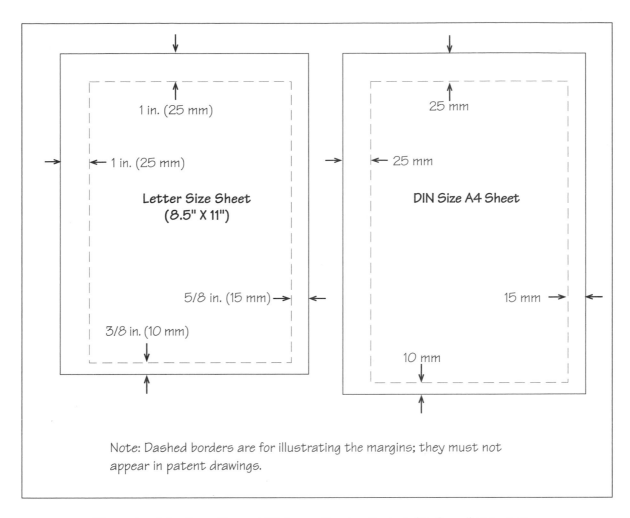

**Illustration 8.1—Paper Size and Minimum Margins, Portrait (Preferred) Orientation**

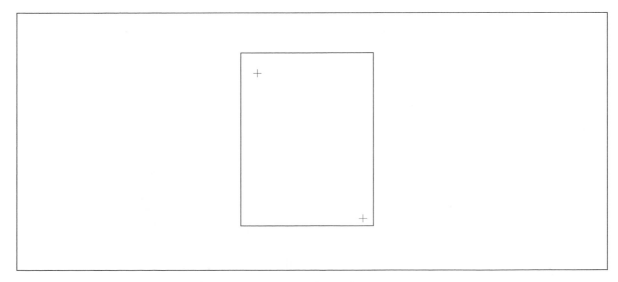

**Illustration 8.2—Crosshairs**

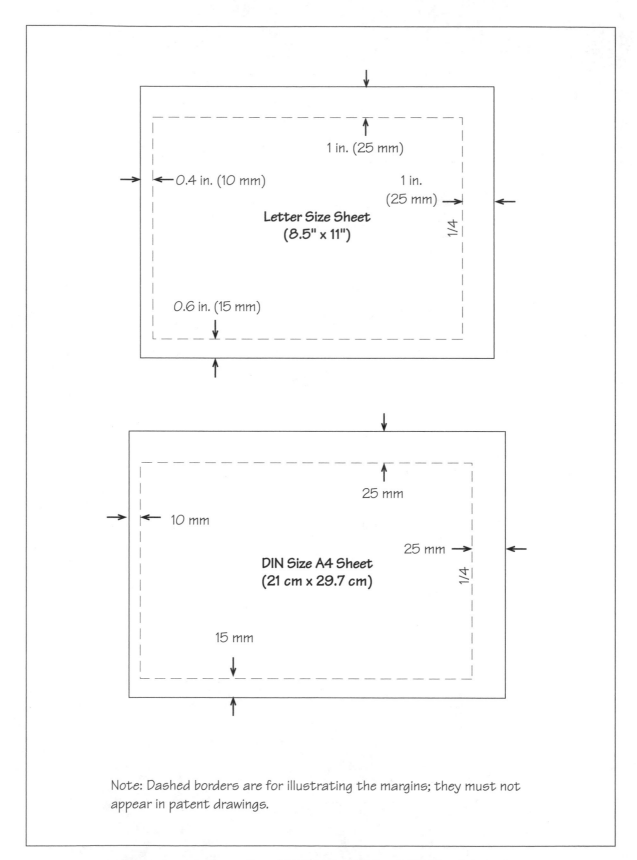

**Illustration 8.3—Paper Size and Minimum Margins, Landscape Orientation**

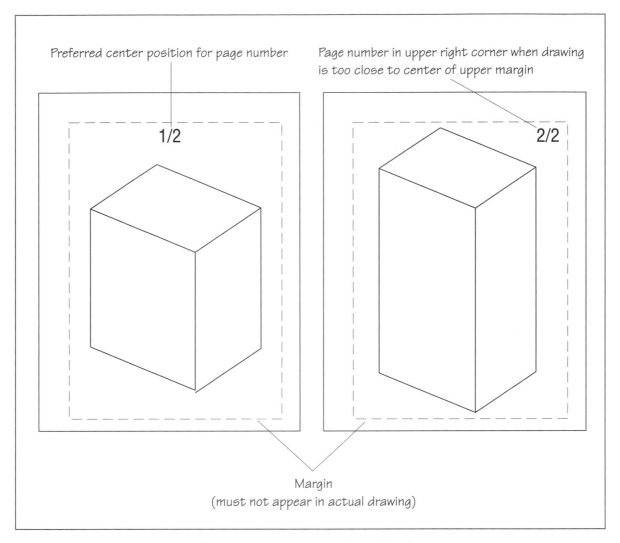

Preferred center position for page number

Page number in upper right corner when drawing is too close to center of upper margin

1/2

2/2

Margin
(must not appear in actual drawing)

**Illustration 8.4—Page Number Positioning**

a sheet must be positioned very close to the top center of the sheet, where the sheet number would normally be, the sheet number may be placed at the upper-right corner of the sight. The sheet numbers must be larger in size than the reference numbers used to identify the parts of the figure—for example, about 5 mm, ⅕", or 22 points in height.

> **TIP**
>
> As shown in Illustration 8.5, making page numbers, figure numbers, and reference numbers **different sizes** allows them to be more easily distinguished.

## Clean Paper

The paper must not be creased or wrinkled, and must be reasonably free of dirty spots, erased lines that remain visible, and other alterations. If you submit photocopies, make sure that they are substantially free of the tiny copier marks or flecks that appear on many photocopies. If a few of these marks are present, you can use white correction fluid to cover them. Or, make new copies after cleaning the copier's glass surface, corona wires, fuser roller, and so on, very thoroughly.

## 2/4
Page number (5 mm, ⅕" or 22 points)

## Fig. 4
Figure number (5 mm, ⅕" or 22 points)

**23**
Reference number (3.2 mm, ⅛" or 14 points)

**Illustration 8.5—Different Number Sizes**

## Mediums

Formal utility and design patent drawings should be black line drawings, but black-and-white photographs, color drawings, or color photographs may be used if necessary, as discussed below. Each type of drawing and the type of invention it is suitable for is discussed below. (See Chapter 5 for additional information on formal and informal drawings.) Plant patents are extremely rare, so they are not discussed here.

### Black Line Drawings

Black line drawings on white paper are normally required for utility and design patent applications; they are suitable for illustrating the vast majority of inventions.

### Black-and-White Photographs

Black-and-white photographs are accepted as formal drawings in utility and design patent applications only if the invention cannot be adequately illustrated with black line drawings (see Chapter 4). For utility applications, acceptable photographs include those for fine and irregular or natural structures and microstructures, such as electrophoresis gels, blots, autoradiographs, cell cultures, histological tissue cross sections, animals, plants, in vivo imaging, thin-layer chromatography plates, and crystalline structures. For design applications, acceptable photographs include those that show subtle ornamental effects. No petition or fee is required for black-and-white photographs.

### Color Drawings or Photographs

Color photos or drawings are accepted as formal drawings in utility and design patent applications if they are the only practical medium for illustrating the invention. They must be of sufficient quality to enable all the details to be clearly reproducible in black-and-white in the printed patent. A petition and a petition fee must accompany them. If the petition is not granted, formal black line drawings must be submitted to replace the color photo or drawings when the application is allowed. Color photos or drawings are approved only on rare occasions. The PTO discourages color photographs and drawings because they are difficult and expensive to reproduce. See Chapter 4 for details on the use of photographs as patent drawings.

Petitions for color photographs or color drawings are granted only if a very good reason is provided to explain why color is necessary. The requirements for submitting color drawings or color photographs as formal drawings are as follows:

- three sets of color drawings or color photographs; color photographs must be developed on double-weight photographic paper, or be permanently mounted on smooth cardboard, and be of sufficient clarity for reproduction.

- a petition (see Illustration 8.6 for a sample petition) that includes an explanation of why the color drawings or color photographs are necessary. (Use the tear-out Petition for Submitting Color Photographs or Drawings in the appendix.) A suitable explanation can read, for example, "The present invention comprises a mosaic assembly method for illustrating images from individual dots of respective colors. Thus it is necessary to provide drawings that show the individual dot colors and how they combine to form the desired image."

- a petition fee ($130 as of this writing), and

- the Brief Description of the Drawings section in the specification (written description of the invention) must contain the following passage as its first paragraph:

  "The file of this patent contains at least one drawing executed in color. Copies of this patent with color drawing(s) will be provided by the Patent and Trademark Office upon request and payment of the necessary fee."

If the petition requesting to submit color drawings or color photographs is filed after the filing date of the application, so that the original specification does not include the above paragraph, a proposed amendment must accompany the petition to insert the paragraph. (See *Patent It Yourself*, Chapter 13, for the procedure for amending an application.) The petition will be granted only if the PTO determines that a color drawing or color photograph is the only viable medium to adequately illustrate your invention.

If your petition for submitting a color drawing or photograph is granted, your patent will be printed with a black-and-white copy. The color drawing will be provided only upon request and payment of a fee, as stated in item four of the requirement above.

If your petition for submitting color drawings or color photographs is denied, the examiner will object to the drawings as being improper and require you to either cancel the color photograph or drawing or provide substitute black line drawings. However, canceling the photo or drawing may not be an option, because the remaining drawings, if any, may not be adequate to allow comprehension of your invention. If this is the case, you must provide substitute black line drawings instead. See Chapter 3 for details on converting photographs into black line drawings.

**EXAMPLE:**

Gladys files an application with three color drawings. Her petition for submitting the color drawings was denied. She cannot cancel the drawings, because the invention cannot be understood with the written description alone. In this situation, she must replace the color drawings with black line drawings. The black line drawings may not contain any details that were not in the color drawings.

## In the United States Patent and Trademark Office

App. No:  _John Smith_

Filing Date:  _Field of dots with hidden image_

Applicant:  _____

App. Title:  _____

Examiner:  _____

Art Unit:  _____

### Petition for Submitting Color Photographs or Drawings

Commissioner for Patents

Alexandria, VA 22313-1450

Sirs:

Applicant hereby respectfully petitions that the color photographs [X] filed herewith ☐ already filed be accepted as formal drawings. The $130 petition fee is enclosed.

These color photographs or drawings are necessary because    _the hidden image cannot be seen if the drawing is rendered in black lines on a white background or as a black-and-white photo._

_____

_____

_____

_____

_____

Sole/First Applicant:  _John Smith_

_John Smith_                              _10-11-11_

Sole/First Applicant Signature                 Date

Joint/Second Applicant:  _____

_____       _____

Joint/Second Applicant Signature               Date

Joint/Third Applicant:  _____

_____       _____

Joint/Third Applicant Signature                Date

Joint/Fourth Applicant:  _____

_____       _____

Joint/Fourth Applicant Signature               Date

Enc.

**Illustration 8.6—Sample Petition for Submitting Color Photographs or Drawings**

# Arrangement and Numbering of Figures

The drawings must be arranged and numbered in particular ways, as discussed below.

## Arrangement of Figures

The drawings must be on sheets that are separate from the written description in the patent specification. The only exceptions are formulas and tables, which may either be submitted as drawings on separate sheets, or be incorporated into the written description as textual information. See Chapter 6 for details on formulas and tables.

Each sheet of paper may contain several drawing figures, also known as views, as shown in Illustration 8.7. Each figure should be shown upright with respect to the top of the paper, depending on whether the paper is in portrait or landscape orientation. The figures must also be far enough apart to be clearly separated, so as to avoid confusion. Separate figures must not be connected by construction lines (dashed lines showing how the parts fit together). An exception to this rule is made for electrical waveforms, which may be connected by dashed lines to show relative timing, as shown in Chapter 6, Illustration 6.43.

> **TIP**
> **Bigger is clearer.** Make full use of all the available space on the paper to make the figures as large as possible. If an object must be drawn so large to show its details that there is no room for another figure, use additional sheets for the other figures. Never crowd the figures. The PTO's fees are the same regardless of the number of drawing sheets in an application.

## Numbering of Figures

All figures must be numbered in consecutive Arabic numerals (the symbols 1, 2, 3, and 4), starting with 1. The figures should preferably be arranged on the sheets so that the lowest numbered views appear on the first sheet, and progress through the sheets as the figure numbers rise. The first figure number of a sheet should continue from the last figure number of a previous sheet, and must not restart from 1 on each sheet. For example, the first sheet may contain Figures 1, 2, and 3; the second sheet may contain Figures 4 and 5; the third sheet may contain Figures 6, 7, and 8; and so on. However, if this is not practical, due to figure sizes, the figures may be arranged out of order on the sheets. The figures on each sheet are preferably, but not necessarily, numbered so that they progress from top to bottom, as shown in Illustration 8.7.

The figure numbers must be preceded by "FIG." or "Fig."—for example, "Fig. 3." Figure numbers may include letter suffixes, such as "Fig. 1A" and "Fig. 1B." However, it is good practice to reserve letter suffixes only for partial views or different views of one embodiment. Each figure number must refer only to a single figure. For example, it is improper to number a sheet "Fig. 3," and number each figure "Fig. 3A," "Fig. 3B," and "Fig. 3C," because "Fig. 3" does not refer to a specific figure. In such a case, just leave out "Fig. 3."

## Numbering of Partial Figures

If a figure is so large and complex that its details are too small if it is made to fit on one sheet, it can be spread across several sheets, as shown in Illustration 8.8. The figure must be arranged on each sheet so that the sheets can be tiled next to each other to assemble the complete figure. A dot-dot-dash line should

1/4

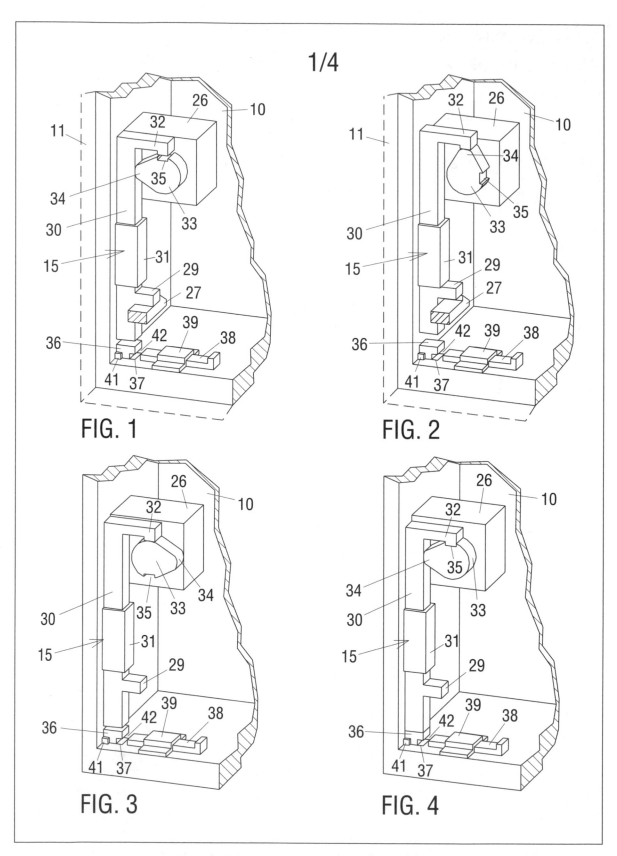

FIG. 1

FIG. 2

FIG. 3

FIG. 4

**Illustration 8.7—Arrangement of Figures**

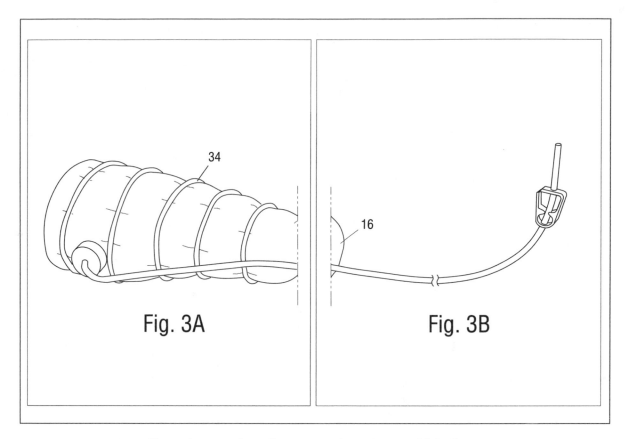

**Illustration 8.8—Spreading a Large Figure Onto Multiple Sheets**

be provided to denote the broken edge of each partial figure. Any arrangement of the sheets can be used—for example, side-to-side, top-to-bottom, and rectangular array as long as the sheets can be assembled without ambiguity. Each partial figure should be labeled with the same figure number having a different letter suffix, for example, Fig. 2A and Fig. 2B.

## Number Size and Style

A simple, easy-to-read lettering style or font should be used, as shown in Illustration 8.9. The ornate type of lettering typically used for the word "Fig." and the figure number in very old patents should be avoided. The figure numbers must be larger in size than the reference numbers to distinguish them. For example, the figure numbers should be about 5 mm, ⅕", or 22 points in height.

## When a Bracket Is Necessary

If a figure includes any elements that are not connected, such as in the exploded view of Illustration 8.10, a bracket must be used to "embrace" the disconnected element to indicate that it is part of the same figure.

Even if a figure is not an exploded view, but it includes a part that is disconnected from the rest of the figure, a bracket must be used (as in Illustration 8.11). However, if an exploded view—or any figure with disconnected parts—is the only figure on a sheet, no bracket is needed, because every element would clearly belong to the same figure.

𝕱𝖎𝖌. 2

Undesirable: Ornate Lettering Style or Font

Fig. 2

Preferable: Simple Lettering Style or Font

**Illustration 8.9—Figure Number Lettering Style or Font**

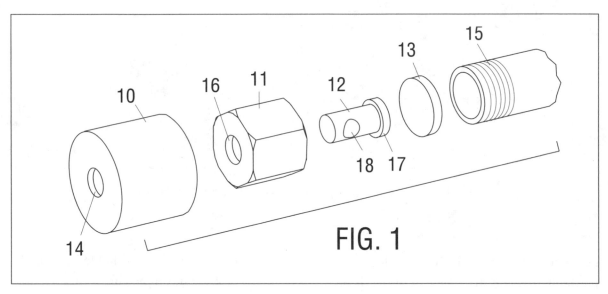

**Illustration 8.10—Bracket in Exploded View**

## Application With Single Figure

If an application includes only one figure, do not give it a figure number. The sheet number is still necessary, though, and should be "1/1."

## Figure Depicting Prior Art

The written description of a utility patent application must include background information, such as a discussion of any relevant prior art (older inventions) of which you are aware. It is usually not necessary to make a drawing of any prior art. If you do, such figures must be numbered in the conventional manner in sequence with the rest of the figures, and the label "Prior Art" must be added next to or below the figure number, such as in Illustration 8.12.

## Reference Numbers

Each part or element of a utility patent drawing mentioned in the written description must be designated by a reference number or letter, although numbers are preferred. They may start with any number and do not have to be consecutive. Design patent drawings must not include reference numbers or letters.

Reference numbers mentioned in the description of the invention in the specification must appear in the drawings, and reference numbers that appear in the drawings must be mentioned in the description. That is, each number must appear in both the specification and the drawings. Let's take a very simple description as an example: "As shown in Fig. 1, a chair includes a seating surface 10; supporting legs 11, 12, 13, and 14; and a seat back 15." For simplicity, consider it to be the entire description in the application. The same reference numbers, which include 10, 11, 12, 13, 14, and 15, must all be shown in the drawings.

## Different Parts Must Have Different Numbers

Each designated component of the invention must have a unique reference number—that is, the same number must not be used to designate different parts of the invention. If the same part appears in separate figures, it must be designated with the same number. For simplicity, the same number may be used to designate separate but identical parts, such as bolts. However, if such parts are referred to separately, different numbers should be used to avoid confusion. For example, "A bolt 13 is removable from the top end of a connecting rod 14, while bolts 15 are permanently attached to the lower end of connecting rod 14."

> ⓘ **CAUTION**
> **Keep your parts and numbers straight.**
> Using different numbers for the same part in different figures, or using the same number for different parts, are two of the most common mistakes.

Proofread the description and drawings carefully to weed out such errors.

## Consecutive Numbers Are Preferable

There is no PTO requirement for reference numbers to appear in any particular order in the written description (specification). Nevertheless, consecutive numbers (for example, 10, 11, 12, and 13), or consecutive odd or even numbers (for example, 11, 13, 15, and 17, or 10, 12, 14, and 16), are preferable, because they are easier for a reader to follow than random numbers that do not follow a logical sequence (for example, 24, 12, 43, 11, and 33). Also, the numbers customarily start with at least 10, or a higher number than the highest figure number, to avoid confusion with the figure numbers. Using every other number, as suggested in *Patent It Yourself*, allows intermediate numbers to be added later, and still maintain the sequence. For example, if after writing much of the specification, you want to number a washer mentioned between a bolt 16 and a nut 18, you can give it the number 17. However, if you used consecutive numbers, and need to add a number, simply use the next higher number or a suffix (16A); don't worry about renumbering everything.

## Reference Letters

Instead of reference numbers, suitable letters may be—but are not necessarily—used for designating nontangible elements, such as "A" for air flow, and should preferably be of the English alphabet. Letters may also be used where they are customarily used, such as in electronics. For example, "R1" and "R2" may be used for designating resistors; "C1" and "C2" may be used for designating capacitors; and so on.

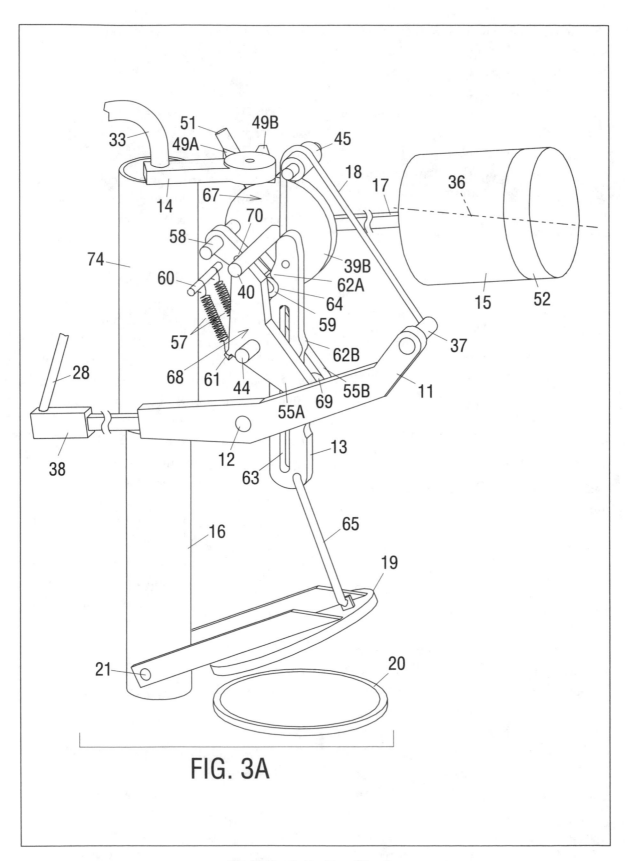

## FIG. 3A

**Illustration 8.11—Use of Bracket**

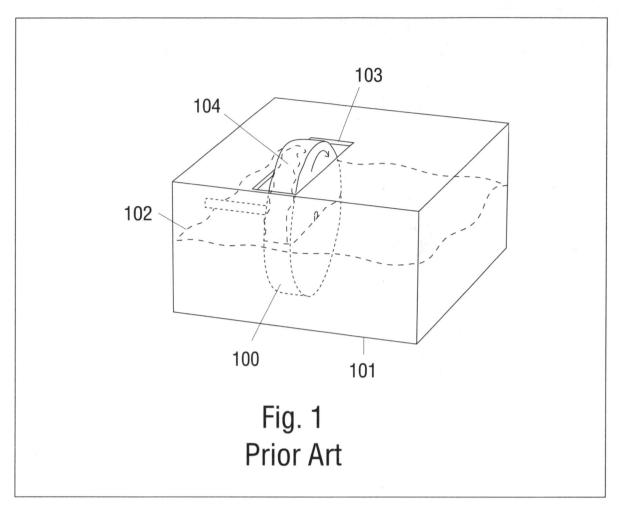

Fig. 1
Prior Art

Illustration 8.12—"Prior Art" Label

## Non-English Letters

Non-English letters are allowed where there is customary usage. For example, Greek letters may be used to indicate mathematical and scientific values in formulas and the labels of graphs, and they may also be used as reference characters in drawings. However, we recommend that you use Latin letters if at all possible, since your examiner or judge may not be familiar with Greek letters.

## Primed Numbers

Primed numbers or characters—that is, numbers with a mark (') to their upper right—for example, 23' and 23'—are not specifically prohibited, but they should be avoided because they tend to be confusing.

## Letter Suffixes

Reference numbers with letter suffixes may be used if the letter suffix helps explain the part, for example "left wheel 12L and right wheel 12R" or "upper surface 14U and lower surface 14L."

## Number Size and Style

Reference numbers or letters must be of a simple lettering style or font and at least 3.2

mm, ⅛" or 12 points in height, as shown in Illustration 8.13. Avoid the very ornate type of lettering used in some old patents. Do not make the reference numbers larger than the required size, otherwise they take up too much room and may make the sheet too crowded for easy reading or may not fit into small spaces. To further save space, use a thin, horizontally compact style or font, which is typically called "condensed."

An exception to the size requirement is that subscripts, such as the "2" in the chemical formula "$CO_2$," may be smaller than 3.2 mm.

**TIP**

**When drawing with a computer-aided drafting (CAD) program,** select the font before applying the reference numbers. This is because if you change the font after the numbers are applied, they will shift position and will no longer line up properly with the lead lines. The amount of shifting depends on the fonts used before and after the change.

**TIP**

**A keystroke saver.** Some CAD programs require the font height to be typed in every time the program is used, so frequently typing in "3.2" gets tiresome. It is more convenient to type in just "3"; a 3 mm font is virtually indistinguishable from a 3.2 mm font, so that it is perfectly acceptable.

## Size of Descriptive Text

In addition to reference numbers and letters, the size requirement applies to all characters, including lowercase letters, used in any descriptive text in the drawings. As stated, all letters must be at least 3.2 mm high. If descriptive text is written in sentence case, such as "Electrical power supply," or title case, such as "Electrical Power Supply," and the shortest lowercase letters must be at least 3.2 mm high, then the uppercase letters will be even taller and take up too much room. Therefore, it is usually best to use all capital letters, such as "ELECTRICAL POWER SUPPLY," so that no letter is over 3.2 mm tall.

53

Undesirable: Ornate number style or font

**53**

Better: Simple number style or font, but too thick and wide

53

Preferable: Simple number style or font

**Illustration 8.13—Reference Number Style or Font**

## Reference Number Positioning

Reference numbers or letters should be positioned a short distance away from the part they are designating, and far enough from other parts and from each other to avoid confusion, as shown in Illustration 8.14. They are preferably positioned outside the figure to avoid cluttering it, but they may be positioned inside if necessary to avoid being too far away. They must never be positioned across any lines of the figure, including hatch lines.

## Reference Numbers Between Different Embodiments

In an application with multiple embodiments or variations that share common parts, the same reference numbers can be used for the common parts between the embodiments. For example, two embodiments of a hand pump include the same pump cylinder, but different handles. The identical pump cylinders may be designated with the same reference number in all the figures—for example, "10"—but the handles must be designated with different numbers, such as "11" in the figure of the first embodiment, and "12" in the figure of the second embodiment.

## Lead Lines

A lead line must extend between each reference number and its corresponding part. One end of the lead line should be very close to the reference number without touching it, and the other end must touch the part of the figure being designated, such as in Illustration 8.15. Lead lines must never cross each other.

## Either Straight or Curved Lines

Lead lines may be straight or curved; a drawing can include both types if you wish. Although straight lines are easier to draw, curved ones can be more easily positioned in tight places, as shown in Illustration 8.15. They should not be too long—that is, the reference numeral should not be positioned unnecessarily far away from the part so as to require a long lead line. They should be positioned at a large angle from adjacent lines of the figure to avoid being confused as lines of the figure. They may cross lines of the figure, but should be positioned so as to cross as few lines as possible to avoid confusion.

**TIP**

**For best appearance, a lead line should be aligned with the imaginary center of the reference number,** as shown in Illustration 8.16. The dashed line is solely for showing alignment; it should not appear in the drawing.

## Correct

Numbers positioned outside figure

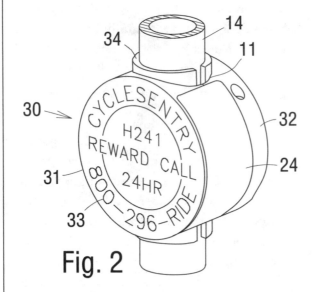

**Fig. 2**

## Correct

Some numbers positioned inside figure without crossing lines of figure

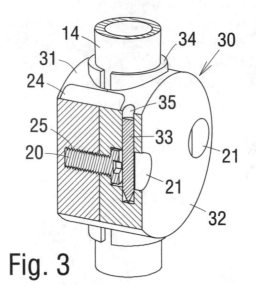

**Fig. 3**

## Incorrect

Numbers positioned over lines of figure

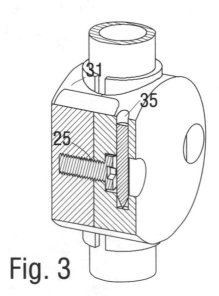

**Fig. 3**

**Illustration 8.14—Reference Number Positioning**

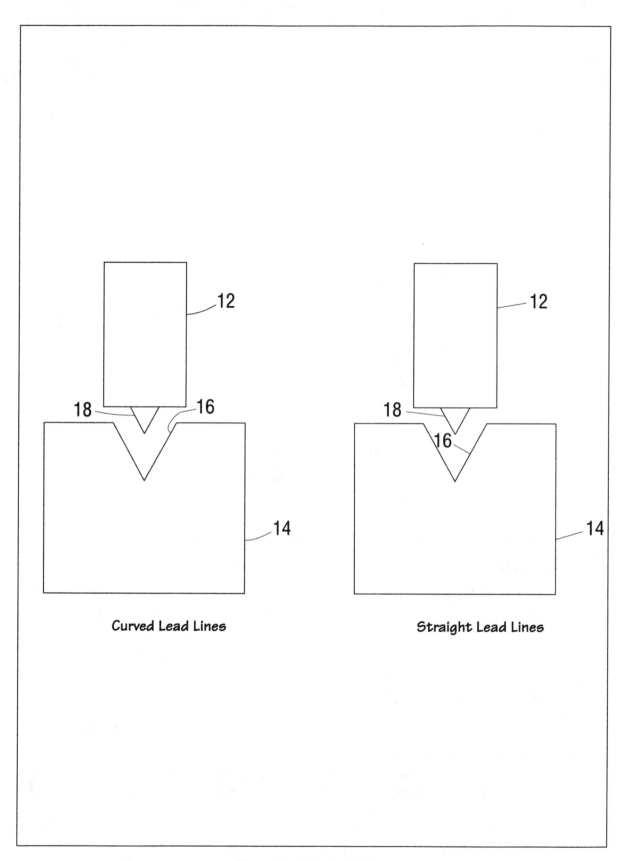

**Illustration 8.15—Lead Lines**

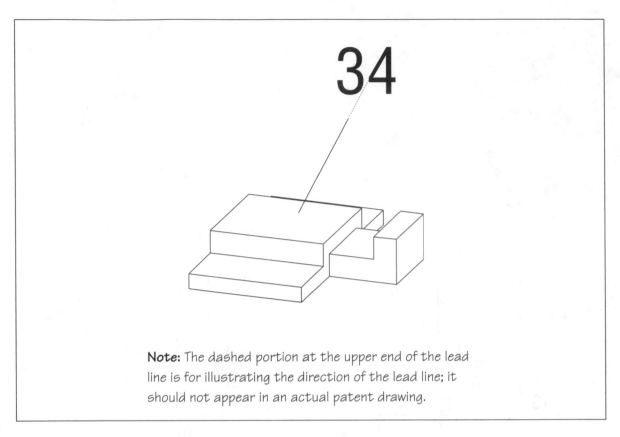

**Note:** The dashed portion at the upper end of the lead line is for illustrating the direction of the lead line; it should not appear in an actual patent drawing.

**Illustration 8.16—Lead Line Positioning**

## Lead Lines Must Not Connect Separate Figures

If an identical part appears in separate figures, it must not be referenced by a single reference numeral with two lead lines. In Illustration 8.17, a badge is shown in different views in Figs. 2 and 3. The top two illustrations show the incorrect usage of lead lines: The pipes in each figure are connected to the same reference number (14) positioned between the figures. The figures are thus considered to be "connected" by the lead lines, which is improper. The bottom two illustrations show the correct usage of lead lines: The pipes in each figure are connected to their own reference numbers, so that the figures are not connected.

## Replacing Lead Lines With Underline

If a reference number lies on a surface or cross section it is meant to designate, the lead line may be replaced with an underline for the number, such as parts 11 and 12 in Illustration 8.18. In fact, part 10 may also be underlined instead of being connected with a lead line. This method may be advantageous in some situations where space is limited. The hatching in the cross section must be interrupted to allow space for the number. However, this type of numbering may be confusing, so it should be used sparingly.

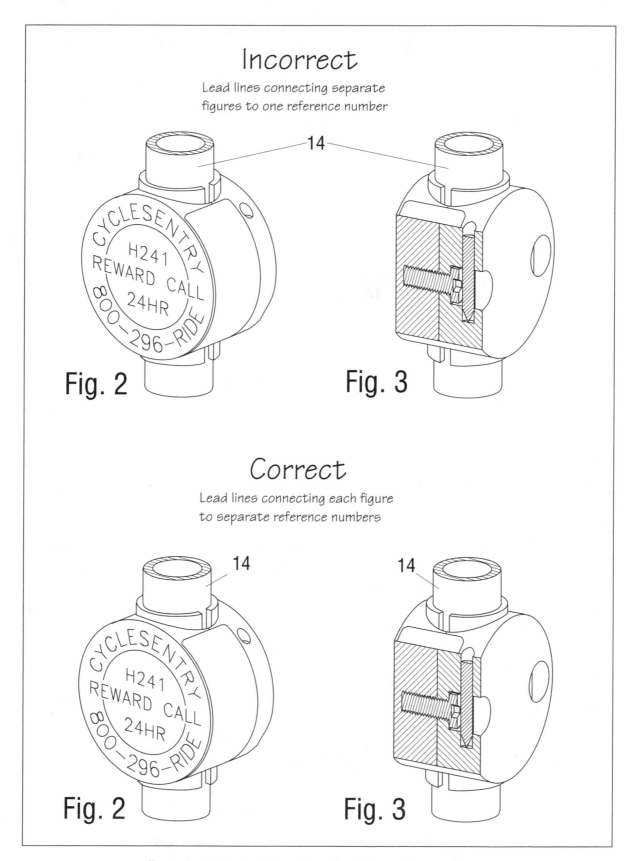

# Incorrect

Lead lines connecting separate
figures to one reference number

14

Fig. 2

Fig. 3

# Correct

Lead lines connecting each figure
to separate reference numbers

14

14

Fig. 2

Fig. 3

**Illustration 8.17—Lead Lines Must Not Connect Separate Figures**

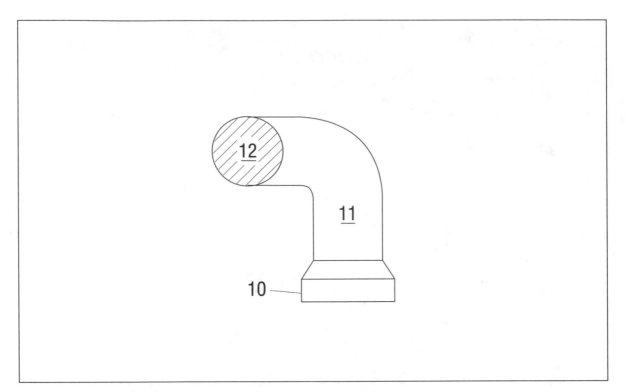

**Illustration 8.18—Underlined Reference Numbers**

## Arrows

Arrows should not be used on drawings except in the following situations:

- to designate a group of parts with a single number, even if each part has its own number, as shown in Illustration 8.19. The arrow should point in the general direction of the group. In the illustration shown, parts 17, 39, 41, 42, and 51 are collectively designated as an assembly 67; and parts 43, 44, 55, and 66 are collectively designated as an assembly 68 (the term "assembly" is chosen arbitrarily). The specification should describe the assembly as including such-and-such constituent parts—for example, "A cam assembly 67 includes arms 17 and 51, a disc 41…."

- to indicate the plane and direction of a sectional view (see Chapter 6 for details), and

- to show the direction of movement, as shown in Illustration 8.20. The purpose of such an arrow should be mentioned in the specification—for example, "a hinged arm 12 pivoting in the direction indicated by the arrow." If there is more than one arrow in a figure, each arrow should be designated with a different reference number to avoid confusion.

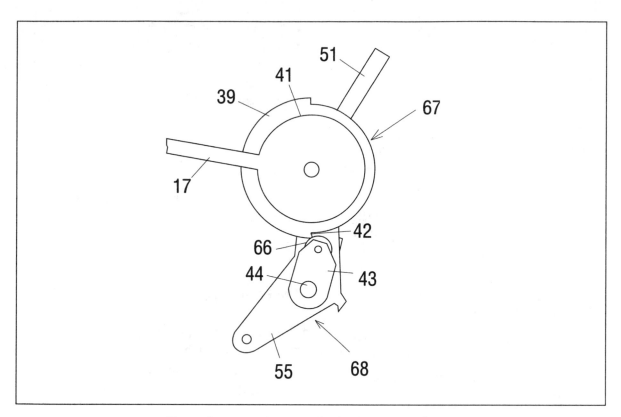

**Illustration 8.19—Arrows to Designate Groups of Parts**

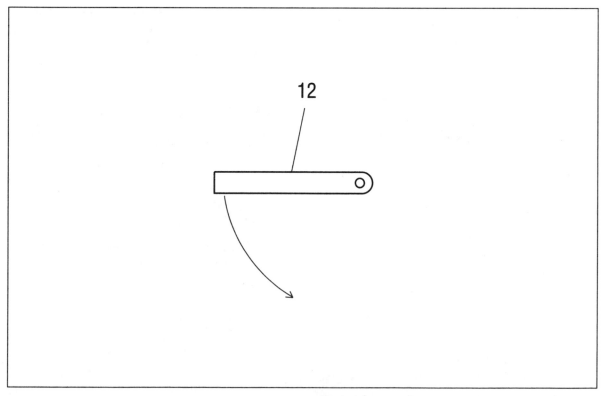

**Illustration 8.20—Arrow to Indicate Movement**

## Line Types

Allowable line types are shown in Illustration 8.21.

**Solid Line.** Use this for edge lines and shading lines.

**Hidden Line (Dashed).** Sometimes it is necessary to show a part hidden behind other parts. Such hidden parts are shown with dashed lines.

**Phantom Line (Dash-Dot-Dot-Dash).** A component that is not part of the invention may be shown in phantom lines. This is absolutely necessary in design patent drawings. Such a component may be shown in solid lines in utility patent drawings.

**Projected Line (Dash-Dot-Dash).** Projected lines may be used to show how separated objects fit together, although such lines are not usually necessary. The use of a projected line in an exploded view eliminates the need for a bracket. (See Chapter 6 for details on exploded views.)

Although technically there are different broken lines (hidden, phantom, and projected) for different applications, the dashed line may be used for any situation that requires a broken line.

## Character of Lines

Except for color drawings and photographs, all drawings must be done in black lines. The lines must be thick enough to allow photocopying without loss of detail, although the thickness of lines may vary according to their roles in a drawing. All lines must be solid black, uniformly thick, and have sharp, smooth edges.

> **CAUTION**
>
> **Common Errors:** Lines that are not dense or black enough, are not uniformly thick throughout, are jagged, or have feathered edges, as shown in Illustration 8.22. These are by far the most common errors found in patent drawings, and are typically made by using the wrong equipment—such as the wrong paper, pen, or computer printer—or by using an improper drafting technique. (See Chapters 2 and 3, on the proper equipment and techniques for making lines.)

Although all the lines in a drawing may be of the same width, the use of different widths for lines in different roles can greatly improve the legibility and aesthetics of a drawing. (See Chapters 6 and 7 for suggested line widths.)

## Descriptive Legends

Descriptive text is permitted in a drawing only when it is absolutely necessary to identify a part or an element whose nature is not apparent from the drawing alone. One situation where it is actually required is within the boxes of flowcharts and block diagrams. Another situation where descriptive text should be used is to indicate a "special" element, such as labeling a container of liquid, "Acid." (Flowcharts and block diagrams are discussed in Chapter 6.)

## Scale of Drawing

The same object should be shown in different figures in the same size if possible. Each figure should be large enough so that all of its essential details are easily comprehensible. Use all of the available space on a sheet to make each figure as large as possible without crowding the figures. Use the whole sheet for a single figure if necessary, as in Illustration 8.23.

> **CAUTION**
>
> **Common Error:** Drawing the figures too small, so that the lines are too close together and the features are too small to be easily discerned, as in Illustration 8.24.

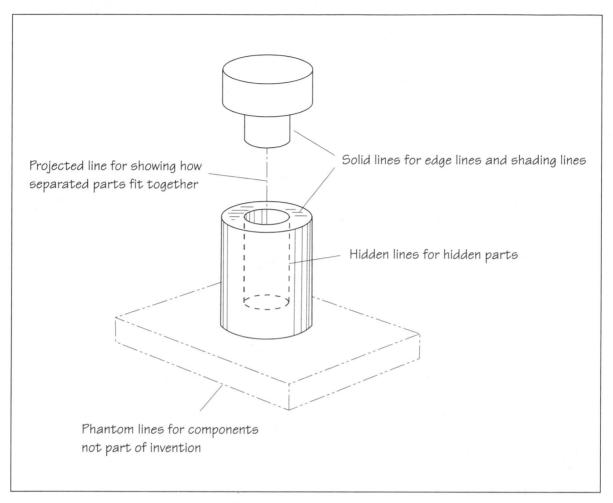

Projected line for showing how separated parts fit together

Solid lines for edge lines and shading lines

Hidden lines for hidden parts

Phantom lines for components not part of invention

**Illustration 8.21—Line Types**

Not Dense Enough

Not Uniformly Thick

Jagged

**Illustration 8.22—Poor Line Quality**

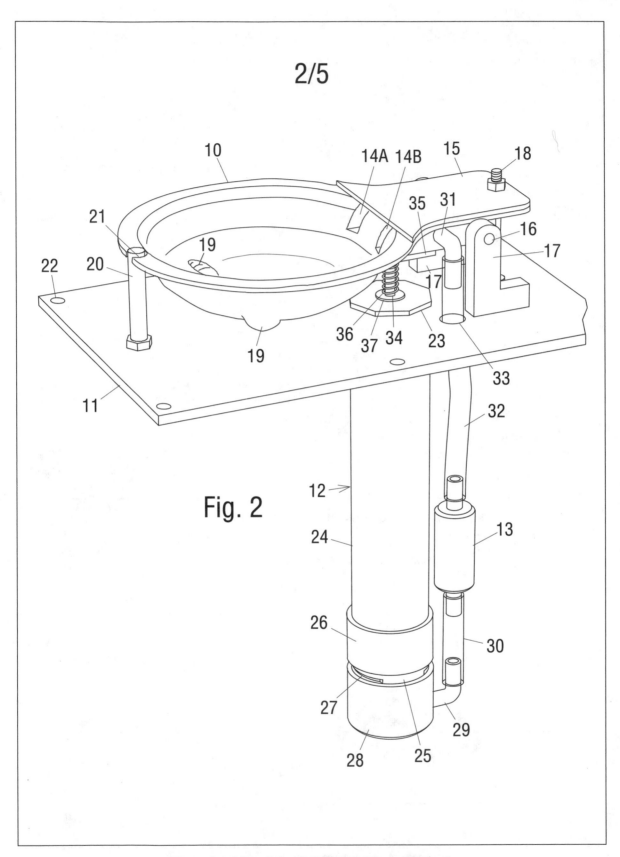

2/5

Fig. 2

**Illustration 8.23—Using Full Sheet to Show All Details**

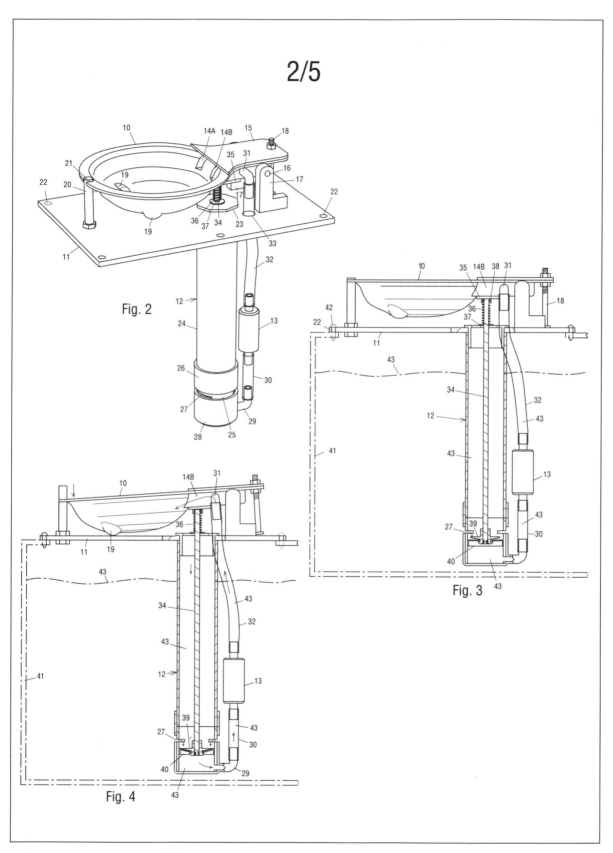

**Illustration 8.24—Figures Too Small and Crowded**

Do not hesitate to enlarge an object in a separate figure for clarity whenever it is necessary. If an object is shown substantially larger in a figure relative to another, the description (specification) should note the different scales to avoid confusion—for example, "mechanism 15 is shown enlarged in Fig. 3 for clarity."

If only part of an object is enlarged in a separate figure, the part of interest should be indicated in the original figure by a dashed circle, as shown in Illustration 8.25, so as to indicate its location within the whole object. However, the PTO rarely objects to the lack of such a dashed circle. Different figure numbers must be used to designate the separate figures.

## Copyright or Mask Work Notice

You may be able to obtain a copyright as well as a utility patent for some inventions, notably objects with aesthetic features and functional parts. Refer to *Patent It Yourself*, Chapter 1, for more information on copyright.

If you are applying for a utility patent for an invention that is also covered by copyright, you may include a copyright notice in the patent drawing. Illustration 8.26 shows a wind vane that uses an electronic position encoder 12, and an ornamental, cat-shaped vane 13. The whole invention (a position encoder attached to a wind vane) may be covered by a utility patent, while the cat-shaped vane alone may be covered by copyright. The proper format of the copyright notice is "© year of copyright your name." The following paragraph must be included at the beginning—preferably as the first paragraph—of the specification:

"A portion of the disclosure of this patent document contains material that is subject to copyright protection. The copyright owner has no objection to the facsimile reproduction by anyone of the patent disclosure, as it appears in the Patent and Trademark Office patent files or records, but otherwise reserves all copyright rights whatsoever."

The copyright notice must be placed below the copyrighted design within the margins—that is, within the sight—of the sheet. The font or lettering must be between 3.2 mm (⅛" or 14 points) and 6.3 mm (¼" or 28 points) high.

A special category of copyright is known as a "mask work," which is a mask used in the making of integrated circuits. If your invention is such a mask, substitute "mask work" for "copyright" in the above paragraph. The proper format for a mask work notice is "*M*," "Ⓜ," or "mask work" followed by your name—for example "*M* John Smith."

If the shape of your invention is considered a trademark (brand name, brand symbol), such as the Fotomat huts in shopping center parking lots, it would be wise to indicate this in the specification (description)—for example, "The shape of building in Fig. 1 is applicant's trademark for a photo finishing service."

## Security Markings

All applications filed in the PTO are screened for subject matter that might impact our national security. If you have invented, for example, a new doomsday weapon, and the PTO and other federal agencies determine that publicizing your invention by granting a patent will be detrimental to our national security, a secrecy order will be placed on your patent application. The PTO will notify you, and the grant of your patent will be withheld for as long as national security requires.

If your invention is subject to a secrecy order, or any other security classification (for

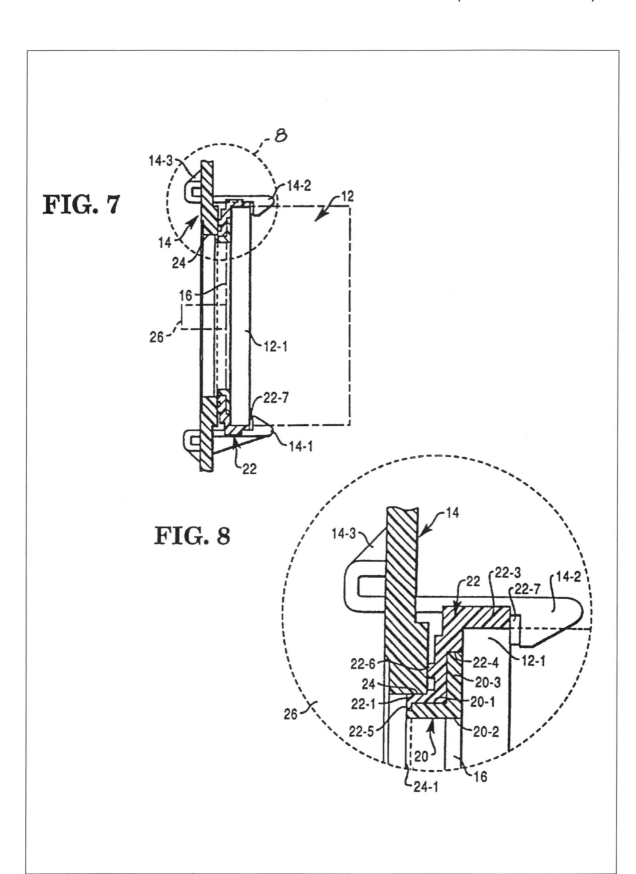

**Illustration 8.25—Enlarged Detail**

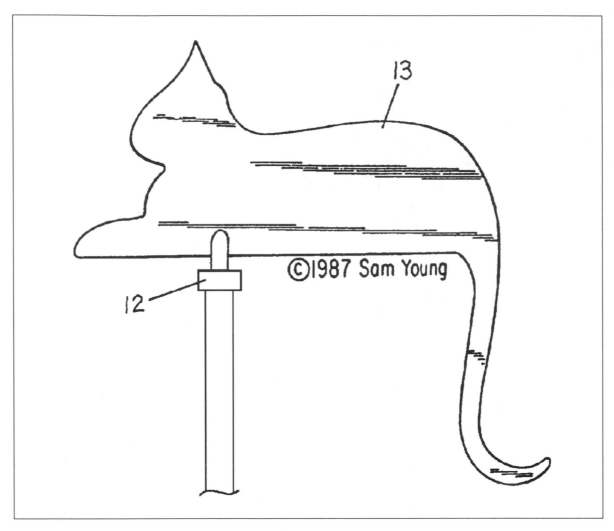

13

12

©1987 Sam Young

**Illustration 8.26—Copyright Notice**

example, you received a secrecy order from the PTO after its security review, or you are working under a government contract, which involves confidential, secret, top secret, or "Q" material), you may place authorized security markings—such as NATO (North Atlantic Treaty Organization), TS (top secret), S (secret), or C (confidential)—in the middle of the upper margin of a sheet, as shown in Illustration 8.27.

## Corrections

Ink drawings may be corrected by erasure or white masking fluid, such as Wite-Out®, as long as erased lines are invisible and the masking fluid is durable, so that it will not crack or flake off. If you use an eraser, be careful when drawing new lines over erased areas, which may become roughened, causing the ink to bleed or feather. If you prefer a masking fluid, select one with a pen-type applicator and avoid those with brush applicators, which tend to dry out quickly and make application difficult. Note that white masking fluid dissolves some inks,

**Illustration 8.27—Security Marking**

which may darken the fluid. Such corrections are not acceptable.

Corrections to a drawing sheet can be avoided if the drawing is made with CAD: The drawing can be corrected on the computer, and a new sheet printed.

## Prohibited Elements

The following elements cannot appear on patent drawings:

- indications regarding the scale of the figures, such as "Actual Size" and "Scale 1:2". This is because the PTO often reduces drawings in size when printing them as part of a patent, so scale indications became inaccurate. Such indications should not appear in the description (specification) either.

- expressions or drawings contrary to morality or public order, such as explicit sexual and violent images (unless necessary to show the invention), or profanity

- trademarks or service marks, such as Coca Cola® or AT&T®, unless you prove that you have a proprietary interest in the mark

- any statement or other matter obviously irrelevant or unnecessary under the circumstances

- descriptive legends (text)—such as "Electrical diagram of widget," "on/off switch," and "serrated surface"—except one or a few words when such words are indispensable—for example, within the individual boxes of flowcharts and schematics

- center lines depicting the center or axis of circular parts. However, this rule is rarely enforced.

- brackets or circles surrounding reference numerals. Although not specifically prohibited, brackets should not surround reference numerals in the description (specification) either.

- any lines connecting separate figures (figures with different figure numbers), except for electrical waveforms

- solid black shading areas, except when used to represent bar graphs, or black color in drawings meant to depict color as a distinguishing feature of an invention, and

- artwork or figures that are covered by copyright, unless you prove that you have a proprietary interest in the mark.

## Identification Information

Optional identification information may be placed on the front or back of each sheet. Although it is optional, such information may become useful if your drawings are separated from your file at the PTO. Such information should include the:

- title of invention
- name of inventor
- application serial number, and
- group art unit.

If on the back, the lettering must not show through on the front of the drawing, so write lightly with a pencil near the edge of each sheet, or print in light gray with a laser printer. If on the front, the lettering must be centered in the top margin. The third and fourth items are known only after the application has been filed and you have received a filing receipt, so they have to be used only when filing corrected drawings, such as in response to Office Actions. (See Chapter 9 for details on filing corrected drawings.)

## Drafting Symbols

In the past, the PTO provided examples of various drafting symbols to illustrate the way it preferred that patent drawings show materials in section, colors, and standard components. However, recent editions of the PTO Rules and guides have not contained these examples. We believe you will find these examples useful, so we are reproducing them here as follows: Illustration 8-28 shows Sectional and Nonsectional Views of Various Materials; Illustration 8-29 shows Electrical Symbols; and Illustration 8-30 shows Mechanical Symbols. Note, however, that some of these symbols are dated and symbols for some modern components are not included, so you may use any standard or descriptive symbols for any modern components that are not shown. Be sure always to number, identify, and describe every component in your specification.

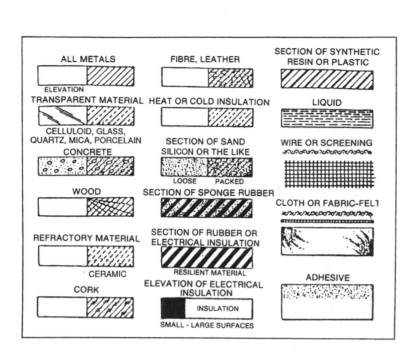

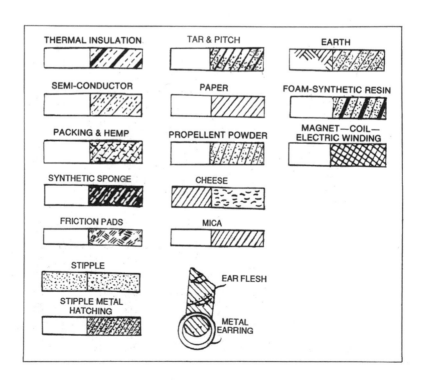

**Illustration 8.28—Sectional and Nonsectional Views of Various Materials**

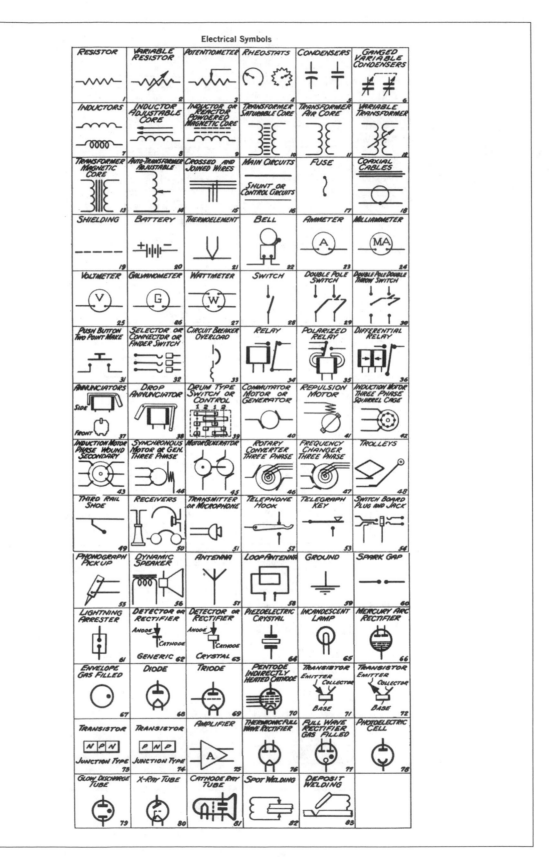

**Illustration 8.29—Electrical Symbols**

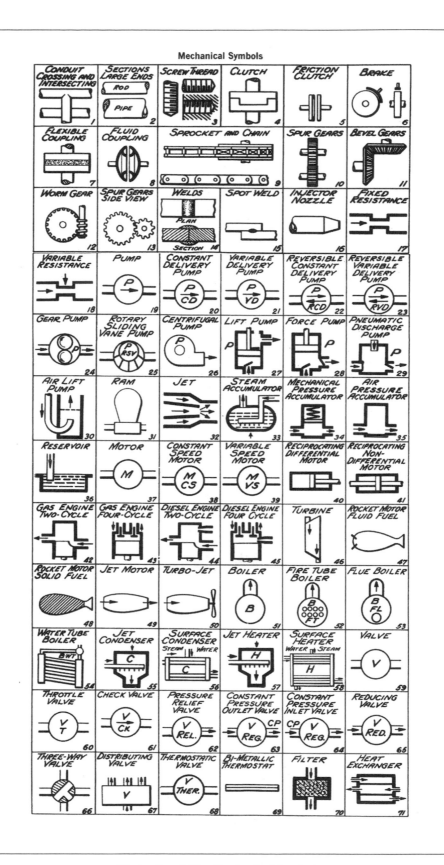

**Illustration 8.30—Mechanical Symbols**

# Responding to Office Actions

After a regular patent application is filed, the first communication from the PTO you will receive is an acknowledgment receipt if you filed on the Internet, or a receipt postcard if you filed by mail, assuming you've followed the instructions in *Patent It Yourself*, Chapter 10. Next, if you've followed all the instructions, you'll receive a filing receipt.

The waiting time for the next communication will vary from one month to as much as two years, depending upon the technological field of the invention and the drawings.

Rule 85(a) (37 C.F.R. 1.85(a)) states that before the application will be assigned to an examiner, the drawings must meet all formalities (compliance with all rules, including size of paper, character of lines, and so on). After the filing receipt is sent, the drawings will be sent to the Drawing Review Branch, where the PTO's draftspersons will study the drawings and usually send a Notice of Draftperson's Patent Drawing Review (PTO 948) form (Illustration 9.1) with a cover letter. The PTO 948 form will indicate any drawing informalities, and the cover letter will state that any informalities must be corrected before the application file will be sent to its examining division. If the drawings are in formal condition and have no errors, no PTO 948 will be sent. If you have done a superb job in preparing the drawings and application, and if the examiner does not find close prior art (older inventions, typically found in existing patents), your next communication will be a Notice of Allowance and Issue Fee Due, which indicates that the application has been approved.

However, if your drawings have one or more informalities, the next communication you may receive will include the PTO 948, in which the PTO will list the informalities, as explained in "Notice of Draftsperson's Patent Drawing Review," below. A cover letter will advise you that you may have to correct the informalities and file corrected drawings before the application can be sent to the examiner for substantive examination. The rest of this chapter explains how to remedy various informalities and file corrected drawings. Once you have satisfied the Drawing Review Branch, the application file will be sent to the examining division. (Sometimes the application will go to the examiner anyway, even with drawing informalities, and the PTO 948 will be sent with the first Office Action.) The Office Action is a multipage letter from an examiner who examined your application. The Office Action will indicate that the application is not approved for one or more reasons.

## Objections and Rejections

The drawings in each regular patent application are examined by two branches of the PTO: the Drawing Review Branch and the Examining Branch. The results of the Drawing Review Branch's examination will be mailed after the filing receipt or with the first Office Action. The results of the Examining Branch's review, if any objections are found, will be included as part of the first Office Action. Typical objections from an examiner are more substantive than those from the Drawing Review Branch—for example, the drawing fails to show one or more features recited in the claims, the reference numerals in the drawing do not coincide with those in the specification, a chemical or mechanical process should be illustrated, or there is some technical inaccuracy in the figures. The drawings in a provisional patent application are not examined; see *Patent It Yourself* for details on provisional applications.

A rejection is made when the claims (the part of an application that defines an invention in legal terms) have substantive defects, such as, they're unpatentable or unclear. An objection, whether made by the examiner or the Drafting Review Branch, is typically applied to nonsubstantive defects of an application, such as incorrect paper size, incorrect line spacing in the specification, misspellings, mismatched reference numbers between the description and drawings, unclear description, inadequate detail in the drawings, and improper claim dependency. All objections and rejections must be overcome by fixing the cited defects, or successfully arguing against them. Otherwise, a patent will not be granted.

New, corrected drawings must be filed to overcome all objections. Refer to *Patent It Yourself*, Chapter 13, for how to handle objections and rejections relating to the specification and claims, and general information on how to prepare a response or an amendment to the Office Action.

There are many possible drawing-related objections. This chapter details how to handle the most common ones. A Notice of Draftsperson's Patent Drawing Review (PTO 948) always gives reasons for any objection, so you will understand it even if you get one that is not covered here. If you do not understand an objection, you may call your examiner or drafting reviewer to ask for clarification; their helpfulness varies from person to person. The phone number of the examiner is provided on the last page of the Office Action, and the phone number of the Drafting Branch is provided on the Notice of Draftsperson's Patent Drawing Review (discussed below), which is included with the Office Action. You should feel free to call these numbers if you have questions, but obviously you should try not to antagonize the person on the other end of the line, as that will hurt your chances.

## Reading the Statute and Rule Numbers

An Office Action always cites specific laws and rules for the objections or rejections, such as 35 U.S.C. § 102; 37 CFR § 1.83, and so on. "35 U.S.C." means Title 35 of the United States Code, which is the patent statutes. "37 CFR" means Title 37 of the Code of Federal Regulations, which is a compilation of the patent rules. "§" is the section symbol, and the number following it is the specific section of the statute or rule that is being applied to the application. Statutes are laws, which are written in relatively broad terms, whereas rules are written to expound on the laws and are more specific.

Both statutes and rules can be found on the PTO's website (www.uspto.gov).

## Objection or Rejection Under 35 U.S.C. § 112

As already stated, an Office Action details objections or rejections to an application under various statutes and rules. An objection or a rejection may be made under 35 U.S.C. § 112, and reads as follows:

"The specification is objected to under 35 U.S.C. § 112, first paragraph, as failing to provide an adequate written description of the invention, and to provide an enabling disclosure." ("Enabling disclosure" means information, including written description and drawings, that are detailed and clear enough to enable someone skilled in the pertinent field to make and use the invention.)

or

"The claim is rejected under 35 U.S.C. § 112, first paragraph, as the claimed invention is not

U.S. DEPARTMENT OF COMMERCE-Patent and Trademark Office          Application No. _____

## NOTICE OF DRAFTSPERSON'S
## PATENT DRAWING REVIEW

The drawing filied (insert date)_____ are:

A. _____ not objected to by the Draftperson under 37 CFR 1.84 or 1.152.

B. _____ objected to by the Draftperson under 37 CFR 1.84 or 1.152 as indicated below. The Examiner will require submission of new, corrected drawings whe necessary. Corrected drawings must be submitted according to the instructions on the back of this notice.

1. DRAWINGS. 37 CFR 1.84(a): Acceptable categories of drawings: Black ink. Color.
_____ Color drawing are not acceptable until petition is granted.
_____ Fig.(s)_____
_____ Pencil and non black ink is not permitted. Fig(s)_____

2. PHOTOGRAPHS. 37 CFR 1.84(b)
_____ Photographs are not acceptable until petition is granted,
_____ 3 full-tone sets are required. Fig(s)_____
_____ Photographs not properly mounted (must brystol board or photographic double-weight paper). Fig(s)_____
_____ Poor quailty (half-tone). Fig(s)_____

3. TYPE OF PAPER. 37 CFR 1.84(e)
_____ Paper not flexible, strong, white and durable. Fig.(s)_____
_____ Erasures, alterations, overwritings, interlineations, folds, copy machine marks not acceptable. (too thin)
_____ Mylar, vellum paper is not acceptable (too thin). Fig.(s)_____

4. SIZE OF PAPER. 37 CFR 1.84(F): Acceptable sizes:
_____ 21.0 cm by 29.7 cm (DIN size A4)
_____ 21.6 cm by 27.9 cm (8 1/2 x 11 inches)
_____ All drawings sheets not the same size. Sheet(s)_____

5. MARGINS. 37 CFR 18.4(g): Acceptable margins:
Top 2.5 cm Left 2.5 cm Right 1.5 cm Bottom 1.0 cm SIZE: A4 Size
Top 2.5 cm Left 2.5 cm Right 1.5 cm Bottom 1.0 cm SIZE: 8 1/2 x 11
_____ Margins not acceptable. Fig(s)_____
_____ Top (T) _____ Left (L)
_____ Right (R) _____ Bottom (B)

6. VIEWS. CFR 1.84(h)
REMINDER: Specification may require revision to correspond to drawing changes.
_____ Views connected by projection lines or lead lines. Fig.(s)_____
Partial views. 37 CFR 1.84(h)(2)
_____ Brackets needed to show figure as one entity. Fig.(s)_____
_____ Views not labeled separately or properly. Fig.(s)_____
_____ Enlarged view not labeled separately or properly. Fig.(s)_____

7. SECTIONAL VIEWS. 37 CFR 1.84(h)(3)
_____ Hatching not indicated for sectional portions of an object. Fig.(s)_____
_____ Sectional designation should be noted with Arabic or Roman numbers. Fig.(s)_____

8. ARRANGEMENT OF VIEWS. 37 CFR 1.84(i)
_____ Words do not appear on a horizontal, left-to-right fashion when page is either upright or turned, so that the top becomes the right side, except for graphs. Fig.(s)_____
_____ Views not on the same plane on drawing sheet. Fig.(s)_____

9. SCALE. 37 CFR 1.84(k)
_____ Scale not large enough to show mechansim with crowding when drawing is reduced in size to two-thirds in reproduction. Fig.(s)_____

10. CHARACTER OF LINES, NUMBERS, & LETTERS. 37 CFR 1.84(l)
_____ Lines, numbers & letters not uniformly thick and well defined, clean, durable and black (poor line quality). Fig.(s)_____

11. SHADING. 37 CFR 1.84(m)
_____ Solid black areas pale. Fig.(s)_____
_____ Solid black shading not permitted. Fig.(s)_____
_____ Shade lines, pale, rough and blurred. Fig.(s)

12. NUMBERS, LETTERS, & REFERENCE CHARACTERS. 37 CFR 1.48(p)
_____ Numbers and reference characters not plain and legible. Fig.(s)_____
_____ Figure legends are poor. Fig.(s)_____
_____ Numbers and reference characters not oriented in the same direction as the view. 37 CFR 1.84(p)(3) Fig.(s)_____
_____ Engligh alphabet not used. 37 CFR 1.84(p)(3) Fig.(s)_____
_____ Numbers, letters and reference characters must be at least .32 cm (1/8 inch) in height. 37 CFR 1.84(p)(3) Fig.(s)_____

13. LEAD LINES. 37 CFR 1.84(q)
_____ Lead lines cross each other. Fig.(s)_____
_____ Lead lines missing. Fig.(s)_____

14. NUMBERING OF SHEETS OF DRAWINGS. 37 CFR 1.48(t)
_____ Sheets not numbered consecutively, and in Ababic numerals beginning with number 1. Fig.(s)_____

15. NUMBERING OF VIEWS. 37 CFR 1.84(u)
_____ Views not numbered consecutively, and in Arabic numerals, beginning with number 1. Fig.(s)_____

16. CORRECTIONS. 37 CFR 1.84(w)
_____ Corrections not made from PTO-948 dated_____

17. DESIGN DRAWINGS. 37 CFR 1.152
_____ Surface shading shown not appropriate. Fig.(s)_____
_____ Solid black shading not used for color contrast. Fig.(s)_____

COMMENTS

REVIEWER _____ DATE_____ TELEPHONE NO. _____

ATTACHMENT TO PAPER NO._____

APPLICANT'S COPY

**Illustration 9.1—Notice of Draftsperson's Patent Drawing Review**

described in such full, clear, concise, and exact terms as to enable any person skilled in the art to make and use the same." ("Art," in this context, means the field of the invention.)

Such an objection or rejection may be applied to utility or design patent applications.

## When Applied to Utility Patent Application

When an objection or rejection under 35 U.S.C. § 112 is made in a utility patent application, the drawings may not be mentioned. However, they are usually also affected, because the drawings and description cooperate to provide the enabling disclosure.

Such an objection or rejection may be overcome if you can argue that the disclosure is in fact enabling—that is, it describes and/or shows the invention clearly enough to enable one skilled in the field to make and use the invention. (Refer to *Patent It Yourself*, Chapter 13, for how to make such arguments.) Otherwise, additional description and/or drawings must be added by filing a continuation-in-part (CIP) application. See below and *Patent It Yourself*, Chapter 14, for details on filing a CIP application.

### EXAMPLE 1:

An application for a stair-climbing, motorized wheelchair describes and shows in detail the mechanism for climbing stairs. The application includes a circuit diagram that does not show a source of electrical power. An inexperienced examiner objects to the specification and drawings, and rejects the claims for failure to provide an enabling disclosure, because a source of electrical power is neither described nor shown. The objection and rejection can be overcome by arguing that anyone skilled in the field, such as an engineer, knows to provide a suitable source of power—such as a battery—and that the power supply is customarily omitted in circuit diagrams.

### EXAMPLE 2:

An application describes a self-healing tire that automatically seals punctures, but does not describe how it is accomplished. The drawings show only the exterior of the tire. The examiner objects to the specification and drawings, and rejects the claims for failure to provide an enabling disclosure, because the application neither describes nor shows how to make the invention. In this case, the objection and rejection can be overcome by filing a CIP application to provide details on how the self-healing works or by citing a previous publication (patent, periodical, textbook) that describes how to make a self-healing tire. Note that there is a serious disadvantage to filing a CIP application: If the original disclosure was inadequate, the CIP will only be entitled to its filing date; it will not be entitled to any benefit of the filing date of the parent case.

## When Applied to Design Patent Application

An objection or rejection under 35 U.S.C. § 112 may also be applied to a design patent application, because the precise or complete appearance of the invention is unclear. The Office Action will specify why the drawings are inadequate—for example, they lack shading, are roughly drawn, or do not show all sides of the invention. It is usually difficult to successfully argue that the drawings are adequate in this situation, so the only response is to fix the drawings to provide the additional information. However, you may add features to a drawing *only* if the information being provided is already shown in some of the other drawings as filed. If the information being added is not shown in any way in the original drawings, you must file a CIP application. See below and *Patent It Yourself*, Chapter 14, for details on CIP applications.

**EXAMPLE:**

The original drawings of an application include a front perspective view of a chair. The figure lacks shading, so that the surface contours of the seat and backrest are not clear. The examiner objects to the figure for lacking shading. Fortunately, the drawings also include a side sectional view that clearly shows the contours of those parts. Surface shading may thus be added to the perspective view to overcome the objection without adding new matter because the contours are already shown in the side sectional view. Additional drawings may also be added to show the chair from different angles if they do not reveal any features that are not in the original drawings. However, if the original drawings do not include a side sectional view, so that the contours of the seat and backrest are not clearly shown in any figure, then the only way to overcome the objection is to file a CIP application to provide the sectional view or shading.

## Objection Under 37 CFR § 1.83(a) for Failure to Show Claimed Feature

In utility or design patent applications, an objection may be made under 37 CFR § 1.83(a). Such an objection reads as follows:

"The drawings are objected to under 37 CFR § 1.83(a). The drawings must show every feature of the invention specified in the claims. Therefore, the [element] in claim [x] must be shown or the feature deleted from the claim. No new matter should be entered."

Such an objection is applied when a claim recites (mentions) a certain element (feature), but such element is not shown in the drawings. The element may be added to the drawings without introducing new matter, provided that what is added to the drawings is no more detailed than what is recited in the specification or claim. That is, as discussed above, unless the element is very simple or readily understood by one skilled in the art—such as a hinge, a switch, or a power supply—the description or claims must be detailed enough to support the changes to the drawings. It may be possible to add a labeled box to the drawing to avoid violating the no-new-matter rule. For example, if a claim recites a jet sprayer and the drawing is objected to for failing to show any jet sprayer, you can simply add a box labeled "jet sprayer" to the drawing in order to overcome this objection without adding new matter; see below. Otherwise, you must delete the element from the claim or file a CIP application to add the element to the drawings. (See below and *Patent It Yourself*, Chapter 14, for details on CIP applications.) Even if the feature may be properly added to the drawings, you may choose to delete it from the claim if it is not important, so as to avoid having to make a new drawing.

## Objection Under 37 CFR § 1.84(p)(4) for Improper Reference Numbers

In utility patent applications, an objection may be made under 37 CFR § 1.84(p)(4). Such an objection reads as follows:

"The drawings are objected to under 37 CFR § 1.84(p)(4). The same part of an invention appearing in more than one view of the drawing must always be designated by the same reference character, and the same reference character must never be used to designate different parts."

Such an objection is applied when there is a mismatch in the reference numbers between the different figures. It may be overcome by changing the numbers in the drawings to ensure that the same parts in different figures have the same number, and that different parts never share the same number. Having a list of reference numbers in the specification may help you keep the numbers straight and avoid this objection.

EXAMPLE 1:

An objection is made because the number 12 is used to designate a bracket in Fig. 1, but the number 18 is used to designate the same bracket in Fig. 2—that is, different numbers are used to designate the same element. The objection can be overcome by changing 12 to 18 in Fig. 1, or changing 18 to 12 in Fig. 2, so that the bracket is designated with the same number in both figures. You will have to file a new sheet of drawings to overcome the objection. The bracket must be also properly numbered in the written description to correspond with the drawings.

EXAMPLE 2:

An objection is made because a lever and a button are both designated with the number 24 in the drawings—that is, the same number is used to designate different elements. The objection can be overcome by changing the drawings so that the lever and the button are designated with different numbers. Again, the elements must also

be numbered in the written description to correspond with the drawings.

# Objection Under 37 CFR § 1.84(p)(5) for Missing Reference Numbers

In utility patent applications, an objection may be made under 37 CFR § 1.84(p)(5). Such an objection reads as follows:

"The drawings are objected to under 37 CFR § 1.84(p)(5). Reference characters not mentioned in the description must not appear in the drawings. Reference characters mentioned in the description must appear in the drawings."

Such an objection is applied when there is a mismatch between the reference numbers in the drawings and those in the written description, so that a reference number is "missing." This objection may be overcome by making changes to either the drawings or description to ensure that each reference number appears in both the description and drawings, and never just one or the other. Again, including a list of reference numbers in the specification may help you keep the numbers straight and avoid this objection.

EXAMPLE 1:

An objection is made because the number 32 is used to designate a cylinder in the drawings, but the number 27 is used to designate the cylinder in the written description—that is, different numbers are used in the drawings and the written description to designate the same element. The objection can be overcome by changing 32 to 27 in the drawings, or changing 27 to 32 in the written description, so that the cylinder is designated with the same number in both the drawings and written description.

**EXAMPLE 2:**

An objection is made because a power cord is designated with the number 19 in the drawings, but the same number does not appear in the written description. The objection can be overcome by either deleting the number 19 from the drawings, or adding the number 19 to the written description to designate the power cord, so that the number 19 is used to designate the same element in both the drawings and the written description.

**EXAMPLE 3:**

An objection is made because a socket is designated with the number 36 in the written description, but the same number does not appear in the drawings. The objection can be overcome by either deleting the number 36 from the written description, or adding the number 36 to the drawings to designate the socket, so that the number 36 is used to designate the socket in both the drawings and the written description.

## Notice of Draftsperson's Patent Drawing Review

A Notice of Draftsperson's Patent Drawing Review, as shown in Illustration 9.1, previously was included with the first Office Action for all applications with drawings. However, as stated, under new Rule 85(a) it may be sent soon after filing, and if so, you must comply with it before the application will be sent to the examiner. It is issued by the Drawing Review Branch. You will get a well-deserved sense of satisfaction if

Part A on the top left of the Notice is checked to indicate that the drawings are acceptable.

If Part B is checked, the drawings have been determined to be out of compliance with one or more rules. As shown in Illustration 9.1, the specific objections are detailed in categories 1 to 17, each of which has several related items. The probable cause and remedy for each objection is discussed below.

## Drawings. 37 CFR 1.84(a): Acceptable categories of drawings: Black ink. Color

___ **Color drawings are not acceptable until petition is granted.**

*Probable cause of objection:* Color drawings or color photographs have been submitted without filing the required petition and fee.

*Remedy:* File a petition and fee, or replace them with black line drawings. If a petition has already been filed, the drawings will be accepted when and if the petition is granted, provided that there are no other objections. You should call the director of your examining group, which is listed on your filing receipt, to make sure the petition was received and will be acted upon soon. It may take several calls to make sure the petition has been acted upon and the objections have been resolved. If the petition is denied, black line drawings must be substituted for them. (See Chapter 8 for details on petitions.)

___ **Pencil and non black ink. Fig(s)_____**

*Probable cause of objection:* The drawings were done with a pencil or other nonblack writing instrument or on an inkjet printer.

## How to File Corrected Drawings in the PTO

If you are a registered eFiler (see *Patent It Yourself*, Chapter 10), you can file new drawings (and any other papers you desire) via the Internet by converting the new drawings to PDF format (by scanning them to PDF or by using a file-conversion utility). Then after logging on, identify your patent application, attach the PDF files of the new drawings, and select the names of the attachments. There is no fee. You should also accompany the new drawings with a transmittal or cover letter (also converted to PDF); use the Submission of Corrected Drawings form in the appendix. You should explain the changes in the space provided in this form. If the changes will not be easy to understand from the cover letter alone, attach a copy of the original drawings marked up to show the changes. Omit the Certificate of Mailing from the cover letter.

If you're not a registered eFiler, you must file the drawings by mail or by fax. Be sure to accompany the new drawings with a transmittal or cover letter; use the Submission of Corrected Drawings form in the appendix. Also type or write "Replacement Drawing, Ser. Nr. ___/_____" [insert your serial number] on the top of each drawing sheet. Be sure to package the drawings carefully so they won't get wrinkled in the mail. You should mail the PTO a good photocopy of the new drawings and keep the originals. If the changes will not be easy to understand from the cover letter alone, you should attach a copy of the original drawings marked up in red ink to show the changes.

If you file by fax, fax the cover letter and the new drawings to the PTO's central fax number (571-273-8300). Make sure that the fax machine or computer you use can transmit crisp, clean drawings. Use the following Certificate of Facsimile Transmission instead of the Certificate of Mailing on the cover letter:

*Certificate of Facsimile Transmission*

I hereby certify that on the date below I will fax this paper and referenced attachments if any, to the Patent and Trademark Office, GAU

_____

at 1-571-273-8300.

Date: 20xx _____

_____

_____,

Applicant Pro Se

*Remedy:* Redo the drawings in solid black lines with a proper black pen or printer.

## Photographs. 37 CFR 1.84(b)

__ **Photographs are not acceptable until petition is granted.**

*Probable cause of objection:* Color photographs have been submitted without filing the required petition.

*Remedy:* File a petition and fee. The petition will be granted or approved only if color photographs are absolutely necessary for adequately illustrating the invention (see Chapter 8). If the petition is denied, the color photographs must be replaced with black line drawings. They may also be replaced with black-and-white photographs if black line drawings cannot adequately illustrate the invention. There is no petition necessary for filing black-and-white photographs, but the conditions for their acceptance are almost as stringent as those for color photographs (see Chapter 4).

__ **3 full-tone sets are required.**
   **Fig.(s)_____**

*Probable cause of objection:* Fewer than three sets of color photographs are filed (three sets of photos are required only when filing color photos).

*Remedy:* File three sets of color photographs. (See Chapter 8).

__ **Photographs not properly mounted (must use Bristol board or photographic double-weight paper). Fig.(s)_____**

*Probable cause of objection:* Photographs not mounted on the proper paper.

*Remedy:* Make new copies of the photos, mount them on the required paper, and file the mounted photos.

__ **Poor quality (half-tone). Fig.(s)_____**

*Probable cause of objection:* Poor quality black-and-white photographs.

*Remedy:* Submit new black-and-white photographs of sufficient quality, or submit black line drawings. (See Chapter 4.)

## Type of Paper. 37 CFR 1.84(e)

__ **Paper not flexible, strong, white, smooth, nonshiny, and durable. Sheet(s)_____**

*Probable cause of objection:* The drawings have been done on poor paper, perhaps yellow notepad paper, grid paper, napkin, wrinkled paper, easily erasable paper, translucent paper, and so on.

*Remedy:* Redo, photocopy, or reprint the drawings on all white, nonshiny, and smooth paper, such as copier or laser printer paper. (See Chapter 8.)

__ **Erasures, alterations, overwritings, interlineations, cracks, creases, and folds not allowed. Sheet(s)_____**

*Probable cause of objection:* The drawings include incomplete erasures, graphic elements or text that has been overwritten with heavy lines, or the paper is cracked, creased, or folded.

*Remedy:* Redo, photocopy, or reprint the drawings to ensure that there are no incomplete erasures and overwriting, and that the paper is not cracked, creased, or folded. (See Chapter 8.)

__ **Mylar, vellum paper is not acceptable.**
  Sheet(s) _____

*Probable cause of objection:* Drawings done on very thin or translucent/transparent sheets.

*Remedy:* Resubmit the drawings on opaque white paper of at least 20 lb. weight. (See Chapter 8.)

## Size of Paper. 37 CFR 1.84(f): Acceptable sizes

__ **21.0 cm by 29.7 cm (DIN size A4) or**
__ **21.6 cm by 27.9 cm (8½ x 11 inches)**

*Probable cause of objection:* The drawing sheets are not one of the indicated sizes.

*Remedy:* Resubmit the drawings on the proper size paper. (See Chapter 8.)

__ **All drawing sheets not the same size.**
  Sheet(s) _____

*Probable cause of objection:* The specific drawing sheets indicated are of a different size from the rest.

*Remedy:* Resubmit the ones indicated to match the size of the remaining sheets. (See Chapter 8.)

## Margins. 37 CFR 1.84(g): Acceptable margins

**Top 2.5 cm Left 2.5 cm Right 1.5 cm Bottom 1.0 cm**
**SIZE: A4 Size**
**Top 2.5 cm Left 2.5 cm Right 1.5 cm Bottom 1.0 cm**
**SIZE: 8½ x 11**

__ **Margins not acceptable. Fig(s) _____**

__ **Top (T) __ Left (L) __ Right (R) __ Bottom (B)**

*Probable cause of objection:* Drawing figures have intruded into the specified margin.

*Remedy:* Move the figures out of the specified margin. (See Chapter 8.) We have received this objection even when the figures are clear of the margins by several millimeters. The PTO drawing reviewers seem to use different rulers than we do, or they may make sloppy measurements. If this happens to you, just move the figures even farther away from the edge. (See below for techniques on making changes.) Alternatively, if you don't mind dealing with a large bureaucracy, you may call the Drafting Review Branch and ask to have your drawing margins measured again.

## Views. 37 CFR 1.84(h)

**REMINDER: Specification may require revision to correspond to drawing changes.**

__ **Views connected by projection or lead lines.**
  Fig.(s)_____

*Probable cause of objection:* Dashed or lead lines extending between figures with different figure numbers.

*Remedy:* Delete the dashed or lead lines. (See Chapter 8.)

### Partial Views. 37 CFR 1.84(h)(2)

__ **Brackets needed to show figure as one entity.**
  Fig.(s)_____

*Probable cause of objection:* An exploded view not enclosed by a bracket.

*Remedy:* Resubmit the drawing sheet with a bracket enclosing the exploded view. (See Chapter 6.)

__ **Views not labeled separately or properly.**
  Fig.(s)_____

*Probable cause of objection:* Parts of a large drawing split onto multiple sheets share the same figure number or are otherwise numbered improperly.

*Remedy:* Renumber the figures with different figure numbers. (See also Chapter 6.)

__ **Enlarged view not labeled separately or properly. Fig.(s)_____**

*Probable cause of objection:* Two figures, one showing an enlarged portion of another, share the same figure number or are otherwise numbered improperly.

*Remedy:* Renumber the figures with different figure numbers. (See also Chapter 6.)

## Sectional Views. 37 CFR 1.84(h)(3)

__ **Hatching not indicated for sectional portions of an object. Fig.(s)_____**

*Probable cause of objection:* Sectioned or cutaway parts lack hatching.

*Remedy:* Provide hatching on the sectioned parts. (See Chapter 6.)

__ **Sectional designation should be noted with Arabic or Roman numbers. Fig.(s)_____**

*Probable cause of objection:* The sectioning plane should be noted in a general view with a double-ended arrow with numbers corresponding to the sectional figures.

*Remedy:* Resubmit the drawing with the sectioning plane arrow and numbers. (See Chapter 6.)

## Arrangement of Views. 37 CFR 1.84(i)

__ **Words do not appear in a horizontal, left-to-right fashion when page is either upright or turned, so that the top becomes the right side, except for graphs.**

Fig.(s)_____

*Probable cause of objection:* Some text not oriented upright or horizontal with respect to the top of the sheet.

*Remedy:* Rearrange the text so that everything is oriented upright and horizontal with respect to the top of the sheet, depending on whether the sheet is in portrait or landscape orientation. (See Chapter 8.)

__ **Views not on the same plane on drawing sheet. Fig.(s)_____**

*Probable cause of objection:* All figures on a sheet are not oriented in the same direction.

*Remedy:* Resubmit the drawing sheet with the figures in the same orientation. (See Chapter 8.)

## Scale. 37 CFR 1.84(k)

__ **Scale not large enough to show mechanism without crowding when drawing is reduced in size to two-thirds in reproduction. Fig.(s)_____**

*Probable cause of objection:* The figure is too small to show details clearly.

*Remedy:* Enlarge the figure to show all of its details clearly. (See Chapter 8.)

## Character of Lines, Numbers, & Letters. 37 CFR 1.84(l)

__ **Lines, numbers & letters not uniformly thick and well-defined, clean, durable, and black (except for color drawings). Fig.(s)_____**

*Probable cause of objection:* Lines or text not sharp, uniformly thick, or black enough. This is the most common objection. Unacceptable lines are usually produced by improper pens, paper, drawing techniques, software, or printer. For example, pencils, ballpoint pens, and rollerball pens usually do not produce acceptable lines, although some good quality roller pens may pass muster. Freehand lines, even if sharp, are usually not acceptable. Rough, highly porous paper will cause the ink to feather (seep out). Bitmap drawing programs usually produce very jagged lines. Dot matrix printers also produce jagged lines. Inkjet printers will not produce acceptable output if a paper not designed for inkjet printers is used; such papers tend to cause the ink to feather or seep out. Inkjet printers may, but do not always, produce acceptable output if special inkjet paper is used. Even laser printers may produce unacceptable lines, usually because the lines are too thin (at or less than 0.1 mm), or because the lines are too jagged, which is typical of 300 dpi printers.

*Remedy:* Redraw the specified figures with the proper pens and techniques, thicken the thinnest lines and reprint the drawings, reprint the drawings with a laser printer instead of an inkjet printer, reprint the drawings with a 600 dpi printer, or use a cleaner or better copier. (See Chapter 8.)

## Shading. 37 CFR 1.84(m)

___ Solid black areas pale. Fig.(s)_____

*Probable cause of objection:* Solid black areas not dark enough—for example, not filled in sufficiently with a pen, or were printed with an ink-jet printer.

*Remedy:* Completely darken the solid black area with a black pen, or print with a laser printer. (See Chapters 7 and 8.)

___ Solid black shading not permitted. Fig.(s)_____

*Probable cause of objection:* Areas are filled with solid black.

*Remedy:* Delete the solid black areas and leave an open outline. In line drawings, solid black areas are permitted only for representing the color black in an invention in which color is important. (See Chapters 7 and 8.)

___ Shade lines pale, rough and blurred. Fig.(s)_____

*Probable cause of objection:* Shading lines not dark and sharp enough, perhaps done with a poor quality pen, pencil, or inkjet printer.

*Remedy:* Use a good quality pen or a laser printer. (See Chapters 7 and 8.)

## Numbers, Letters, & Reference Characters. 37 CFR 1.84(p)

___ Numbers and reference characters not plain and legible. Fig.(s)_____

*Probable cause of objection:* Text is poorly formed, either due to an improper pen, technique, software, printer, or copier. As stated, pencils, ballpoint pens, and rollerball pens usually do not produce acceptable text. Freehand text is usually not acceptable, unless done extremely neatly and professionally. Fonts or writing with very thin lines (at or less than 0.1 mm) are usually not acceptable. Bitmap drawing programs usually produce very jagged text. Dot matrix printers also produce jagged text. Inkjet printers may, but do not always, produce acceptable text if special inkjet paper is used. All 600 dpi laser printers should produce acceptable text.

*Remedy:* Redraw the specified figures with the proper pens and techniques, use a thicker font or pen, print on special inkjet paper, reprint the drawings with a 600 dpi laser printer instead of an inkjet printer, or use a cleaner or better copier. (See Chapters 2 and 3.)

___ Figure legends are poor.
Fig.(s)_____

*Probable cause of objection:* Characters are poorly drawn, perhaps by hand.

*Remedy:* Redraw the characters very carefully with a template or lettering set. (See Chapter 2.)

___ **Numbers and reference characters not oriented in same direction as the view. 37 CFR 1.84(p)(3).**
Fig.(s)_____

*Probable cause of objection:* Some text not oriented upright or horizontal with respect to the top of the sheet.

*Remedy:* Rearrange the text so that all of it is oriented upright and horizontal with respect to the top of the sheet, depending on whether the sheet is in portrait or landscape orientation. (See Chapter 8.)

___ **English alphabet not used. 37 CFR 1.84(p)(3). Fig.(s)_____**

*Probable cause of objection:* Non-English letters are used.

*Remedy:* Use English letters, or use numbers. (See Chapter 8.)

___ **Numbers, letters, and reference characters must be at least .32 cm (⅛ inch) in height. 37 CFR 1.84(p)(3). Fig.(s)_____**

*Probable cause of objection:* Text is too small.

*Remedy:* Make all text, including lowercase letters, at least ⅛", 3.2 mm, or 14 points tall. (See Chapter 8.)

## Lead Lines. 37 CFR 1.84(q)

___ **Lead lines cross each other.**
Fig.(s)_____

*Probable cause of objection:* Some lead lines cross each other.

*Remedy:* Reposition the lead lines, and also reference numbers if necessary, so that the lines do not cross each other. (See Chapter 8.)

___ **Lead lines missing. Fig.(s)_____**

*Probable cause of objection:* One or more lead lines are missing for some reference numbers.

*Remedy:* Provide a lead line between each reference number or letter and its corresponding part in the drawings. (See Chapter 8.)

## Numbering of Sheets of Drawings. 37 CFR 1.84(t)

___ **Sheets not numbered consecutively, and in Arabic numerals, beginning with number 1. Fig.(s)_____**

*Probable cause of objection:* Drawing sheets not numbered consecutively, are in non-Arabic numerals (something other than 1, 2, or 3), or do not start with 1.

*Remedy:* Renumber the sheets in consecutive Arabic numerals, starting with 1. (See Chapter 8.)

## Corrections. 37 CFR 1.84(w)

___ **Corrections not made from Patent and Trademark Office-948 dated _____**

*Probable cause of objection:* Objections listed on a previous Notice of Draftsperson's Patent Drawing Review form have not been made.

*Remedy:* Make the corrections indicated on the previous form.

## Design Drawings. 37 CFR 1.152

\_\_ **Surface shading shown not appropriate. Fig.(s)**_____

*Probable cause of objection:* Inappropriate shading that does not properly depict the surface shape or contour, or shading of an inappropriate type.

*Remedy:* Redo the shading according to accepted techniques and to properly depict the desired shape. (See Chapter 7.)

\_\_ **Solid black shading not used for color contrast. Fig.(s)**_____

*Probable cause of objection:* Solid black areas are used.

*Remedy:* Delete the solid black areas and leave an open outline. (See Chapter 8.)

## Do Not Add New Matter

Many defects cited by the objections and rejections, such as unclear description or drawings that lack sufficient detail, are seemingly curable by changing the description or drawings. However, after an application is filed, no new matter can be added to the same application. (New matter is any technical information not in the description, claims, or drawings as originally filed.) The objections and rejections cannot be overcome by substantively changing the information in the application, no matter how slightly; they must be overcome by relying on the information provided in the original application.

## Changing Drawings Without Introducing New Matter

The new matter prohibition does not mean that the drawings cannot be changed. In a utility patent application, if a feature is not shown in the original drawings, but is specified in the original description and/or claims, it is not new matter, so it may be properly added to the drawings if necessary.

**EXAMPLE:**

An application includes original drawings that show a portable CD player, but without a speaker. Fortunately, the written description states that a speaker is used. In this case, a speaker can be added to the drawings without violating the new matter prohibition.

Unless the element being added is very simple or readily understood by one skilled in the art—such as a hinge, a switch, or a power supply—the original description must be detailed enough to support the changes to the drawings. However, the feature added to the drawings cannot have any more detail than the original description.

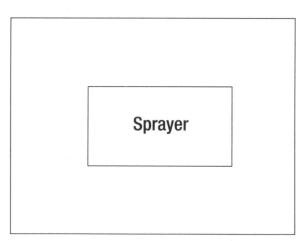

**Illustration 9.2—Labeled Box**

EXAMPLE:

The written description of a carpet cleaning method states that "a sprayer can be used" to apply a cleaning solution, but no sprayer is shown in the original drawings. The drawings can be changed to show only the most basic, rudimentary sprayer. Alternatively, the sprayer may be represented with a labeled rectangular box to avoid any question of new matter, as in Illustration 9.2.

Generally, features cannot be added to design patent drawings, because there is no detailed description or claims to support them.

## Adding New Matter by CIP

Although new matter cannot be added to the same application, it may be added to a *new* application, known as a "continuation-in-part" (CIP) application. (See *Patent It Yourself*, Chapter 14, for more on CIP applications.) However, any claims to the new matter will not get the benefit of the original filing date, so any relevant invention that predates the new matter may be used by the PTO to reject the CIP application.

EXAMPLE:

Maria Spinoza invented a chair on Jan. 1, 1996, and filed a patent application for it on the same day. On June 1, 1996, she added casters (wheels) to the legs of the chair; she then filed a CIP application on the same day to include the casters. However, on May 30, 1996, another inventor, Lucy Kant, created an identical chair with casters, and filed an application for it on that same day. Maria was unable to obtain a patent on a chair with casters because Lucy's chair with casters predated Maria's CIP application.

Also, under the 20-year-from-filing patent term, any patent based on a CIP application will expire 20 years from the filing date of the original (parent) application. The CIP application can lengthen the time it takes to get a patent from several months to a couple of years, so the patent term is effectively reduced by the same amount. For these reasons, CIP applications should be avoided by ensuring that the original drawings, as well as the original written description, include enough information to enable one skilled in the pertinent field to make and use the invention. Alternatively, it may make sense to file an entirely new application if you feel that relevant prior art has not been issued in the meantime. You should consult with a patent agent or an attorney for advice in this situation.

## Removing Features

Removing a feature may be considered as introducing new matter if its removal changes the invention. For design inventions, *nothing may be removed*, because the appearance of a design invention cannot be changed after filing, not even slightly. However, if the feature was described in the original application as not being part of the invention, or if the feature was shown in dashed lines (which are used to illustrate features that are not part of the invention; see Chapter 7) in the original drawings, it may be removed without introducing new matter—that is, altering the design.

EXAMPLE 1:

A utility application for a lamp describes and shows a switch for turning the lamp on and off at will. The switch cannot be deleted from the application, because its removal will substantively change the invention— that is, the lamp will turn on and stay on all the time when it is plugged in—and introduce new matter.

**EXAMPLE 2:**

A design application for a clock shows a plain clock face with a single round dot at the 12 o'clock position. The dot cannot be deleted from the drawings without introducing new matter. The application also shows a power cord. If the power cord is shown in solid lines, it cannot be deleted from the drawings without introducing new matter. However, if the power cord is shown in solid lines, but the description for the figures states that the power cord is not part of the invention, it may be deleted from the drawings without introducing new matter. Also, if the power cord is shown in dashed lines, even if there is no statement indicating that it is not part of the invention, it may be deleted from the drawings without introducing new matter.

## Correcting the Drawings

The PTO will not correct the drawings for you or return them to you. New drawings or corrected copies must be submitted. Therefore, if you made the drawings by hand, you should keep the originals in case corrections are required. If you made them with a computer, keep the computer file and make a backup so you may make changes later. (It's always a good idea to keep backups.) Be careful not to introduce new matter; see above for details.

### Correcting Ink Drawings

If you made the drawings by hand, you must correct the original and submit a good quality photocopy free of copier specks. Drawings made on bristol board, vellum, or Mylar film, which is a durable and substantially nonporous plastic sheet, may be erased with a suitable eraser (see Chapter 2) without damaging the surface. The elements to be deleted must be completely erased, so that no trace of such elements appear on a photocopy.

Drawings made on porous paper cannot be erased without damaging or fraying the paper. Ink applied on the frayed areas will feather, so the drawings will again be objected to. Therefore, it is best to use white correction fluid on porous paper. Correction fluid does not provide an ideal surface for ink; so if large areas are covered, the lines applied over it will probably be poor, which may again be objected to. Redoing the entire sheet may be preferable in such a situation.

If the figures on a sheet must be repositioned, they may be cut out, taped, or glued onto a new sheet, and photocopied. Make sure that the edges of the pasted pieces do not appear on the photocopy. If they do, try taping or gluing down the offending edge, or covering the unwanted lines of the photocopy with white correction fluid.

### Correcting CAD Drawings

Correcting CAD drawings is easy. Just open the drawing file, make the necessary changes on screen, and print a new copy. This is one of the greatest advantages of making drawings with a computer.

### Adding an Element to a Drawing

If an element is specified in the description but not shown in the original drawings, it may optionally be added to the drawings. If the element is specified in the claims but not shown in the original drawings, it must be added to the drawings, or the element must be deleted from the claims. Such a requirement is typically stated in an Office Action.

Prior to making any changes to the drawings (other than to make minor corrections, or corrections in response to the Notice of

Draftsperson's Drawing Review), you must first obtain permission from the examiner. To obtain permission, file a copy of the drawing sheet to be changed, with the element being added shown in red, along with a copy of the Submission of Corrected Drawings which is in the appendix.

You can make a photocopy of the original drawing and draw the element in red ink. If you are drawing with a computer, you may print the drawing with the new element in black and trace over or circle it with red ink. It is expedient to concurrently submit an extra copy of the drawing sheet with the new element properly executed in black lines. If you do this, check the box next to the following sentence in the request: "A formal copy of the drawing with the proposed changes is also enclosed."

## Making Voluntary Changes

After filing, or after receiving an office action, you may feel the need to make voluntary changes to the drawings. These changes can include adding or changing elements, deleting elements, correcting reference numerals, and so forth. These changes (and all other changes) must be done by filing new "corrected" drawings. Formerly, applicants had to obtain permission from the examiner to file corrected drawings, but now you may file the corrected drawings without permission. However, you must be sure these new drawings don't contain any new matter. Otherwise the examiner will object to them and require you to eliminate the new matter.

You may make voluntary changes anytime before the application is allowed. You may even be able to make them after allowance before the issue fee is paid under Rule 312—see *Patent It Yourself*, Chapter 13.

## Filing Corrected Drawings

Subject to approval by the examiner, voluntary changes may be filed any time before the application is allowed. Under new Rule 85(a), corrections required by the Drawing Review Branch must usually be made before the application is sent to the examiner for examination. Corrections required by the examiner may be filed with the written response (see *Patent It Yourself*, Chapter 13, for details on Office Action responses). Applicants are no longer allowed to defer drawing corrections until after allowance unless the examiner gives permission to do so. If the examiner does give such permission, the corrected drawings must be filed within three months from the mailing date of the Notice of Allowance (a notice indicating that the application is allowable). They should be filed as soon as possible after allowance, because if the drawings are again objected to, another set of corrected drawings must be filed within the same three-month period. Otherwise you will have to buy an extension to submit the corrected drawings after the three-month period. (The issue fee must be filed within the three-month period; it cannot be extended.) Whenever you submit a new (replacement) drawing sheet, clearly write or print "Replacement Drawing" and include the application serial number and the inventor's name on the front side of each sheet, centered within the top margin. (See Chapter 8 for margin requirements.) Send in the drawings with the Submission of Corrected Drawings form in the appendix. (This form is not required if you're a registered eFiler and you submit the drawings by EFS-Web.)

## Summary

Congratulations on finishing the book! As with any endeavor that requires a new skill, you may not be able to turn out patent drawings immediately. There are learning curves associated with ink drafting and computer drafting. Be patient in your efforts to get the equipment together and in your initial attempts to use them. Reread the relevant sections of the book as necessary. In the end, you will find that your work will pay off in savings—and in having the satisfaction of being able to create professional-looking patent drawings yourself. ●

# Tear-Out Forms

Petition for Submitting Color Photographs or Drawings

Submission of Corrected Drawings

# In the United States Patent and Trademark Office

App. No: _____

Filing Date: _____

Applicant: _____

App. Title: _____

Examiner: _____

Art Unit: _____

## Petition for Submitting Color Photographs or Drawings

Commissioner for Patents
P.O. Box 1450
Alexandria, VA 22313-1450

Sir:

Applicant hereby respectfully petitions that the color photographs ☐ filed herewith ☐ already filed be accepted as formal drawings. The $130 petition fee is enclosed.

These color photographs or drawings are necessary because _____

_____

_____

_____

_____

_____

_____

Very respectfully,

Sole/First Applicant: _____

_____     _____
Sole/First Applicant Signature                        Date

Joint/Second Applicant: _____

_____     _____
Joint/Second Applicant Signature                     Date

Joint/Third Applicant: _____

_____     _____
Joint/Third Applicant Signature                        Date

Joint/Fourth Applicant: _____

_____     _____
Joint/Fourth Applicant Signature                      Date

Enc.

# In the United States Patent and Trademark Office

Serial No: _____

Appn. Filed: _____

Applicants: _____

App. Title: _____

Examiner: _____

Group Art Unit: _____

Mailed: _____

At: _____

## Submission of Corrected Drawings

Commissioner for Patents
P.O. Box 1450
Alexandria, VA 22313-1450

Attn: Chief Draftsperson

Sir:

New drawing sheet(s) _____ for the above application is/are enclosed, corrected as necessary. Please substitute this/these for the corresponding sheet(s) on file.

The new drawing sheet(s) are all marked "Replacement Sheet, Ser. Nr. _____/_____,_____."

The new sheets contain the following changes; these changes do not introduce any new matter into the drawings:

Fig __:

[ ] Attached is/are copy(ies) of the original drawing sheets marked up to show the changes.

Very respectfully,

_____

Applicant

## Certificate of Mailing

I hereby certify that this correspondence will be deposited with the United States Postal Service as First Class Mail, postage prepaid, in an envelope addressed to "Commissioner for Patents, P.O. Box 1450, Alexandria, VA 22313-1450" on the date below.

_____    _____
Person Depositing Paper          Date

# Index

 **NOLO** *Keep Up to Date*

Go to Nolo.com/newsletters to sign up for free newsletters and discounts on Nolo products.

- **Nolo Briefs.** Our monthly email newsletter with great deals and free information.

- **Nolo's Special Offer.** A monthly newsletter with the biggest Nolo discounts around.

- **BizBriefs.** Tips and discounts on Nolo products for business owners and managers.

- **Landlord's Quarterly.** Deals and free tips just for landlords and property managers, too.

Don't forget to check for updates. Find this book at **Nolo.com** and click "Legal Updates."

## *Let Us Hear From You*

Register your Nolo product and give us your feedback at Nolo.com/book-registration.

- Once you've registered, you qualify for technical support if you have any trouble with a download or CD (though most folks don't).

- We'll also drop you an email when a new edition of your book is released—and we'll send you a coupon for 15% off your next Nolo.com order!

DRAW6

 **Lawyer Directory**

## Find an Intellectual Property Attorney

- *Qualified lawyers*
- *In-depth profiles*
- *A pledge of respectful service*

When you want help protecting your intellectual property, you don't want just any lawyer—you want an expert in the field, who can give you and your family up-to-the-minute advice. You need a lawyer who has the experience and knowledge to answer your questions, whether they're about provisional patents, trademark, patent, copyright or trade secret law.

**Nolo's Lawyer Directory** is unique because it provides an extensive profile of every lawyer. You'll learn about not only each lawyer's education, professional history, legal specialties, credentials and fees, but also about their philosophy of practicing law and how they like to work with clients.

All lawyers listed in Nolo's directory are in good standing with their state bar association. Many will review Nolo documents, such as a will or living trust, for a fixed fee. They all pledge to work diligently and respectfully with clients—communicating regularly, providing a written agreement about how legal matters will be handled, sending clear and detailed bills and more.

## www.nolo.com

The photos above are illustrative only. Any resemblance to an actual attorney is purely coincidental.